Scott O'Hara

Autopornography:
A Memoir of Life
in the Lust Lane

*Pre-publication
REVIEWS,
COMMENTARIES,
EVALUATIONS . . .*

"**S**cott O'Hara is one of the few figures able to come out of porn with an articulate, honest take on it. After so many important writings on the culture and politics of sex, his notoriety as a writer/editor has eclipsed his porno career, and *Autopornography* sets the stage for O'Hara's role as an important writer and sex advocate. O'Hara does tell all on the mid- to late-'80s porn industry, but this is only one section, 'The Good Parts.' I like the background, the childhood, the bookworm. It is intriguing that O'Hara wasn't a poor young male who had no options but to perform sexually for money. He happened to be intelligent and self-sufficient. His world still revolves and evolves around his sexual experimentation.

Autopornography is also about O'Hara's life before AIDS, life with AIDS, and surviving lymphoma. Not throwing a socially acceptable blanket over the issue, O'Hara dares to tell his truth–many people with HIV's truth–that he's not abstaining from sex, and furthermore, with consenting, mostly HIV-positive adults.

While much of Scott O'Hara's life story is outlandish, either in content or concept, he tells it in a relatively low-key tone. He is also fearless about investigating a few of his innermost dark thoughts, or unpleasant realities, and serving them up undiluted. There is no cry for acceptance, no whitewashing of the facts, in *Autopornography*. I have to agree with O'Hara, that most of us have an inherent need for pornography."

Ron Athey
Writer, Performance Artist

More pre-publication
REVIEWS, COMMENTARIES, EVALUATIONS . . .

"**S**cott O'Hara's *Autopornography* is a work of intelligence and passion that shakes the very boundaries of how we think and act about sex. It is the culmination of many things, the foremost of which is O'Hara's lifelong dedication to exploring the potential and extremes of sexual experience. But *Autopornography* is also the blossoming of three decades of social change and radical thinking about sexuality. The experimentation of the 1960s, the sexual extravagance of the 1970s, and activism of the 1980s and '90s find their apotheosis here. *Autopornography* is a record of pleasure and struggle, redemption and exhilaration, set against the tumultuous changes of the late twentieth century; it is a vision of history that shows us the way into the future."

Michael Bronski
Author of *Culture Clash: The Making of Gay Sensibility*

"**S**cott O'Hara is a *rara avis*–a unique combination of the unapologetically sex-positive and the warmly articulate and literate. *Autopornography* is essential reading for anyone who has ever wanted to peek behind the veil obscuring the true nature of America's sex industry from view."

Alistair Williamson
Associate Editor,
The Harvard Gay & Lesbian Review,
Boston, Massachusetts

The Haworth Press, Inc.

Autopornography
A Memoir of Life in the Lust Lane

HAWORTH Gay & Lesbian Studies
John P. De Cecco, PhD
Editor in Chief

Autopornography
A Memoir of Life in the Lust Lane

Scott O'Hara

The Haworth Press
New York • London

The Haworth Press, Inc., 10 Alice Street, Binghamton, NY 13904-1580

Front cover photo of Scott O'Hara by David Lebe. © 1990. Used with permission.

Cover design by Donna M. Brooks.

Library of Congress Cataloging-in-Publication Data

O'Hara, Scott.
    Autopornography: a memoir of life in the lust lane / Scott O'Hara.
      p. cm.
      ISBN 0-7890-0144-6 (alk. paper).
    1. O'Hara, Scott. 2. Pornography—United States—Case studies. 3. Sex oriented businesses—United States—Employees—Biography. I. Title.
HQ472.U6033 1997
363.47—dc20
                                                     96-41442
                                                       CIP

For Claudia

ABOUT THE AUTHOR

Scott "Spunk" O'Hara, appeared in 26 pornographic movies between 1983 and 1992. Since then, he has been the editor of the sex journal *STEAM* ("the literate queer's guide to sex and controversy") and has been published in numerous anthologies and magazines. His first book of short stories, *Do-It-Yourself Piston Polishing (for Non-Mechanics),* was released in August 1996 by Badboy. A long-term "Person With AIDS," Scott's writings on the subject have raised some eyebrows, as has his "HIV+" tattoo. He currently lives in San Francisco.

CONTENTS

Preface

SCOTT REVEALS ALL!

Most of you already know who Scott O'Hara is. A few of you may even realize that the Scott O'Hara you "know" is not necessarily related to the Scott O'Hara who brushes his teeth most mornings (but seldom flosses). Everyone has a myriad of different personas for the different parts of their lives; in my case, this was taken to an extreme because my personas were created for me by directors and art directors, each of whom had his own private fantasies and demons to bring to life with my body. Yet, there are many of my fans out there who seem to think that the attitude I projected in *Below the Belt*, or the hairstyle I wore in *Oversize Load*, must be the "real" me. Well, yes. They're all "real." They're all me. But no single persona has exclusive rights.

For the past ten years or so, I've been struggling to integrate these various personas with my own private life–to give a holistic, integral image to the world. Because that is, in a nutshell, the major criticism I have of modern civilization: we've allowed our sexuality to become separated from our personality. We've become fragmented, compartmentalized persons. No, sex is really not the all-important subject that my writing would seem to imply. (I'll admit to having had a one-string harp for the past decade.) All I want is for sex and porn to take their proper places in life, alongside eating and writing letters–enjoyable activities, not for everyone perhaps, but normal, beneficial, and quite, quite harmless to children. Nothing to get excited about.

So I tried, in the last half of my video career, to visibly convey the pleasure of sex: I smiled. (In the first half, it wasn't yet a conscious decision; I was just enjoying myself.) In my writing since then, mostly in *STEAM* magazine, I've tried to let people know that it's okay to laugh during sex. Orgasm is really not the serious business that some people would like to make it. Every time I go out in the bushes, I feel like I'm spreading the gospel of sexual integration. Yes, you can enjoy nature in all its wonderful forms simultaneously. Sex really doesn't need to be hidden away in a darkened bedroom. It's not that important, and doing it out in the open is the best way of eliminating shame. Keeping sex secret is bad for the soul.

This book was written as a last-ditch effort–a way to open up all my closets, let you in on all the dark corners of my life, and give you a better picture of what goes into the making of a pornstar. Because if there's one profession that arouses people's curiosity, it's that one. Am I a "unique" person? Well, obviously. But I'm sure most of you will find points of reference in my life, and wonder, "Could I have done it. . . ?" The answer is probably "Yes, you could have." But before you fire off that resignation letter to your boss, take a good long look at yourself and your goals, and examine what place sex has in your life. Porn really is for everyone–everyone human, that is–but I'm afraid it can't be a career for everyone. We need a few plumbers to make sure we can shower off afterward.

Acknowledgments

With gratitude to my many mentors: Claudia Scott, Frode Jensen, Gregg Sylvester, Richard Howard, Douglas Cantrall, Walt Killeen, Dennis Forbes, Mark I. Chester, Bob Chesley, Drew Okun, John Rowberry, Howard Cruse, David Lebe, Kerry O'Quinn, Philip Core, John Gaines, Howard Roffman, John Preston, Mike Shearer, Eric Garber, Keith Griffith, pansy, Chip Delany, Melissa Murphy, Steve Zeeland, Bruce Shaw, and all those nosy audience members out there who, ultimately, made this book both possible and necessary.

Something in the Water

To spend my days in transit
to find a man in every town
and see myself as river trout:
caught, presumed dead
only to make a spectacular leap
disappearing in the stream.
Nothing new to me: I've been hooked
thrown back or escaped
more times than I can count
and seeing now the trusting face
of each past fisherman in every other . . .
this is my life, this is my goal
I want no more than this
I wish they all could eat me.

Soap Gets in My Eyes

Timmy, who had just turned eighteen, was just coming out of the locker room of his junior high school, where he had just jerked off for the first time in his life, when he ran into his coach.

"Gee, Mr. Hawkins, I'm sorry–I didn't see you. I must've been daydreaming again."

"All that daydreaming's not good for a kid, son–why don't you come to my office and we'll have a nice father-and-son-type chat–we'll see if we can't work some of these daydreams out; whaddya say?"

All right, I'll give it up. I don't have the stamina to keep up with that sort of writing, no matter how amusing it may be. Besides, I spent too much of my adolescence jerking off fantasizing about something uncomfortably close to the scene I was trying to capture. Let me try again, a bit nearer to reality this time. . .

When you're a horny kid, without any available outlet for your frustrated libido except your fist–well, you spend a lot of time jerking off and a lot of energy doing more physical things, to tire yourself out so you can sleep. Me, I used to go out running at night. Yeah, I know, most of you grew up in cities, and it wasn't safe or legal for a boy to be out at night. I grew up on a farm in the Applegate Valley, the prettiest little valley in southern Oregon, and I used to love to go out jogging at midnight after the rest of the family was asleep. There was very little traffic on that road at that time of night; for the occasional passing car, I'd usually put on a show by rubbing my stomach while patting my head, or tying my T-shirt around my face to impersonate a ghost, or jogging backward. Depending on where I was and how secretive I felt, I might jump the ditch and hide in the woods. I'd jog the three miles to the corner store, then turn around and go home. If I felt particularly energetic, I might take a detour up Board Shanty Road, a steep climb—and then turn around and run back down when I couldn't climb anymore. Once, I made it all the way to Grants Pass, a ten-mile run—and then my legs gave out. I lay down immobilized on the lawn of the Free Methodist Church, and it was nearly dawn before I could make my wobbly way home. So, yeah, running was an important physical outlet for me.

Running, as anyone who does it will tell you, provides prime time for thinking. The things I thought about, though, could sometimes get me into trouble since I often had to dash into the woods to pump off a load, just to get my hard-on to go away. All right, I'll admit it, that was the real purpose of going out jogging in the first place. Sure, I could jerk off at home anytime, but there was something special about doing it in the woods at midnight, especially someone else's woods. The occasional passing car, its headlights briefly blinding me, only made it more exciting—there was this terrific ambivalence in my mind over whether I wanted to be seen or not. My fantasies varied, but they tended to center around a classmate named Jeff Southern.

Jeff was the school jock; I was more in the "brainy" camp. Jeff had a steady girlfriend; I couldn't have been less interested in girls. We didn't really have a lot in common. Still, I thought he was the cat's pajamas. His main sport was basketball—he was very tall and skinny, a perfect basketball player—but he also wrestled, played football, and was pretty good at track and field events, too. He was a regular Renaissance man of the sports department. Through every year of junior high, we had the same phys ed class, and whenever I could, I'd sneak looks at him in the locker room. Dicks were what fascinated me then (all right, they still do, but they were more mysterious and a great novelty then, due in large part to the puritanism of my family), and I tried to memorize all the different possibilities. There was, for instance, only one guy in my class who didn't fit the WASP stereotype—John Aiassa was his name. Southern Italian, Greek, I don't know, but I had the locker next to him, thankyoujesus, and I spent lots of time "struggling" with getting my sweater off, just so I could take long, searching looks at that delicious-looking, dark-brown, floppy thing. (Hell, that was the reason I always wore pullovers!) I wanted John in the worst way. I wanted him to catch me spying on him and say, "All right, you like my dick–here it is, cocksucker; lick it!" and stick it in my face. I wanted him to sneer at me and tell me that if I really wanted to suck him off (even the words "suck me off," if seen in printed form, were enough to get my nut!), I could meet him that night, down by the river, and he'd be there with his three older brothers, and they'd . . . do something. Unfortunately, John was a shy and retiring type, as was I, and whether or not he ever noticed my insatiable voyeurism, in three years I don't think I exchanged five words with him. And I never got to touch his dick.

Jeff was another matter. He was a star, after all, and immensely popular; he could talk to anyone, and did. In spite of being a jock, Jeff was basically nice, and he would often encourage me in phys ed when I looked like I needed some encouragement. Once he asked me why I didn't have a 4.0. I told him it was because of phys ed, a subject that I'd given up as a lost cause years earlier. Jeff assured me that I could get an A in phys ed if I really tried–the coach wasn't that strict. From then on, I did try–how can you not try when you feel as if your Jeff Southern is watching your every move?–and I guess the coach noticed because that semester I moved up to a 4.0. Wow.

So it's only natural that I should spend a lot of quality time fantasizing about Jeff. (In fact, I still do.) For instance, he'd be driving by some night, on his way home from one of the many adult sorts of things that jocks undoubtedly were allowed to do; he'd see a glimpse of someone off in the trees, he'd stop and come to investigate–and there I'd be, leaning against a tree, beating off to beat the band. What would he do at that point? Generally speaking, my imagination didn't go very far. He'd pull out his dick–that dick that I never recall actually seeing, throughout all those years of furtive locker-room glances, because his locker was always across the locker room from mine–and take a piss. Some of it would hit my bare leg, and I would cum, dissolving into a warm puddle of romantic goo under his gaze. Or, he would walk directly up to me, grab both my hands and force them above my head–then, holding them there easily with one hand, he would smile knowingly, slowly lower his other hand and cup my balls in it–and I would spontaneously explode while he looked down, astonished. Or–and this was a fantasy so precious I hardly dared use it, for fear of tarnishing it–he would just come up to me, take me in his arms, and kiss me. And I would probably pass out, hyperventilating, and go directly to heaven: Do not pass go, do not collect $200.

If all of these seem excessively innocent, you have to recall that I *was* innocent. In fact, if not in fantasy. Oh, I would often drink my own piss and fantasize that it was someone else's; I collected quite a number of old, stretched-out jockstraps from the locker-room waste-basket and jerked off in them (especially the one marked "AIASSA"–of course, I knew it was John's older brother's, but that was close enough); I had a collection of swimwear catalogs, which I had creatively cut and pasted and altered to make the nearly naked hunks appear to be doing nasty things to each other. And on several occasions, I even tried sucking off the family's billy goat (he was never very cooperative, but I'll never forget the wonderful silken feeling of his balls–which really *were* the size of tangerines). Perverse? No, I would just say that I was desperate. These are things that every country boy does, for want of more "traditional" outlets. Had sex been more readily available to me–had Jeff, or John, or Mike, or Larry, or any of my other buddies "initiated" me into what were, I am quite sure, their nightly circle-jerks out behind the bleachers–why, I wouldn't have had to stretch so far to find my erotic thrills. And therefore, I might never have learned the erotic potential of feet and earlobes and jockstraps and pine trees–and therefore might never have become Scott O'Hara, star of stage and screen. Who's to say? I know that, oppressed as it seemed to me then, I had a relatively good childhood, and the only regrets I have are the things I never got to do . . . like jerking off with Jeff Southern.

"So you see, Timmy, it's better for young boys to work out their frustrations in creative ways, together. You haven't tried out for track, have you? Well, why don't you? Our track team could teach you a thing or two. Oh, and when you get home tonight, be sure to ask your father about the fun times we had when *he* was on my basketball team–especially the weekends at the cabin in the woods, and what the other boys made him do whenever they went swimming. Okay?"

"Gee, thanks, Coach! My balls feel better already!"

June

One of my first memories is of driving cross-country with my family, in a camper and a VW bus. We were enroute to the Montreal World's Fair, and if you don't already know what year it was held, I don't choose to enlighten you. Of the fair itself, I remember virtually nothing; of the trip cross-country, I have only confused impressions, but I can categorically state that I liked it. Travel excited me. I was a good traveler, too, even at that age: I never had to stop to pee, I could sit mesmerized by the passing scenery for hours at a time, and I even had the idea (or perhaps my mother subtly suggested it to me) of memorizing the slogans and colors of all the license plates I saw. I think I can date my love of travel to that journey. Oh, there were other family trips—to Big Bend in Texas, to Los Angeles practically every summer, and once to Yosemite—but that fabulous caravan across the continent serves as my model. I remember the firefall on Mt. Rushmore (or was it Yosemite?); sitting around the campfire while one of my older cousins sang mildly risqué songs, accompanying himself on the guitar; and me lying curled up under a blanket in the back of the van for what seemed like hours, trying to delude my parents into thinking they'd left me at the last gas station (I was the seventh child—they were already wise to such tricks). While I doubt that I actually jerked off under that blanket, I know there was an embryonic erotic thrill in my groin, feeling the engine vibrating underneath me and the car swaying around me, that I still feel sometimes in a well-planned bathhouse or a Felliniesque public cruising area—or on a Greyhound™ bus.

Maybe I'm being too Freudian. Travel is essentially enjoyable to most people, isn't it? Who needs adolescent fantasies to explain the urge to see faraway places? But you see, it isn't the faraway places that thrill me. I've been to London a dozen times, and I don't recall ever going to the Tower or Big Ben or Westminster Abbey or the British Museum. Two things thrill me about travel: the people I meet there (who are generally the same type of people I would meet if I stayed home) and the process of getting there. The process is the part that really makes the trip memorable.

My first big solo trip was during the summer when I was seventeen. Two weeks after graduating from high school, I took off on my bicycle, traveling south from Oregon to San Francisco, hot for a reunion with Douglas, the man who'd deflowered me (nervously) two years previously. I rode four hundred miles in four days, and I arrived on Saturday afternoon–the day before Gay Pride Day. I had a place to stay and a guide; I don't think he was thrilled about showing around a piece of jailbait like myself, but he consented. He took me down Castro Street, and even into one of the bars, briefly, until someone spotted me and asked for my ID. The crowds were pretty intense for this country boy, and I could certainly understand the appeal–wow, all these gay men in one place! Everyone must be getting laid every ten minutes! Don't ask me how I knew that all these men were gay. Douglas certainly didn't have to tell me. I just *knew*, even though I'd met fewer than a dozen (known) homosexuals at that point in my life. What I didn't understand, though, was why all these gorgeous men had to pack themselves into *bars* when they could do just as much cruising on the streets (this still puzzles me). I stayed with Douglas for another week, and then took off for Chicago–armed with a Damron guide to the gay world.

I stopped in Sacramento the first night and tried getting into the Steamworks, but of course they weren't about to admit a seventeen-year-old, especially one who looked fifteen. The attendant was real nice, though–told me "Come back in six months, and I'd be happy to let you in!"

Instead, I wandered the K Street Mall, listed in Damron as a "cruisy area." I guess it was; inside of ten minutes, I had someone following me around. Don't ask me to describe him at this late date; my concise travel journal merely describes him as "neat," and says his name was Ed. His pick-up line, which I thought charmingly direct, was "Do you, uh, go for guys?" I said that I thought I did. He guided me to a deserted stairwell–I think it was next to the Sears at the west end of the mall–where we stood in the gloom and jerked each other off. Yes, this was a first for me–this public aspect of sex–and I recall feeling let down by it. I mean, I'd had so many fantasies about locker-room sex all through high school–was this what it would've been like if it'd happened? Depressing thought. The orgasm was perfectly satisfying, but where was the erotic thrill that was supposed to accompany it? The intensity, the compulsion? It all seemed too ordinary and even tawdry for words, not much different than jerking off by myself–and nowhere near as intense as the sex I'd been having out in the fields with the Radical Faeries up at Wolf Creek for the past two years. This impression has stayed with me to this day; I felt and still feel similarly let down by an alarming number of my sexual encounters. I'm not sure what proportion of it has to do with my expectations going into the fuck, the situation, or possibly my partner. I hesitate to blame it all on *him*.

I went back down to the mall, had some lunch, shopped a bit (bought a windbreaker), and when I saw Ed again, two hours later, both our batteries had been recharged. This time, he took me to a restroom, which I found even less stimulating than the stairwell had been.

Several hours later, tiring of the mall scene, I accepted an offer from an attractive young man named Ken, went home with him, and spent the night.

The next day, I headed east again–up the Sierras. Somewhere past Auburn, just as the mountain was getting steep, I noticed that I'd lost a nut from my rear luggage rack–not good. I was sitting by the side of the road, trying to jury-rig a clothespin into a sort of cotter pin, when one of the last surviving hippies stopped and asked if I needed help. We ended up strapping my bike to the top of his VW bug, and he gave me a ride right over the mountains, into Reno. First, though, we stopped off for a wild weekend in the woods at Lake Tahoe–he had the use of a small cabin for three days, and I was on no particular schedule, so I was more than willing. Pete was what I would call "of indeterminate age"–meaning that his shoulder-length hair was greying, but it might have been prematurely grey; he still dressed and acted the part of a hippie and/or faerie, and had a childlike attitude and some very impressive muscles. I'm guessing he was in his forties. We slept together, but I don't believe we had sex that night.

The next morning, Pete suggested a hike up Maggie Peak. I was game. We set off, and after an hour or more of climbing, found snow (in July!). This is the part I remember vividly: an alpine meadow, strewn with gigantic granite boulders and the occasional patch of snow, and that's where Pete laid me down on a sun-warmed boulder and gently, oh so gently, fucked me. For most of the morning. Oh, I'd been fucked before (though not many times), but this one stands out in memory as one of the standards. Sex belongs in the outdoors, I firmly believe: It is a natural function, as natural as sunlight and grass, and restricting it to the bedroom is insane. I wish I had a better memory for the specifics: I don't remember anything about what positions he fucked me in, or how big his cock was, or anything else; I just remember being incredibly happy while he was moving in me, and the birds were all singing around us.

Late that afternoon, sunburned in intimate places, we headed down the mountain, stopped at a mountain stream, washed ourselves off, and then he took me down to Reno, where we spent the night. In the morning, he headed back to San Francisco; I continued east.

The desert and the mountains were not filled with sexual adventures, as you might expect. The next episode didn't occur until Cheyenne, where I picked up (or was picked up by, I suppose— though as aggressive as I remember myself being, it's hard to accept that terminology) a thirtyish man named Frank, whose lover was away for the week. I'd actually spent the afternoon and evening chatting with another boy, named Matt, who had my hormones in a whirl, but he wouldn't, or couldn't, take me home. Nor was he willing to have sex in the park. He did introduce me to a friend of his, whose name I don't remember. This boy was still in high school, but he had a car, so we went to his car and jerked off together. I remember being slightly freaked at the thought of having sex with someone younger than myself; he was the first. Then I went back to the park, and waited. Eventually Frank showed up, and we connected. We loaded my bike into the trunk of his Buick. I spent the night with him, rubbed his back, and was fucked by him (quite well). In the middle of having sex, his parents dropped in for a visit. I hid in the basement, but they'd seen my bicycle, and Frank had to devise an explanation off the top of his head—he said it was his lover's little brother's bike. How strange, I thought, he's not hiding from his family the fact that he fucks guys; he's hiding from them the fact that he's cheating on his lover. Now *that's* novel. The New Family Values–at least, in Cheyenne.

I was on my way again in the morning. Two days later, in Sutherland, Nebraska, while sitting in the park eating a light dinner of bread, cheese, and fruit, a man approached me and asked me if I needed a place to spend the night. I was cautious–I'd been proselytized by christians before, and I wasn't about to subject myself to an evening of preaching–but it eventually turned out that his intentions were strictly dishonorable, so I went along with him. John was his name. He worked for the phone company, was in his early thirties, and was, he claimed, "Just sampling the other side of the fence." When he told me he'd never been fucked, but hinted that he wanted to try, I was dubious–I mean, my dick has never been described as a "trainer" size–but I went ahead, and it slipped in as easy as you please. I didn't say anything, but afterward, when we'd both cum and were rested up, and he started giving subtle signals that he'd like to fuck me, I told him the same thing: "I dunno, guy–y'know, I've never actually had anything up my ass . . . well, okay . . ." and I was right, it turned him on like gangbusters. He was damned good at it, too–when he was finished with me, I knew I'd been fucked. And I slept like a baby.

That was that. Two days later, most of the way across Nebraska (do you have any idea of how *big* that state is, by bicycle?), I gave up and hopped an Amtrak to Chicago. Once there, with fake ID, I found my way into various bars, was passed around from leash to leash, and became the toast of a certain backroom (no longer in existence). By the time I headed for college in late August, my horizons had broadened considerably.

The following spring, I was on a motorcycle. I'd made reservations in Provincetown for Memorial Day week, and I had tickets to the Stratford Festival, in Ontario, in mid-June. Nothing about that trip worked out quite the way it was supposed to. I was planning on stopping in Philadelphia to stay with a friend of my sister's, but I wasn't familiar with the local freeways, and before I knew it, I was past Philly and heading for Atlantic City. "Why argue?" I asked myself, and went down to the shore. I parked the bike and walked along the boardwalk, and before you could say "Jackpot!" I'd been picked up and whisked into the Grand Central Resort, which, I was vaguely aware, was more of a bathhouse than a hotel (Yes, the rooms had real walls, a real bed, and even a sink; but we had to go through a turnstile at the front desk, and most guys left their doors open). I fondly remember a man named James, from Atlanta; I kept thinking, how appropriate!—given the peach fuzz on his face. I spent that weekend in his room, in somewhat of a haze.

Sunday afternoon, I found myself back out on the street, dazed and confused, but smiling. I headed back into Philly, spent a night with Claudia's friend, and went north.

P-town . . . well, I wasn't prepared. Yeah, I went out to the beach on my first day there, and I was promptly set upon by a couple, Rob and Donald. They were about thirty and forty-five, very forceful, and both rode motorcycles. They took me back into town, and we played some at their motel room; then they gave me some acid and got ready to go out on the town. There was a big-name entertainer at one of the clubs that night, and they were eager to attend.

Just so you're not misled: this wasn't the first acid I'd had. I was eager. My previous acid trips (two? three? not many) had been fabulous. But I wasn't counting on the changed circumstances. They were taking me out onto a street crowded with throngs of raucous partiers, into a club with deafening music . . . almost from the second we stepped out of their room, the trip started to get weird. If you've never experienced a "bad trip," you really can't imagine. I became paranoid and fearful of absolutely everything; my heart began palpitating so that I thought I was dying. The crowds of men turned into a gauntlet of grinning goblins. When we got to the club, I guess I looked like a lost child; the bouncer carded me, and I discovered that I'd left my wallet back at their room. So I couldn't get in, and since I looked like I was panicking, Rob agreed to stay outside with me (Donald had already gone in, and was lost in the crowd). We went out to the parking lot, and Rob stood there with his arm around my waist, looking at the moon, saying how beautiful it was. And (this is the acid speaking) all I could think was: Someone's been murdered in the parking lot behind us, and he's trying to keep me from looking around to see it.

By the time we got back to the motel room, I was a wreck. I finally managed to convey to those two that this was a bad trip, that

I couldn't take any more stimulation. So we went to sleep. Maybe I slept; I can't remember.

What could be more natural after an intro like this than canceling my reservations for the rest of the week and riding back to Boston with them? Perhaps if I'd stayed longer, I would have had more positive impressions of P-town.

I stayed two days in Boston. I'm sure I had lots of sex with both of them. (They both tried to fist me, separately, but neither one was successful). I remember Donald showing me how to make poppers—he was a professional chemist, with a lab in his basement, and when he mixed up a batch and then shoved my face next to the beaker, I went stratospheric. This was the pure stuff. Next stop was Rochester, New York, where I spent the night at a bathhouse that's now known as the Rochester Spa & Body Club (it seems to me that it had a different name then). Suddenly, my eyes were opened. Oh, the nights in Atlantic City had been impressive, but that wasn't officially a bathhouse. Now I knew what these places were called, and I knew that I liked them. Imagine: a milieu where sex is unabashedly the goal, the reason why every man is there. It took my breath away. Yeah, I'd heard about baths before that (remember I'd tried to get into the Steamworks in Sacramento), but I hadn't really imagined they could be this wonderful.

I spent much of that night watching porn movies, in between visits to private rooms. A few nights later, I was in Toronto, at the Club Baths Toronto. I can't remember which other baths I checked out in that city. I know that when I got to Stratford, a few days later, I was worn out, and ready for a little quiet culture.

I saw about six plays while I was there; the only ones I remember are *Virginia* (a show featuring Maggie Smith, about Virginia Woolf) and one of Shakespeare's bloodier plays, either *Titus Andronicus* or *Coriolanus*—I can never remember. What I remember is going down to London after the last play to visit Upstairs/Downstairs, the local gay bar. I met Marc, and that started a whole chain of events . . . more on that later.

June was just about over; I was thinking nostalgically about Chicago, and I remembered that Duane's annual Cellar Party was coming up . . . so I headed west again. I don't think I even stopped in Detroit, even though I knew there was a bathhouse there. I knew that with a motorcycle, I had my perpetual freedom; I could always hit the road, so for the time being, I was ready to settle down and be domestic.

Next June found me on the road again—as has nearly every June since. Whether it's hormonal, or just a temperature-change thing, I won't speculate. I just know I start yearning for a different climate every year at about that time . . . not to mention the adventures that come with the territory.

The Family:
Hard to Live With

[Those of you who couldn't care less about my formative years should now "skip to the good parts." The good parts begin on page 55.]

My parents, like most parents, hoped that I would be unexceptional. All they really wanted me to be was a good christian and a good husband. I'm delighted to say that they've been bitterly disappointed; disappointing my parents was, for the five years or so that I continued to notice them, one of my chief pleasures. Nevertheless, given some of the eccentricities my parents engaged in, it's really not all that surprising where I ended up. You might say I was well prepared for a life at the margins of society. A few examples:

I do not recall ever sleeping in a bed as a child. In fact, the first time I regularly used one was when I went off to college. Oh, when I first moved into my own bedroom (age four? five?) there was a bed in there, formerly used by my brother Jim, but I was already sleeping out on the lawn, in a sleeping bag, with my dad and older brothers (just like the big boys! Woof!). After a year or two, to make more space, I moved the bed out.

This simple fact–sleeping outdoors–dumbfounds most people. As I grow older, it's one of the few memories of childhood that I cherish: listening to my dad describe the constellations and tell tales about flying saucers, getting up in the middle of the night to pee, and only stepping to the edge of the lawn, dew soaking my bare feet; sleeping out in the barn with the goats on wet or wintry nights, with that magical, musty smell of old hay and manure. But to other people, when I relate it, it's an instant sign of extreme poverty: "They couldn't afford a bed?"

Another couple of anecdotes indicate something about what my parents could and couldn't afford. First, neither of them ever held real jobs. (Both did lots of volunteer work for the church and the local chapter of the John Birch Society.) It wasn't until I reached junior high that I began to realize how unusual this was. My father was always available, on summer afternoons, to help me with my current project: building a boat, a miniature golf course, or a go-cart. This in itself probably left me scarred for life. It did not, however, seem unusual to me.

Second, one afternoon when I was in third or fourth grade, I came home to find a box in my room. About 15" × 15" × 20", it was quite heavy for its size, and was addressed to my father. I didn't say anything; I just began using it as a seat when I was reading or watching my fish tanks. It was just the right height. (Why didn't I ask questions? I don't know. It just wasn't something I felt comfortable asking about. If Dad wanted me to know, he'd tell me.) After a few years of being sat upon and kicked around the room, one of the top seams finally split open, and one day I noticed a piece of paper inside. I fished it out, and as I did so, I felt a roll of coins. The paper was an invoice: this box that I'd been kicking around (the contents of which my father had never even bothered to check!) contained about 20 pounds in gold and silver. Let's just say, in rounded off figures, $50,000. I have no idea if he intended them for me or not; I never asked. No, I didn't take any.

I think that was the first moment that I realized (and I'm what, fourteen or fifteen by then?) that I probably didn't need to prepare for a typical career.

My parents, as I guess should be clear, did not lead lives of conspicuous consumption. They drove Volkswagen vans, we ate off of Melmac, and when my mom wanted the kitchen redecorated, she did all the painting and wallpapering herself (with some help from her interior decorator son, yours truly). My father, when he saw a freshly killed rabbit or squirrel on the road, would stop to pick it up . . . and take it home, broil it, and eat it. (Yeah, that thought does a number on my stomach, too. He always had a stronger stomach than anyone else: he actually ate comfrey. Still does.) Luxurious living would have been totally contrary to their moral code. They were good Presbyterians. They paid cash for the family farm (bought the year before my birth, it was registered in my six siblings' names; although I do love the place where I spent the first seventeen years of my life, I am grateful, now, that I have no legal ties to it). A mortgage would have been immoral. They also, to this day, have never owned a television. In my formative years, this was a difference I felt acutely; all my friends at school talked incessantly about their favorite shows, which I never saw. The only thing I could talk about was books. Once a month or so, the family would make an excursion over to a neighbor's house to watch (please don't gag) *Wild Kingdom*. This was the only show that my parents could be certain would be clean enough for our innocent ears, and I considered these trips to be major events.

But by and large, I didn't object to being "deprived" of television. We had thirty-eight acres of untamed farmland on a wild and scenic river; I had regular access to the school library and the county library, not to mention the sizable home library accumulated by six older siblings. When I wasn't out building myself little forts in the forest, I could usually be found curled up with a book or cleaning a fish tank. There were far, far better things than TV. In this, I concur with my parents, both then and now.

One of the lesser ways in which my childhood was unusual: my parents acquiesced, when I was quite young, to my sister Nancy's demand for a vegetarian diet. Now, I can never remember steak being served in that house (except minute steak); that sort of food was much too extravagant for them. Hamburgers, sometimes, or bacon; pork chops, once or twice a year. Mostly, it was macaroni and cheese, tuna casserole, lots of salads and vegetables. It fails the "white trash cooking" test largely by virtue of the fact that junk food was not allowed in the house. The macaroni and cheese was not from a Kraft™ box. We always had a garden; Mom canned lots of beans and tomatoes and fruits. And of course, every July and August, we ate blackberries in every conceivable dish. In southern Oregon, you can't beat the berries (they're like kudzu), so you have to take advantage of them. Occasionally, one of us would get butch with a fishing pole, and we'd have fresh fish. I made that mistake once. Dad said, "You caught it; you clean it." Yeccch! It was a bullhead catfish, and it kept staring at me long after it was decapitated and eviscerated. It made my flesh crawl.

Okay, so growing up vegetarian in the 1960s is not exactly shocking, but for that locale, it was fairly unusual. As a result, I've never felt much need for meat in my life (except, of course, trouser trout).

One more tidbit about my family life that always gets lots of attention: I had (have) twin brothers, David Alexander and Donald Fredrick. They are identical, born precisely four years before me; yet, if one of them were in the room with me, a stranger might ask if we were twins. I was tall for my age; they were short. There was a time during my childhood when I actually weighed more than they did. One night, when I was probably about ten, when we had friends of the family staying with us, and the adults had stayed indoors talking while the kids retired to our sleeping bags, one of the visitors suggested that we all take turns running around the lawn naked. I guess he was as interested in comparing dicks as I was. Alas, it was too dark for me to see much of anything, and they all ran much too fast, as if they didn't really want to be seen. One of our guests made the somewhat indelicate observation, after we'd all gone on display, that "You've got twice as much dick as they do. Maybe since they were twins, they had to share it!" I've never been altogether sure, but I probably had a hard-on at the time, which would explain the comment. I know I found it immensely exciting to run naked around the yard, showing off to the other boys. Funny: I still do.

The only other opportunity for such shenanigans came on Boy Scout camping trips. Now, I was never much of a Scout; I don't think I ever earned a single merit badge. But since my mom was the Cub Scout den mother, my dad was the scoutmaster, and Dave and Don were both Eagle Scouts by the time they were twelve, I went along on every scouting event, willy-nilly. I didn't mind. Oh, I wasn't a very butch camper, but I did like building campfires. I vividly remember the camp out where some of the guys were sitting around the fire late at night, and they started daring each other to strip, run down to the river, and skinnydip. Then, of course, as soon as they were in the water, everyone else would shine flashlights at their crotch–highly homoerotic, in retrospect, but at the time, it was "just kidding around." Is the simple act of skinnydipping titillating to every child, or just to those raised in homes with ironclad nudity taboos? I remember being achingly, blazingly aroused; when my turn came, although I knew that they'd do something terribly embarrassing to me like hiding my clothes, I'm sure I had a hard-on. That put a damper on things. I guess I made the sexuality of the situation a little too plain. The circle-jerk that I'd been eagerly anticipating never materialized . . . or perhaps it did, later, after I was asleep. That's what I've always suspected, anyway.

A year or so later, on another Boy Scout Jamboree: René Paré, a year younger than me but taller and ever-so-much butcher, cornered me against a tree and started making fun of my sissified ways. I don't remember any of what he said, until he finally challenged me, asking, "Are you gay?" I responded, quite seriously, "I try to stay cheerful, yes." This threw him right off stride; I'm sure he'd been expecting a blanket denial. He ran off telling all the other campers that I was a faggot, and that I'd even admitted to it. Now, I wasn't altogether clear on what I'd admitted to (neither was I quite as innocent as I pretended to be), but I knew that I would be lying if I said "No," and I tried very hard to avoid lying.

Need I add that from that time on, my reputation at school was made?

David and Donald, of course, were my idols. What boy doesn't idolize his older brothers, even if they don't necessarily get along? They shared a bedroom, and as often as I could, I snuck in there to breathe in their aromas. When they started wearing jockstraps in phys ed, I immediately developed a jock fetish. (I remember hearing Don telling Mom that he needed one. I wasn't sure yet what a jock was, I'd only heard the phys ed coach tell us that we didn't need them yet, but the tone of his voice told me that I wanted to know.) Whenever they developed a new hobby (which they usually did in tandem), I tagged along. In one of my first memories (age three or four), I recall collecting insects for a collection just like David and Donald's. They took up photography; I begged and pleaded until my mom gave me a Brownie camera, and I shot endless rolls of bleak, fuzzy photos of snowbirds. When they chose different instruments in the school band, I was eventually faced with a dilemma: trombone or trumpet? I chose trumpet largely because I'd always liked Donald better (the younger twin, he was somehow gentler, softer, more communicative). Finally, I tried, repeatedly but with no success, to emulate their expertise in woodshop.

Everyone wants to know, of course: Did they have sex with each other? Well, I'd like to know, too. Alas, if they did, the world is unlikely to ever know. Today, both are married; both graduated from christian colleges and immediately went off to third world countries to spread the gospel among the heathens . . . in short, even if they'd fucked each other nightly for ten years, I suspect they would both have thoroughly repressed the memory by now. I will admit to having occasional fantasies about them; the last time I saw David (about five years ago), his formerly dark hair had turned mostly grey, and he was a stunning specimen. No "married flab" for that boy. He'd been doing construction work–hands-on construction work–for the past decade, and had a body that finally made me understand the appeal of incest.

All that aside, I hear you asking, "How could identical twins, boys who shared *everything* in their lives, boys who slept in the same room, who went through puberty simultaneously–how could they *not* have sex, whether or not they ended up gay?" Surely they jerked off. Surely they talked about it. It makes me wish I were one of them. Oh, to know what the experience of being a twin is really like! Maybe someday I can convince them to let me ghostwrite a book for them. With just a few slightly salacious segments, it would sell like hotcakes to gay men. I'd title it *The Testicle Twins*.

Having three children's birthdays on the same day could be seen as convenient for parents, but it left us feeling a little cheated, I think. We alternated years; one year DaveyDonny (for most practical purposes, they were one person) would choose the party venue, and the next year I'd get to choose it. I don't vividly remember many of my birthday parties; like xmas, they always struck me as a little suspicious. "You vill haf fun now, ja? Or ve vill make you verrrry sorry!" But there are two years that stand out. I'm guessing they were my ninth and tenth birthdays. For one of them, I asked to have the party at our local roller rink. It was lots of fun. For once, I really enjoyed myself. Until I fell down and broke my arm. I spent about thirty minutes pretending I was okay (who wants to be taken away from their birthday party to go to the hospital?), but when it came time to cut the cake and I couldn't hold the knife, they knew something was up. It wasn't a terribly serious break–I think I only spent six weeks in a cast–but it was memorable.

The next year, we went to a football game. Thrilling, huh? Davey-Donny were, of course, playing in the band. I don't think I'd ever been to a football game before (and I haven't been to one since, and goddess willing, I can die without going to another), and it all seemed very exotic and mysterious. I spent a lot of the time running around in the passageways underneath the stadium, hanging out in the men's room. No, I didn't know why I liked the place; I just did. It had a wonderful subterranean feel to it. I've always liked basements and tunnels...and urinals.

The memorable parts of the evening were before and after the football game. We opened our presents before we left; the gift that thrilled me the most was my very own instamatic camera (a cheap one, but hey, it was a step up from the Brownie). I took an entire roll of photos that night at the football game. What didn't excite me too much at the time, but in retrospect gives me a shiver of anticipation, was Claudia's gift: *Old Possum's Book of Practical Cats* and *The Red Badge of Courage*. I never grew too fond of the latter, but the former became one of my most beloved books. I was greatly offended, fifteen years later, when someone stole "my" book for a popular musical. Up to that point, it took a special sort of person to know who Skimbleshanks was. Now, about forty million people have seen him onstage. It robs me of my sense of exclusivity.

After the game . . . well, it's hard to say why this sticks in my memory. We came home; I continued to snap photos of everyone, and we started eating. "Foodwalks," as Nancy called them, were not uncommon in our household, especially late at night; the only reason this one stands out is that it was documented on film. Everyone would grab something from the refrigerator–yogurt, veggies, cold cereal, sandwich fixings, donuts–and eat while walking around the kitchen table. If this sounds ritualized, it wasn't; it was perfect chaos, with everyone grabbing bites of everyone else's food. It stands out as one of the few "family" activities that I really enjoyed. Coincidentally, these foodwalks only took place after my parents were in bed, so "family" usually consisted of Nancy, Patty, Davey-Donny, and me.

When I was fourteen, I began to seriously rebel. I guess this is the one aspect of my life that was absolutely typical–though most of my siblings displayed remarkably low Rebellion Quotients. One of the first ways in which I tried to escape the Family Values ethos, of course, was to spend as little time with them as possible. I began bicycling to school instead of taking the bus, because it meant I could stay after school and study in the library (And yes, I did some studying; mostly I went into the private study rooms and jacked off, though). The librarians loved me because I was a model student, and they'd just close up around me, saying, "You know where the light switch is." Eventually, through means that were certainly unethical and quite possibly illegal, I acquired a complete set of keys to the school, and began altering my schedule. Instead of staying after school, I'd rush right home and go straight to bed–thus avoiding dinner with the family, a truly deadly affair. I'd wake up at midnight, make myself a meal, then hop on my bicycle and head for school. I'd let myself in, and spend the next six hours "studying." One night, just to satisfy my curiosity, I spent several hours roaming the unfamiliar portions of the school: locker room, woodshop, and (holy of holies, territory which I had never before penetrated) autoshop. I was strongly tempted to scrawl in the dust on one of the old autobodies, "Scott Was Here" or some such, but I refrained.

More than once, during this period, I slept at school, curled up in one of the practice rooms. Anything to avoid contact with the despised family.

It didn't take them long to catch on to this new routine. Within a month, I began encountering family members "accidentally" in the kitchen at 1 a.m.–mostly Dad, but sometimes David or Donald. They'd try to engage me in conversation; I'd sulk. I felt like I was being spied upon, and it enraged me. I took to leaving my room by the window, so I wouldn't have to run the gauntlet of the kitchen. They obviously disapproved, but since my bizarre schedule was all in the interest of academic advancement, they couldn't say much.

Does all of this sound like a comic opera, or perhaps an Italian farce?

There was only one further element to complete my rebellion, and my mother unwittingly provided it. She issued an ultimatum: I *would* attend church every Sunday, as long as I lived in their house.

I have to backtrack a bit, here. Yes, for most of my childhood, my parents were good Presbyterians. Go to church on Sunday, tithe, live modestly . . . and that's all. Potlucks once a month. I don't recall ever having the slightest flicker of belief in a deity. Yes, I loved reading those *Bible Story* books, but mostly so that I could stare, enrapt, at the beautiful illustrations of Samson bringing down the temple and Jacob wrestling with the angel. But when I was ten, there was a schism in our local church, caused by a reform-minded pastor; my parents were among the disenchanted. They spent the next year shopping around for a new church, during which time they did not insist that I join them. By the time they joined the Free Methodists (the most conservative church available in Grants Pass, hangout of most of the John Birch Society members), my independence had been established. I went with them once or twice, but after that I refused. For the next four years, until my mother's ultimatum, I had Sundays all to myself. I'd usually spend them in prolonged jack-off sessions–in the living room, in the kitchen, often outdoors; sometimes I'd sunbathe naked on the lawn. Oh, joy! Later, I learned to bicycle into town and cruise the library tearoom. This gave me the added benefit of being able to spend time around my best friend Shawn Gibbs, who had a part-time job at the library.

So when my mom laid down the law, inspiration struck. She hadn't, after all, specified a particular church . . . and Shawn's family were Jehovah's Witnesses. I was sure they'd welcome a young convert.

My mother was suitably appalled, but said nothing.

For the next year, I went with the Gibbs to Kingdom Hall. I learned all the Witness's quaint habits and beliefs, and pretended, like the wide-eyed innocent I wasn't quite, to swallow them. Then, after the state convention, Mrs. Gibbs started making noises that it was time for me to be baptized. I agreed wholeheartedly, hoping that it would give my mother a coronary. That's the point at which Shawn had an unexpected attack of morals.

Well, not morals, exactly. Pragmatism is more like it. He had just heard the news from another of his friends that I was queer. This was not news to Shawn; we'd talked about it rather intensively over the past two years, and he had no problem with it. But he suddenly realized that if I became widely known as a queer . . . and he was widely known to spend a lot of time with me . . . well, it wouldn't look good for him. So he made a preemptive strike: he told his mom what his friend had told him. She asked me if it were true; I gladly admitted it, and the next weekend I was officially disfellowshipped. This is a JW term; it means that you are anathema, that no member of the church is allowed to speak to you.

I was heartsick. Shawn was my major support system, and, well, a major crush, too. (He had the cutest way of blushing deep, deep red whenever I'd tell him he had a nice ass.) But I quickly rebounded: I asked Mike King, one of my secondary crushes, what that medal around his neck was. "A St. Anthony medal," he said. Aha! Catholic. Okay, I thought, I'll give Rome a try. I quickly read *The Cardinal* for some background, and bicycled into town on three successive Sundays for 10 o'clock mass. (Mrs. Gibbs had been in the habit of picking me up at home, since she thought it was inappropriate for me to show up all sweaty.) I never saw Mike. Maybe he attended a different Mass, maybe he didn't go at all. Catholics are notoriously careless about that, I've learned. I quickly lost interest.

Fortunately, my classmate Doug quickly jumped into the breach, with an invitation to join him. Now, Doug was serious about his religion, unlike Shawn and Mike. He also knew I was gay (as did everyone at school by this time),* but thought that Jesus could save me. He was Born Again, charismatically; at his church, they talked in tongues. I viewed it as a test of my acting abilities, and was jabbering away with the best of them inside of two months. It was fun. But what really "converted" me, naturally, was the youth group. Particularly Les. And, later, Don. I joined Bible Bowl, their version of College Bowl. Teams from around the country compete to see who had the most encyclopedic grasp of one particular book of the Bible. That year it was John. We did okay, had a lot of fun, and we got to go on a lot of overnight trips, staying in college dormitories. No sexual adventures, alas. I also joined the choir, and started going to Wednesday night services. In other words, I'd found a very effective way of staying away from my family, four nights a week.

The First Assembly of God church (the acronym was the other reason I chose them) was about twelve miles from home. Summer evenings, instead of riding home, I'd often sneak into the meeting hall, grab something from the fridge, and curl up on the floor. Until,

---

*Had word gotten back to my parents? Frankly, I don't know. They had strong suspicions and lots of evidence, but I wasn't about to discuss it with them.

of course, one night my parents missed me, and called the pastor, who came down to the church . . . it wasn't pretty. The church elders were unamused.

They were even less pleased about six months later, when Doug had the same attack of morals that Shawn had suffered. Doug had been having progressively more serious doubts about my commitment to overcoming my affliction; when I let slip an incautious word about my intentions toward Les and Don, his moral fire alarm went off. I was asked to a counseling session with the pastor the next week. "Is it true that you're a homosexual?" "Yes." "Will you join me in prayer to ask Jesus Christ to cast out this demon?" "No." "Don't slam the door as you leave." And that was that.

I was over religion by this time, and I think my mom had learned her lesson too. She didn't insist that I find another church. I only had a few months left before graduation, anyway. I spent the evenings at rehearsals for a community theater production of *Bells Are Ringing*.

I made reference, some pages back, to my father's belief in flying saucers. This was kind of a running joke in our house, always treated very seriously but never really taken seriously. I don't think my mother ever shared his beliefs; she probably thought they were sacrilegious. But like any "successful" (i.e., long-running) marriage, there were areas of disagreement that were tacitly off-limits to discussion, and this was one of them. Dad wouldn't talk about saucers in front of Mom, but with just the kids around, he could go on for hours—where the saucers came from (from inside the earth, which was hollow; the ports of entry were the North Pole and the caverns on Mount Shasta), how they were powered (he'd mail-ordered, sometime in my very early childhood, detailed plans for building a "whoosher," as he called it, powered by the earth's magnetic field, capable of traveling thousands of miles per hour and landing in a backyard; he's never made any serious progress on building it), what their motivations were (benevolent), and even their religion. He had a book, about six inches thick, with a very odd name: *Ouishy*, or *Ouadji*, or some such. It was essentially a bible, describing these beings and their philosophy. He would read this book in his leisure time when Mom wasn't around, but I doubt that he ever finished it. My father was intelligent and well educated, but he wasn't a fast reader. His eyesight was also poor; he really needed reading glasses, but he refused to get them.

This was due to his distrust of doctors. I don't think he ever saw a dentist. (This is an area in which I've inherited my father's skepticism. I have about as much faith in the medical profession as I do in god.) Whenever he had medical problems, he preferred to visit a long series of quacks . . . pardon me, alternative therapists. I can recall being taken to a man who tried to correct the shape and/or arrangement of my sinuses by inserting balloons into them and inflating them. As the years have gone on, the infrequent letters from my father have grown increasingly predictable; he spends a couple of paragraphs telling me about the status of the whoosher project, then a few notes from around the farm (we've got three new doe kids; Don is cultivating the back forty; Tanya just got married), then he'll mention his health problems and what he's doing for them. Hyperoxygenation, hydrogen peroxide, electromagnetic fields, sleeping under a pyramid, and a myriad of other miracle cures have been mentioned in his letters. Since I told him I had AIDS, in 1988, he's described most of these treatments as potential AIDS cures. I remind myself, reading these sections, that I've visited my share of quacks too. I share his dislike for medicine, but his choices don't seem to be much better.

The most recent letter I received took on a somewhat pitiful tone: he described how his hips were no longer able to support him, so he can only get around with crutches. He describes hip replacement surgery as "invasive," and refuses to have it done. My emotions, upon reading this letter, were mixed: pain, at thinking of my father, that man I admire, hobbling around on crutches; and pride, knowing that maintaining his independence means more to him than anything else. I think I inherited that trait from him. Or maybe it's just a male thing.

My father's resistance to doctors can't be blamed on simple cheapness, either. Oh, he occasionally uses that excuse, but the fact is, when he really wants something, he buys it. He just doesn't allow himself to want things very often. I recall being so proud, as a ten-year-old, when he brought home a pair of Mercedes sedans. ("I got a better deal on the pair.") They were '56 and '57, very unfashionable years in the early 1970s, so they were dirt cheap, but I was ecstatic. Leather upholstery! Walnut burl instrument panels! Wow!

None of the other family cars even approached them for luxury. Whenever we were going into town, I always asked if we could drive them.

Perhaps he only bought them because he saw them as orphans. He always had a thing for unpopular cars. He still has the rusting hulks of six Nashes from the early 1950s and the slightly more preserved bodies of several early Corvairs. (The last time I visited, one of the Corvairs was actually running, courtesy of brother Don.) Sometime after I left home, just to complete the collection, Dad started acquiring Studebakers, much to my mother's displeasure. That's the disadvantage of having thirty-eight acres and a barn: there's very little incentive to get rid of things. Easier to just store them. I once counted twenty-eight cars around the place–twenty-five of them nonfunctional.

The previous description may lead some of you to think that my father was certifiably insane, really Looney Tunes. And yes, it's clear that he did not live entirely in the real world, but I maintain that he was one of the sanest people I've known. He was always a gentle man, as well as a gentleman; I never saw him lift his hand in anger, and virtually the only time he raised his voice was when he was delivering a polemic against government intrusion (usually by the IRS) into his life. It took me a number of years to realize it, but I admire him wholeheartedly. The only area of his life that seems crazy to me is his (to date) fifty-year marriage to my mother. Why anyone would want to stay married to that frozen mackerel is quite beyond me. I've never seen any sign of love, or even affection, between them. In my opinion, he took those marriage vows a little too seriously. But I guess I shouldn't complain; if they'd divorced when I was a kid, my mom would certainly have gotten custody, and I would have been forced into matricide.

I've been distracted, I fear. I was discussing my father. His history: a father who had extremely puritanical notions about life (a photo of Granddad, hand on Bible, staring belligerently at the camera like Jehovah, still sits in my parents' living room); an older brother who had four kids and then, shockingly, got a divorce once they were grown; a childhood spent in Pittsburgh, moving to Orange County, California, in the early 1930s when it was still all orange groves. He worked at the post office in his twenties, went into the military during WWII (he served as a dental assistant on some remote Pacific island), and then retired to raise kids upon receiving his grandfather's inheritance. By the time I was born, there were only two surviving members of the preceding generation: his father, who died when I was about ten, and Aunt Marian, whose actual relationship to me was unclear (my grandfather's cousin's half-sister, or something). Marian fascinated me. First, she lived the sybaritic lifestyle that my parents shunned: she had a house in Palm Springs and condos in San Francisco and New York City, and spent half her time traveling around the world. Second, she was the only woman of her age I'd ever met who had remained unmarried. She had, however, had a "female companion" for the past forty years or so. I was intrigued. My mother tried hard to hide her disapproval, but it was patent in her voice whenever Marian's name was raised.

I only saw Marian three times: once at the farm, once in San Francisco, and once in Palm Springs. They're three vivid memories. She played Bridge-It with me, one of my favorite games; and on the visit to the farm, we picked cherries together. And then . . . she disappeared. No more contact. For years, I asked my various relatives if they knew her present whereabouts; none of them admitted to it. David once went to visit her when he was in college and writing a term paper on our family's history. Since Marian wasn't at home, he knocked on her neighbor's door and asked them some questions. When Marian found out about this, she was furious, and wrote my father a scathing note telling him not to send his brats around "snooping" into her life. Hence, I've always been somewhat reluctant to look her up. She's not listed in the Palm Springs directory—not that that means anything. I assume she's no longer alive (I guess she'd be over a hundred years old by now), but I wish I could find out for sure.

As for Mom—well, I'm afraid I can't enlighten you very much. I never learned very much about her background; I never felt the slightest friendship or love for her. Sometime in the 1980s when I was visiting my parents, I recall her anguished question to me: "What happened between us? We used to be so close!" I was speechless; I couldn't believe she was serious. Different worlds, I swear.

Let me move on to brother Jim. James Wilbur Thompson, that is. Twelve years my senior, I didn't see much of him in my childhood;

he got married to Glenna before they were out of high school (I was the ring bearer), then they joined the Peace Corps and went off to Jamaica. About five years later, they had their first kid, Ciara. That name amazed me; it demonstrated that there really was a spark of imagination somewhere in the family. Another five years, and Glenna finally got pregnant again. Twin boys, this time: Stanley and Steven Lee. I've never seen them, or even photos of them.

As I said, I didn't have much contact with Jim. He was a puritanical prude who reminded me of that photo of my grandfather. I never really trusted him. The last time I saw him was at a family reunion in 1985 or so. I was already in porn, and proudly defending it to anyone who would listen. The family didn't quite know how to react. I also admitted, when asked, that yes, I occasionally used drugs. (The ironic thing is that by that time, I'd given up drugs; I continued defending them merely on principle, as I still do.) This engendered what was probably the most heated discussion over Sunday dinner that's ever been heard in that house. By the end of the meal, I was overdosed on togetherness; I wandered into the living room, alone, figuring no one would really want to join me. Ciara followed me. At ten years old, she was quite capable of saying what her elders were restraining themselves from saying. "My mommy and daddy say that you're a sinner, and that unless you accept Jesus Christ as your personal savior, you're going to burn in hell." She said this in a tone of deepest concern.

I saw red. I mean, this business of child indoctrination is one of the things that makes me most certain that the traditional family is a mistake. It also makes me want to start haunting schoolyards, to open those poor kids' eyes. I thought for a moment, remembering the curious acoustics of this house (virtually any noise in the living room can be clearly heard in the kitchen), and said, loudly and distinctly, "Well, Ciara, that's because your mommy and daddy are fools. Someday, when you're older, you'll know better." After that, I walked back out into the dead silence of the kitchen. Glenna looked over at me, anger pinching her face, and said sweetly, "Beaten by a ten-year-old, Scott?"

Given all of this, you understand my glee when, a couple of years back, I was informed by my cousin Bill that Jim and Glenna were getting a divorce. Oh, scandal! Oh, tragedy! Oh (giggle, giggle) horror! Naturally, I never learned the details. I like to fantasize that Glenna caught him in bed with a man. Doesn't seem altogether unlikely. These repressed types, you know? I also have occasional fantasies about looking up Steven and Stanley after they've gone off to college in 1998. Given the ignorance of their parents, I'm sure they'll be in need of a *real* education.

Next on the list is Patty. Patricia Louise. She's the one I always hated. Seven years older than I, she often got baby-sitting duty when I was growing up, and she resented it. Nevertheless, there was a time beyond memory when I must have had some fondness for her; when I was three or four, my first christmas memory is of giving her a present. My first christmas present. Of course I didn't have any money, and I hadn't yet quite grasped the true spirit of christmas; I just gave her the most valuable thing I owned. Valuable to me, that is. My insect collection, which I'd spent all summer collecting. Of course, they weren't pinned to a board or anything, just dumped together in a box with cotton batting, and none of them looked very stunning. I wrapped it carefully, and didn't let anyone know it was from me. Patty opened it, shrieked with disgust, and ran outside and dumped them out in the snow. I burst into tears and ran bawling to my room, refusing to come out for the rest of the day, even for christmas dinner. Eventually, Patty came knocking at my door. Apparently, my parents had made her go out and collect the bugs, and she brought them back to me and apologized. I told her I forgave her. I lied. I never have. She never forgave me, either.

And that's my first christmas memory. Is it any wonder I don't much like the holiday?

As I grew older, Patty continued to torture me at every opportunity. I vividly remember another occasion, just a couple years later. I was supposed to bring in the newspaper every afternoon; sometimes I forgot, and had to be reminded. I sometimes balked, if it was after dark, since it was a 200-yard walk to the mailbox, unlighted, and I was terrified of the dark. Everyone knew how scaredy-cat I was, of course, and mostly they treated my phobia with respect–but they still made me go get the paper. Children need to be forced to *face* their fears, you know? One night in particular, I don't know why, I was especially scared. I crept along the driveway, trying not to alert the monsters to my presence, heart beating violently. I still occasionally get these terrors when I'm alone in a dark house at night; now, however, I mostly associate them with an excess of caffeine during the day.

I made it safely to the mailbox, picked up the paper, and was trying to calm myself on the return journey, deliberately slowing my breathing, walking slowly and carefully . . . when a monster leapt at me out of the hedge beside the driveway, making horrible sounds. I dropped the paper and ran, screaming and sobbing, to the house. Of course, I knew after only a second or two that it was really Patty (I've referred to her ever since as The Monster), but I still couldn't stop bawling and shaking. And yes, my mom scolded her, and made her go pick up the paper, but this was one more brick that I'd like to throw at her.

It wasn't very long after this that Patty started dating. She was enthusiastic about it. She had lots of boyfriends. I remember one in particular: Dick Brainerd. I liked him. He was tall and thin, and good with kids. His father owned the camera shop in town, so I viewed him as "a good catch." Every time he came to pick up Patty, I'd hear his car arrive (his dad's car actually), and I'd wait, poised by the front door, for his footstep on the porch, and then yank open the door just before he could knock. I thought this was funny, somehow. He played along, pretending to be surprised.

My parents saw an opportunity, here, to reconcile Patty and me. Oh, they didn't phrase it thus; they just suggested that I go along on some of Patty and Dick's dates, as chaperone. Patty, obviously, didn't care for this. I think she was already fucking him. (One night, for some reason, he slept in the guest bedroom; I got up for a midnight snack, as I often did, and happened to see Patty slipping silently out. She gave me a black, don't-you-dare-tell-anyone look. I didn't tell, of course, figuring it was better to know and keep quiet. The threat is greater than its execution.) I went to several drive-in movies with them and on a couple of hikes up the Rogue River. It didn't do anything to improve relations between me and my sister, but I loved spending time with Dick. (In some ways, nothing's changed . . .)

I don't remember who came after Dick—a long string of unmemorable boyfriends. I was getting old enough to have a life of my own and didn't have to depend on her for fantasy boyfriends. That's the point when Nancy met Steve, too. More about that later.

I don't remember where Patty met Larry Small, but he was the final boyfriend. Shortly thereafter, they got married. No, she didn't have a child six months later, but I think it's entirely possible she had an abortion. She never really had any respect for my parents' religious convictions.

Larry never appealed to me. Oh, not unattractive, but not very interesting. So when, a couple years after their marriage, I began to notice that he'd developed very conservative religious tendencies (for instance, he wanted to go off to darkest Africa to save the heathens), I could do nothing but giggle. I felt like Patty had got what was coming to her. With her first pregnancy, she was forced to give up her Porsche, being no longer able to fit behind the steering wheel. We never talked about it, of course, but I was sure she was chafing under his newfound religion. She eventually had lots of kids (whose names I don't know, and don't want to know), and became a hausfrau.

One final anecdote about Patty, the episode that came this close to throwing the household into civil war: She always had a thing about "etiquette"–table manners, especially. She would comment cuttingly about the fact that I refused to learn to use a knife and fork (I preferred a spoon). One day, when I was fifteen, she was sitting on a stool in the hallway, talking on the phone, with her legs propped up on the opposite wall, when I came tearing down the hall. She didn't move, pretending not to see me. I came to a screeching halt, uncertain of what to do. Considering my intense hatred of her, the thought of begging her to move her feet was unthinkable, and it was obviously precisely what she wanted me to do. So I ducked under her legs. She promptly brought down her legs on top of me, collared me, and began lecturing me on "polite" behavior. I tore myself away from her; I may have slapped her, I don't know. I ducked into my room, which was handy, and tried to close the door, but she was behind me, fuming and raging at me. I sat down and tried to ignore her. She stuck her hand into one of my aquaria and grabbed a fish–as it happened, a fish that had been born in that tank–and held it up to get my attention. That's when I attacked her. I don't remember anything of that fight: I was never much of a fighter, but I know I didn't hold anything back. I wanted to kill her, and I did my best. Other family members eventually pried us apart. She wasn't any worse for wear, but we were both pretty wild-eyed. Mom sent me back into my room while she talked to Patty. A few minutes later, she called me out into the kitchen, where the whole family was gathered. (This, as I mentioned, was a nonviolent family. I don't think there had been a physical fight amongst us in my lifetime. This was a serious matter.) Mom didn't ask for any explanations; she ordered me, "Apologize to Patty." I said, "No." Saying "No" to a parent was pretty unthinkable in their world, too; she looked outraged, and slapped me. Not too hard, but enough to let me know she meant business. I waited a second, and then slapped her back, trying to give it exactly the same force. The entire family jumped two feet closer to us, since I'd clearly lost my mind, but nothing else happened. Everyone stayed silent for a few seconds. Then Mom, with pursed lips, said, "Well, you're certainly not going to France, then."

This was her trump card. For the past few months, she'd been using it, anytime she wanted me to do anything: "If you really wanted to go to France, you'd do the dishes"; "If you really wanted to go to France, you'd show up for dinner on time," etc. I was getting heartily sick of it, and even regretting that I'd ever made it obvious to her how important that summer trip was to me. (It was supposed to be nothing less than my liberation, my deflowering, my blossoming; it didn't quite turn out that way, but at the time I was still fantasizing.) So, I'd put myself into this situation, where I was being blackmailed with the one thing that was most important to me right then . . . the thought of having to spend the entire summer with my family flashed through my head, and I blanched with horror. I swallowed my pride (temporarily, I assured myself: I'll get her yet, preferably when she's asleep) and turned to Patty and said, "I'm sorry if I was rude." She said something similar to me, and the whole family relaxed and went back to pretending that we were happy and loving and there was no such thing as murderous thoughts blazing in our minds. I went to France that summer–but that's another story.

And now we come to Nancy, saved for last because she was the best. (Claudia, the eldest, is talked about at length elsewhere in the book.) Nancy was just a year older than Patty; she shared babysitting duties, but unlike Patty, she seemed to love it. She read us

The Once and Future King; she played all the Gilbert and Sullivan operettas, and we'd all sing along on the patter-songs. Sometimes she'd take us on long excursions up into the mountains. I loved her, and thought she was the most beautiful girl in the world. Later, I learned that by contemporary standards of femininity, she wasn't particularly attractive. I've never understood those standards.

When I was in fourth grade, Nancy got a fish tank, and I was immediately enchanted. I tried to spend all my time in her room (a fancifully decorated room, with a gorgeous flower-patterned curtain dividing it: one side of the room painted chartreuse, the other side sky blue), I got her to let me do some of the aquarium maintenance, and eventually, when her collection had grown to three tanks but her enthusiasm had waned, she gave me one of them. (By the time I graduated from high school, I had seventeen of them.)

That was the summer she went off to summer school at UCLA. Or was it USC? I'll never know. She was taking classes in modern dance. She'd gone through the local possibilities, and wanted more professional instruction. Besides, one of her fellow students at the community college was a boy named Steve Eissinger, and he was going down to the summer session, and she wanted to spend the summer with him.

As did I. Steve was stocky, dark, extremely muscular, with a furry chest and heavy eyebrows; his almost-black hair was long and wavy. He looked fabulous when he danced, sweat flying everywhere. He loved spending time around me, too. I'd help him wash their car (he and Nancy had bought a VW bus together, to drive down to L.A.; they painted it with flowers, and named it Positively), he would spray me with water, and we'd sort of wrestle in the back of the van, and get all sweaty, and I'd get light-headed from the smell of his armpits . . . no, we never actually "did it." I knew I wanted him, in lots of ways, but I didn't know quite what those ways were, yet. I think I was ten years old. He gave me what he called "wet, sloppy kisses" whenever we met–and somehow, I thought they were nothing more than friendly hugs. But I liked them... a lot. No one in our family had ever been affectionate with me that way, and I was starved for it.

So they drove down to L.A., leaving me in charge of Nancy's fish tanks. That meant that I spent several hours every day in her room, reading her books: *Everything You Always Wanted To Know About Sex, The Naked Ape, King Solomon's Ring, Seven Arrows*. It's funny, but I don't recall being shocked or even surprised by anything I read there; I viewed them basically as pornography, and jerked off endlessly to the clinical description of sex in *The Naked Ape*. I also read Nancy's letters to Patty, on one occasion when Patty was away from the house for a couple of days. I don't remember much of what was written, but Nancy wrote that she had gotten a prescription for a diaphragm. Steve was fucking her! Talk about a thrilling revelation. I started imagining the scene . . . not her, specifically, but Steve fucking . . . someone . . . okay, I guess you could say this was my first big crush.

Toward the end of the summer, Nancy suggested to Mom that I come down to L.A. for a week and stay with her. I was thrilled. We'd been exchanging letters weekly; occasionally, Steve would add a PS, and he'd always send "wet, sloppy kisses." I was gonna get to spend a week in a small apartment with them! Maybe I'd get to hear their bed squeaking as they fucked! Yes, I was excited.

Oddly enough, I don't remember anything of that week. Oh, I remember being taken around to all the tropical fish stores in the area; I remember seeing my first cockroach, in their Venice Beach apartment (I was horrified), but I don't think Steve and I interacted in any meaningful way.

Sometime shortly after that, Steve and Nancy broke up. I was heartbroken. I know that my mom had a long, knife-to-heart talk with Nancy about how mixed marriages never work (was he Jewish? I always assumed he was a pagan/atheist, just because of his pure animalistic sensuality, but I really don't know), in which she all but forbade the proposed marriage. I know that they'd taken a trip to visit my sister Claudia in Chicago, and Steve had stopped off in Mankato to visit his family . . . and he never returned.

Nancy didn't stay single long. Within the year, she'd met and married a man named Bill Eicher. Now, this was a man I truly disliked. A tall, thin, awkward man with no sense of humor–exactly the opposite of Steve. This man had no redeeming characteristics at all, in fact. I have no idea what brought them together. But shortly after they met, they started taking church seriously, and within a couple of years, they were hosanna-ing with the rest of the family.

Nancy started popping out kids, and stopped smiling. The last few times I saw her, she'd completely lost whatever spark it was that I used to love in her. She looked dead. I mourn her loss. She could've been fabulous.

I moved away from the family farm immediately after high school graduation (which I refused to attend, merely because I knew that seeing me graduate would give my parents pleasure), and haven't spent any significant chunk of time there since. I've dropped in for a visit nearly every year, up to 1992; most of them have been just a quick lunch, a walk around the place to see what buildings have fallen down, what cars have been added to the collection, and then outta there. There's always a short heart-to-heart with my dad; he tries to say something along the lines of "But aren't you worried about the life to come?" but I don't think he really means it, he just thinks he has a responsibility to try to convert me. One time he shocked me by taking me over to a neighbor's house, a widower of Dad's age who was a raving atheist and who had a cellar full of homemade plum wine. Dad actually drank some! I'd never seen him touch alcohol before. Apparently, he and this neighbor made a habit of getting together and arguing and drinking . . . all of which was kept a secret from my mom, of course.

When I talk about this family, I often feel like I'm contradicting myself. I say that I have nothing in common with them; then I praise them for having raised me without television. I say that I detest their Family Values, but the most basic of their values is simple Integrity, a characteristic that I feel is far too rare these days. I say that I wish they would just forget about me (and I've done my best to disappear from their landscape), but I am aware that my father's respect means (would mean) a great deal to me. Does he respect me and the choices I've made with my life? I don't know. It's not a question you can ask, at least not in my family.

Chrysanthemum Tea

When I was a boy, like most rural-raised boys, I dreamed of living in the city. I would often get presents from my glamorous older sister Claudia, who'd moved first to St. Louis, then Dallas, then–gasp!–Chicago; she was sort of like a fairy godmother to me. I didn't see her except at holidays, but I thought she was wonderful, and therefore, cities must be wonderful. Now, my parents had emigrated from Orange County, California, about a year before I was born, because it was getting too "congested" (remember, 1960–that meant the lots were down to half-acre size, and they were in danger of putting in sidewalks) and crime-ridden. They had no illusions about city life. But whenever we went to visit the cousins, back at the old homestead, or family friends in Portland, I got very excited.

I don't actually remember visiting very many other cities when I was a kid. Most family vacations (and by many people's standards, we were compulsive vacationers) were to places like Yellowstone and Yosemite; when we went to Hawaii, we only spent one night in Honolulu, and the rest of the two weeks on the outlying islands. But I remember stopping in San Francisco, once, to visit Aunt Marian, and being absolutely fascinated with her lifestyle. She had a condo on the nineteenth floor; on the one hand, I envied her view and the worldly amenities of city life, but I think I was also mystified how anyone could live without a garden and a river in their backyard.

Enough background. When I was about eleven years old (I think it was the summer after we'd gone to Hawaii), my mother's family–the Farwells–had a reunion in Kalamazoo, Michigan. My mother decided to go, and invited all of us to join her. I took her up on it for the sole reason that we would be flying into Chicago, where my sister Claudia lived. I really wanted to see Chicago and to see Claudia; this impetus was even enough to make me endure the time I'd have to spend alone with my mom. (I can never remember a time when I felt comfortable around her. She always made me nervous and uptight, largely because I was always aware of her uptightness about anything body-oriented.)

A little more background: Claudia was thirteen years older than I; she'd left for college immediately after graduating as valedictorian of her high school class. She was the oldest child, and she set a high academic standard for the rest of us to equal. I've never regretted having that standard. She'd done five years or so of college, never graduating, changing her major from medicine to literature to whatever—until she finally gave up and moved to Chicago, where she started writing poetry and doing volunteer work at small theaters. At one of those small theaters, I believe, is where she met Stephanie.

Stephanie and Claudia picked us up at the airport. I was enthralled/appalled by Stephanie; I'd never seen a woman so large. Oh, today I see people larger than her everyday, on the bus; it's not that uncommon in any large city. But in rural Oregon, extreme obesity was pretty much unknown. So . . . you might say I was intimidated by her size. (It didn't help that she was about 5′ 5″.) Driving into the city, I was equally fascinated by her driving style (fast, dangerous, and loudly abusive toward the other drivers) and by the city around us. My mother was more furious than fascinated—reason enough for me to like Stephanie instantly. Anything my mother hated . . .

I don't remember much of that visit. I remember Stephanie's apartment: it was, quite frankly, a pigsty. The kitchen floor was sticky and black with old spilled food; I'd never seen such squalor. I remember the el: Stephanie took us on a tour of the city by elevated train, which thrilled me and disgusted my mother. I remember driving out to the northwest suburbs (Skokie?) to visit a couple of fish stores. Stephanie drove us out there (it's funny, but much as I liked Claudia, I don't remember doing anything with her on this trip), and was as enthusiastic as I was. She had a ten-gallon tank of her own in the bathroom, which didn't contain anything interesting, but we'd established a bond of common interest immediately.

And that was Chicago. Claudia came with us to Kalamazoo (which made the drive tolerable), and we reunioned at a house on the lake surrounded by vacation homes. My mental snapshot of the event is of about a dozen long tables set up on a sloping lawn, kids swimming, adults milling about with plates, and endless photo ops of different groupings of relatives–not exactly my scene. After-wards, we visited the local cemetery to see some of our ancestors' graves. I stayed in the car.

About a week after we got home, I got a letter from Stephanie. (She told me, years later, that after my mom and I had left, she'd turned to Claudia and said, "That boy's going to grow up to be one of the great faggots of the world. Someone's got to save him from those people!" Of course, still later in our relationship, I learned that Stephanie valued a good line, a good story, much more highly than accuracy. I suspect that wasn't quite the way it went. But it does make a good story.) The letter talked mostly about fish. It asked my advice ("What does it mean when the catfish has been hanging upside down from the surface for two days?"). It included very childish drawings of some of them. I responded, in laborious detail, of course. She wrote back with more questions. Eventually, other subjects entered our sphere of common interest: French, which I was enthusiastically learning, and my sexuality, which was busting out all over. I don't think Stephanie ever wrote, in her letters, of being a lesbian, but I also know that it wasn't any revelation to me when she asked me in person, a couple years later, if I knew. I said, "Sure, I've always known," and it seemed like I had.

That visit–when Claudia and Stephanie came to the family farm for a week–wasn't particularly memorable for me. Claudia brought me some books, as she always did when she visited, but I don't remember which ones. The only vivid memory I have of the occa-sion is a drive that Stephanie took me on; we went to some scenic spot and talked, which was when she asked me that question. I was a little bit embarrassed, but I think I responded with some ambigu-ous comments that confirmed in her the suspicion that I was gonna be queer. My mother, however, apparently saw their visit as an assault by all the forces of Satan. After just a couple of days, Clau-dia and Stephanie moved to a motel. When they left, Mom's advice to Claudia (again, this is as reported by Stephanie, years later) was, "Next time, if you bring that woman with you, don't bother com-ing." In retrospect, although I have no love for my mother, I find it easier to believe that Stephanie fabricated this line than that my mother would speak it.

Our correspondence continued; it was when I was thirteen, I think (some months after Stephanie and Claudia had finally broken up, and Claudia had moved to Philadelphia to be with her new lover), that I first hinted to Stephanie that I was wondering whether I might be gay. (In fact, I'd reached that conclusion quite definitively about a year before.) She was supportive, of course, and asked me why I thought that. I went into my lusts for the boys in the locker room, and she said, "Yeah, seems likely, but give yourself some time. No one has to make decisions forever and for aye." Good advice. She also advised me to start writing to Claudia, getting her input, which I did, and those letters (which I still have) are extremely precious to me. Claudia, as a poet, had a way with words; she was also a continuous world traveler. She wrote of Notre Dame and British country churches and sent me postcards from various art galleries. Stephanie exposed me to gay life, to the rough, gritty world of the city, and many other things, but it was Claudia who taught me my love of language, and who gave me whatever cultural background I had from those early years. And I loved her handwriting! My father, when he occasionally got letters from her, had to get out a magnifying glass to read it; it was exquisite, but tiny–perfect for postcards.

Throughout the next four years, I wrote to both Stephanie and Claudia about once a week. It was Stephanie who arranged for her friend Douglas to stop by for a visit, on his round-the-country bicycle tour; knowing in advance that he was gay, I jumped on him, and got myself deflowered. About time: I was a very horny fifteen-year-old. Douglas was a very frightened twenty-eight-year-old; my father, after all, was sleeping just a couple of rooms away. Douglas hopped on his bicycle bright and early the next morning, and headed straight for the California border. He told me later that it wasn't until he'd crossed the border that he allowed himself to stop long enough to call Stephanie and ask her why, oh why she'd sicced a horny teenager on him. Of course, I heard this story through the filtering medium of Stephanie's letters, but according to her, the first thing Douglas said was, "You didn't tell me he was so beautiful!" Was I beautiful? If I was, I was totally, naïvely unaware of it. I know that I thought Douglas was the most beautiful man I'd ever seen, and he treated me so gently that he made me cry.

When I graduated from high school and told my parents I was riding my bicycle to college in Dallas, it seemed only natural to me that I should leave immediately, stop over in San Francisco, then head for Chicago to spend a month with Stephanie. No, I didn't quite ride all the way–I took the train across Nevada, and then again across part of the Great Plains–but I hit Chicago rarin' to go.

Nothing had changed at Casa Stephanie. I spent my first week there scrubbing floors, vacuuming, washing dishes, and alphabetizing her record collection. She spent the entire month of August giving me the sexual culture that I'd been missing. The first full day I was there, she took a critical assessment of me, took me down to a trendy salon in Boys' Town, got my hair cut, and bought me a pair of tight khaki shorts that showed off everything I had. That night, she took me to her workplace–she worked as a typesetter–and fabricated an ID card for me which said I was twenty-five years old. Took until about 10 p.m. On the way home, she stopped the car on a dark side street. "See that door over there?" she said, pointing across the street at an isolated, forbidding-looking building. "Get out. Go over there. Go in. You'll like it. Here's my transit pass, so you can get home in the morning. Take the Ravenswood train to the Lawrence stop." Need I mention that this was a gay bar? Probably not. But not just any gay bar; this was the Gold Coast, possibly the most notorious leather bar outside of New York. The habitués, however, didn't seem to mind a bit of chicken wandering through the door. I don't think the bouncer even checked my ID; I guess I had the "right" look. I don't remember the name of the guy I left with that night (it didn't take very long for me to get picked up, I said yes to the first guy who made an offer), but we just went back across the street to a very sleazy fleabag hotel, where he rented a room and fucked me silly. He also introduced me to poppers.

The next night, I was back–and many of the following nights. I tried other leather bars: The Redoubt a couple of times (had less luck there, for some reason), and Touché (more friendly, but less cruisy); and I met a lot of guys, collected a lot of phone numbers. I'm not in touch with any of them today. This was my month to make up for four years of frustrated near-abstinence; I got fucked almost every night, sometimes more than once. And I loved it.

I don't remember much of what we did during the days, that month. Oh, there were a couple of walks along the lakefront; and Stephanie took me to the Art Institute and the zoo, she filled in a few of the major gaps in my cultural heritage by playing some of her records for me: *Mame, Godspell, Gypsy, Candide,* and, most importantly, *Pacific Overtures.* I didn't instantly fall in love with that one (I don't think anyone does), but ultimately, it's had as much influence on my life as any musical I've heard since. Okay, I'd already heard "Send in the Clowns" about a million times in the previous year, as had everyone in the country, but aside from that, I think *Pacific Overtures* was my first Sondheim. That's a crucial turning point in anyone's cultural education.

When I left for Dallas, toward the end of August, I felt (and looked) like a new man.

School had been, up to that point, my main social outlet. Is that true for every teenager? I'm not sure; most of them claim to despise school. I loved it. I was a straight-A student, always getting academic awards–all without any special effort on my part. I felt more closely allied to all my teachers than to most of my peers. Mr. Weddle, the drama teacher, was my big crush; but Frode Jensen, Gregg Sylvester, Mr. Beaubien, and all the rest–they were my friends. So somehow I expected this to continue at college. Why'd I choose University of Dallas, a Catholic school? Well, I didn't, exactly. They chose me. I wanted to go to Northwestern, but they weren't impressed by my academic record. At least, not enough to give me a scholarship, and my parents had made plain that they'd never pay for my tuition at a hedonistic institution such as that. University of Dallas had a national contest, and I won a half-scholarship, based on an essay I wrote. That, and it was 2,000 miles away from Grants Pass. That was a big consideration, in my mind. My parents wanted me, really, to stay at home and go to community college–a thought which froze my blood. But they couldn't say no to UD.

That first semester at college was relatively quiet. Oh, I got my parents to buy me a motorcycle after a month or so, and after that, I spent a couple nights per week in Oak Lawn, mostly at the two leather bars (I'd bought my first leather jacket when I got the motorcycle). And of course, I wrote long letters to Stephanie about each new sexual discovery, until she eventually got sufficiently annoyed by my one-track mind that she actually asked something along the lines of, "Yes, but what are you studying?"

Maybe a few words are in order, here, about this gravitation to the leather scene. It all seemed completely natural to me at the time, but in the years since, I've come to realize that most gayboys don't come out in a leather bar. Well, I repeat: it was all Stephanie's doing. She was quite the leatherdyke herself, a gender-crossing man-fucking dyke in the days before that subgenre had incorporated itself into "queerdom." She told me a lot of tales about her various boyfriends–her favorite, whom she called "Mr. Savage," was a married Pakistani man who liked being extremely rough with her. I tried to imagine a man (or anyone, for that matter) finding Stephanie physically attractive; it stretched my imagination beyond the limits. Just looking at her stretched-out size sixty-three lace underwear was enough to make me feel slightly nauseous. I wondered whether, even with a ten-inch dick (which she claimed for Mr. Savage), it would be possible to find her cunt through all that extra flesh. Not pleasant thoughts for a fagboy, but it did eventually force me to the realization that everyone has a sex life, even those people who seem totally unsuited for it. That's another lesson that proved useful later in life.

But I digress. Along with Stephanie's stories of her various roughsex boyfriends, she also had quite a stack of *Drummer* magazines at her apartment. When I left for Dallas, she gave them to me, saying that I might be able to learn something from them. I don't recall how much I learned, but I did contact several of the men in the Personals section, one of whom definitely educated me in odd and wonderful ways; so yes, I can credit both Stephanie and *Drummer* with that part of my education. I'll add one more observation about why I liked leather bars: Stephanie did take me to a couple of other bars in Chicago, "sweater bars," where we stood around and talked. I tried, one night, to go to a disco; I was denied entry, presumably because I was wearing polyester pants. In leather bars, I could count on going home with someone and getting fucked. Sometimes, we didn't even have to go home. That made me very happy. I was a boy who knew what I wanted.

My next direct interaction with Stephanie came at christmas of that year. Two days before the holiday, Claudia, in a fit of depression, offed herself. Reasons: a failing relationship with Frances, a recent rejection of her latest manuscript, and a disastrous Thanksgiving dinner at my brother's house, which ended with my parents leaving in a self-righteous huff because they didn't want to be at the same table with a woman "like that." So Claudia couldn't take it any longer. She got herself good and drunk, and then rigged up a hose from the exhaust pipe of her car. I found out on christmas eve; the family gathered in Philadelphia the day after christmas. (Doncha love holidays?) Why? Good question. Because we do odd things when we're crazy with grief. Because we all wanted to see the garage where she did the deed. Because we wanted to see her physical surroundings, her possessions; that's what it takes, sometimes, to convince yourself of the unthinkable. My function: liaison between the family (with whom I still had a tenuous relationship) and Frances, who clearly needed my support.

Fortunately, Claudia had a well-written will. Frances got most everything, I got a smaller share, and Stephanie got the car. (Her response, when informed of this fact on the phone: "Do I get the hose, too?" Such tact.) The rest of the family got nothing. They did the gracious thing, at my insistence, and sent Stephanie a plane ticket so she could join us.

Then there was the trip back to Oregon. Stephanie came with us. (Claudia was finally bringing "that woman" back with her, conditions slightly changed.) The funeral was, well, bleak. I haven't been to another funeral since; I can do without that sort of maudlin moaning. But Stephanie kept her spirits up, and kept me going. Following that, we stopped over in San Francisco for three days of recreation before heading back to our respective cities.

One of the first things Stephanie did in San Francisco was look up her old boss, Jan, who was now doing typesetting for—yes!—*Drummer* magazine. I think they were on Harriet Street at that point. While Stephanie chatted with Jan (who was industriously typing away at her big clunky machine, an early word processor that took up most of the desk), I was watching, fascinated. You see, ever since Stephanie had taken me to that place in Chicago and produced an ID for me, I'd been fascinated with the process of typesetting, layout, and design—the production of printed pages. Before long, Jan noticed my interest, and said, "Here, wanna try?" I sat down at my first computer, and entered several pages of copy for the next issue of *Drummer*. It was very exciting for me.

The rest of that trip, nothing much happened. I saw Douglas, the bicyclist who'd cured my virginity; he broke the news that he had a lover, and broke my heart (it mended, eventually). I then went back to school in Dallas, and over the next five months, slowly went to pieces. I still don't know why. Sure, Claudia's death had something to do with it, and kinky sex gave me a new area of education that I liked a helluva lot more than Philosophy 101. Finally, when one instructor told me (with great relish) that he was gonna flunk me, and the guidance counselor told me that would void my scholarship, I said the hell with it and got on my motorcycle. Two days later, I was back in Chicago at Stephanie's.

There were a lot of people, during the four years after I finished high school, on whom I imposed. I had this habit of showing up on the doorstep of casual acquaintances, friends, tricks, friends of friends, and saying, "Here I am; I'm staying a week (or two)." To their immense credit, none of these people reacted with the outrage that they were, realistically, entitled to express at such chutzpah. But Stephanie was the only one of my friends who was close enough to me that there wasn't really any doubt; I was welcome there anytime, and for any length of time.

After spending June on the road (Philadelphia, Provincetown, Boston, Rochester, Toronto, Stratford, London, and Detroit), I landed back in Chicago "for good." I moved in with Stephanie, got a job at a messenger service, and started going to the baths regularly, whenever she had Mr. Savage or another of her boyfriends over. (It's funny, but in all the time I knew Stephanie, although she self-identified as a dyke, Claudia was her only female partner, either brief or long-term.) I helped her tear out a couple of walls in her basement apartment; then, when the space proved to be too small for the two of us, I got another apartment about a mile east of hers (and two blocks east of Manscountry, my favorite baths). And yes, we still spent most of our time together, but this was an attempt at independence, by someone who was starting to feel his personality overwhelmed.

In November, we took a quick trip up to Madison, Wisconsin together. No particular reason; she had a friend up there, I needed a break. We went to Rod's, the main gay bar, which at that time was somewhat leathery, somewhat collegiate. I got picked up by a man in leather who took me home, fisted me, and told me all about his dog, who would've fucked me if he'd been there—a very hot fantasy for me. I had a fabulous time, and told him I wanted to make a return visit, sometime when he had custody of the dog. Unfortunately, I was never able to schedule it.

The next day . . . oh, I don't know what we did. I know we stopped in Milwaukee that evening, and went to a Chinese restaurant. I know that shortly thereafter, I was struck by the worst stomach cramps I've ever had. While Stephanie drove, I lay curled up on the floorboards, whimpering in pain. By the time we got home, they'd subsided somewhat; by morning, when we were able to see a doctor, I was almost back to normal. MSG poisoning was the ruling. And really, don't ask me what the connection was, but it was that day when, on a whim, I suggested to Stephanie that we ought to get married.

Have I not quite conveyed to you the sense of closeness, of camaraderie, that we shared, which made this suggestion seem perfectly logical? Perhaps subsequent events make it difficult for me to describe her in sympathetic terms. But it's true that at the time, we were best buddies, pals, "life-partners"—we did everything together except have sex, and we shared a similar sense of camp, and that seemed as good a basis for marriage as anything straight society could invent. Somehow, I thought it would be good for me, tax-wise (it wasn't). I also had fears, given my family's fanaticism, of what would happen to me should I become incapacitated, and they were to take charge of me. Those "deprogramming" "ex-gay" ministries were starting to make news at the time.

Stephanie agreed instantly, and we went directly down to City Hall and got a marriage license. Along the way, we stopped at a pet store and bought a dog collar, which she asked me to put on her at the conclusion of the ceremony, in lieu of a ring.

It was some weeks before we told anyone about this new development. My parents, of course, had mixed feelings about it, but once again, they did the "right" thing and invited us both home for Christmas. We went. They showered us with wedding gifts—nothing too expensive, but enough to make me feel embarrassed. (Really, I

mean, it's not as if we took this marriage seriously or anything . . .)
What Stephanie felt, I have no idea. Since she ended up with most of
the loot, she was probably gloating.

Once again, we stopped over in San Francisco on our way home
to Chicago. (Hey, it's the easiest air connection from Medford.) I
promptly stepped out to the baths, and broke my foot in a pitch-dark
orgy room, and had to have a knee-high cast. Stephanie tended me,
to the extent that she was a tender, for the next month; I wasn't quite
bedbound, but the icy streets of Chicago clearly weren't safe for me
on crutches. (Tony, my then-current romantic liaison, brought me a
dozen red roses; I was touched.) In February, with the first thaw, I
ripped off the remaining shreds of cast and got on my motorcycle
again. I immediately made plans (with Stephanie's full consent and
cooperation) to move to San Diego, a place where the sidewalks
don't get icy in winter.

This is where it all starts falling apart. Now, Stephanie had taken
the Motorcycle Safety Training course with me the previous summer, and she'd ridden a little bit around town, but she'd never been
out on a long road trip. Yet somehow—possibly just because I
thought she was omnipotent—it hadn't occurred to me that this
would be a problem. I mean, I'd ridden all over the eastern half of
the United States without any special training; why couldn't she? I'd
be riding my GoldWing; she could ride the smaller Honda CB500T.
What could be simpler? So we had a moving company pick up our
worldly goods, and hit the road.

We only made it to southern Illinois the first day. Stephanie
complained of extreme fatigue, and wanted a hot tub. Seemed silly
to me; I mean, we'd barely ridden 200 miles. The second day, we
did make it to Memphis, which had been my goal for the first day.
You see, I had a boyfriend in Memphis—described elsewhere in this
book—named Marc, with whom I was head over heels in love, and I
wanted to spend some time with him before heading west. Marc
lived with his parents, but he had surreptitiously rented a small,
ramshackle bungalow in the bad part of town as a "trick pad."
Stephanie and I moved in—and two weeks later, after major screaming matches and bitchfights, she moved out, saying, "I'm going
home to mother!" I put her on the bus without any particular regret.
She'd been increasingly jealous and emotional, taking lots of seda-

tives and god knows what other pills, claiming I was abandoning her in a strange town; she even used the word "infidelity" to describe my affair with Marc. Somehow, I never expected to hear anyone apply that word to me; it comes from a worldview that I would rather avoid. But there you are; jealousy can make people do strange things.

After Stephanie went storming back to Chicago, Marc and I lived a life of adulterous bliss for about six more weeks. I sold the smaller bike, and rode the GoldWing back up to Chicago to sell it and try to make peace with Stephanie (I was only partially successful). I then went back down to Memphis, bought an MGB, and drove out to San Francisco with Marc.

When I eventually ransomed the household goods that Stephanie and I had shipped to San Diego, I realized how stupid we'd been. At least three-quarters of it was easily replaceable, and should have been sold. So I had a garage sale–first inviting Stephanie to come out and rescue anything she wanted to keep. My parents even offered to give her a Volkswagen van to drive her things back to Chicago, if she wanted. She did. She felt wounded, betrayed; she spent most of her week-long visit trying to convince me that Marc was only with me for my money, that he was "cheating" on me, and that he was a terrible, evil person. Alas, by the time she huffed back to Chicago (this was August by now), the seeds of doubt were sown; I'd lost my trust. I left for Hawaii in late September, with hardly a word of goodbye to Marc. It was one of the few decisions in my life that I really regret. I did love Marc, and he loved me; the problem, really, was that I didn't have the foggiest notion of how lovers should behave toward each other. After all, the only models we had were heterosexual marriages, most of which would be better models for war games.

I didn't see Stephanie again for almost two years. During the time I lived in Hawaii, we talked occasionally on the phone, and wrote some letters; she never got over her pique, and her letters and her voice took on a whining, wheedling, sometimes psychotic tone: could I send her $200 for the rent, could I buy her a swimsuit (and frankly, even though I did buy it for her, the thought of her in a swimsuit gave me nightmares), why didn't I ever come to visit, didn't I love her anymore? I learned, later, that she'd made many of the same appeals to my family, and they'd established a monthly stipend for her.

When I moved back to the mainland, in February of 1983, I went to visit her. She was living pretty well, it seemed to me, although her car had been impounded for parking in front of a fire hydrant on the night when the adjacent building burned down; the city had even threatened her with "accessory to manslaughter" charges, but never followed through. I stayed for a few days; our relations were cordial. She was working as a switchboard operator now, with a regular schedule, and still using antidepressants. I somehow didn't expect to see her again when I left, but I did, that summer, when I was visiting my parents, and my father insisted on flying her out, hoping for a reconciliation. (Although my parents didn't really approve of her, we were married, by gum, and it was up to them to make sure we stayed married.) It wasn't a pretty visit. She cried a lot, I was silent a lot. That was, in fact, the last time I saw her.

The next fall–well, you remember that fall. That was the year that Ronald Reagan was reelected. I'd exchanged a couple of letters with Stephanie over the previous year, but we'd fallen mostly out of touch (and better that way). After Reagan was reelected, though, I decided I wanted to emigrate to Australia. Safer, I reasoned. Not because of possible nuclear war (though there's that, too), but because of the very real chance of concentration camps for AIDS folk. (No, I didn't yet know I was HIV positive, but I did think it was quite likely. I wasn't about to get tested.) It seemed quite possible, given the Aussies' strict immigration policies, that the only way I'd be able to stay there was by marrying an agreeable female. So . . . it was time for a divorce. (Imagine: me, a thoroughly out and proud gay male, well-documented on video having sex with lots of other men, divorcing his wife in order to marry another woman. Ironic, ain't it?) So I visited an attorney, and advised her of the situation; she thought there would be no problem, given the fact that Stephanie and I hadn't lived together in two years, but I told her I wanted to talk it over with Stephanie first, rather than just having the papers served on her out of the blue. I called up Stephanie, explained the situation to her; she snuffled a bit, and tried to make me feel guiltier, and then said, tearfully, that she still loved me, but she would sign any divorce agreement my lawyer drew up. I was relieved; I told my lawyer to go ahead.

Two days later, I was served with papers. Stephanie had seen her own lawyer, and was asking for half of everything, plus alimony. And since she filed first, her suit had precedence.

Now, there's a reason why I've never written anything about this whole, sordid story. In the gay (and especially lesbian) community, men who whine about the way they've gotten shafted by their ex-wives do not have a very good reputation. The fact is, I've listened to enough divorce stories. The storyteller is never at fault; the ex is always the villain. I don't want to sound like that. And yet, if I write honestly about how I feel about the ensuing two years, that's how it's going to come out. I feel, frankly, that Stephanie agreed to marry me with strictly mercenary motives, calculating that I'd be good for alimony at the very least, and quite possibly a small fortune. (She'd lived with Claudia, remember, and seen the distribution of her will; she knew just how much we'd each inherited from the grandparents.) Those two years were made pretty miserable by her continual actions of discovery, petitions and charges, and general harassment. This is when thoughts of chrysanthemum tea kept crossing my mind: I began wishing I knew someone in Chicago who could solicitously visit her on a daily basis, bringing her a soothing cup of something sweet . . . with poison in it.

Two years later, it was finally over; I settled out of court. She got a lump sum payment of $8,000; the attorneys' fees were about $10,000. And you wonder why ex-husbands are bitter?

As I've mentioned, I've never seen Stephanie (or, "the Bitch," as I began calling her during the course of the legal battle) again. I've been back to Chicago many times since then. On several occasions, I've visited socially with Duane, a mutual acquaintance. He never fails to update me on her status. One time, he told me she'd been declared "a ward of the state, incapable of taking care of herself." I could've told them that. What was news was that apparently she'd failed to find another sugar daddy to maintain her in the style to which she'd become accustomed. (Did I mention that she'd had two husbands, I believe, before me? No? Not relevant, I suppose . . . but what amazed me, in the end, was that she was still on speaking terms with one of them. I guess he didn't have enough money to make divorce court worthwhile.) Duane couldn't tell me anything else. He just said she was "as crazy as ever."

I wish I could say that I'd learned my lesson about "committed relationships"–that people who enter them ought to be committed. But alas, there's evidence to the contrary elsewhere in this book. Treat it as a cautionary tale, okay? You can call me bitter, if you like.

Re-creation

Because the sky was amber-red
because I saw a shooting star
because a perfect summer night compelled me—
how many, do you think, can I expect to see?
I walked along the beach and out the pier
The pier—
where headlamps of arriving cars, circling,
hunting, played like searchlights. I went out
in search of Slavic dick, and love.
And found—Trpnje's not the place
for midnight assignations on the pier.
The men were there, so I suppose their dicks
were present too. I couldn't prove it, though.
Moonless nights
with wind the shade of possible romance
and just the right amount of fishiness
may always make me think of men:
of those I've had—the best, the finest
group of men I could imagine—
and those I've just imagined, walking on the pier,
unzipped—phosphorescent fishes flashing back—
inviting as the Real seldom is.
And Jugoslavian men,
impossible to catch, provide themselves
—a living, willing sacrifice to sex—
as subjects for the perfect fantasy.

The Good Parts

BILL FINDLAY

Bill's family moved into the neighborhood (meaning two miles away, in our rural area) just after I'd finished second grade. I don't remember much of that summer; I do remember meeting Bill and his little brother, Wade. I was going to Bible Summer Camp, of course–every year!–and Bill and Wade were enrolled, too, before they'd even settled in. My family, being the sociable types they are, offered to share driving duties. One night, after a few days of this, Bill's parents invited me over to spend the night. Oh, I doubt that it was as simple as that. My parents probably had some late-night function to attend, and suggested the sleepover. Anyhow, I went. It stands out in my memory like a beacon. It was a hot summer night. Bill and Wade slept in the same room; I was in Bill's bed, of course. None of us felt sleepy. I think I had a hard-on; or if I didn't to begin with, I know I did later. All I remember is Bill daring me to put my mouth on his dick. Wade, across the room, was sitting up watching. I said, "Uh-uh–you'll pee in my mouth!"–which I felt somehow obliged to say, though I wouldn't really have minded if he had. Piss was already a fascinating substance to me, I recall. He promised that he wouldn't; I still wasn't convinced, so he added that he'd do it to me if I did it to him. That convinced me that he was serious, so I ducked down, quick as a wink, and sucked it into my mouth. I don't really remember too much about how it felt, except that I liked it. I wanted to keep it in my mouth all night, but Wade burst out laughing at that point and said "He did it!"–obviously derisively–and Bill pulled his dick out of my mouth as if he were afraid I was going to bite it. Why didn't I just smack my lips and say "Mmm-mmm! Tasty!"–which was what I felt? Well, I wasn't that self-confident. Need I add that at that point, Bill went back on his deal, and refused to return the "favor?" Perhaps I should have felt betrayed; instead, I remember feeling that I got the better end of the deal, and wondered how I could get him to challenge me to a repeat. I just wished he hadn't pulled it out of my mouth so fast.

We didn't repeat that particular experience, but we did become friends. Bill wasn't the most intellectual sort of person–he ended up repeating third grade–but since he was the nearest kid my age in the neighborhood, we spent a good deal of the following summer together. I remember roaming the hills behind his house, finding a female coyote and kits, and having pissing contests at the edge of a small cliff. It wasn't until two years later, when Bill "testified" to some of his christian friends that I had been "saved" (and was therefore an okay person to associate with)–and then asked me, "Isn't that right, Scott?"–and I refused to back him up, that he and I sort of drifted apart. Later that year, for reasons that are quite obscure to me, we actually got in a physical fistfight–only the second time I had ever fought someone–and visited the principal's office together. (He told me later, in penitent tones, that he "forgave" me.) The next year, he and Wade were transferred to a private christian school up the road (where my parents threatened to send me as well–I told them,"Uh-uh, no way, not a chance in hell. I'll run away if you do"), and I don't think I ever saw him again. I still wonder if he remembers that delightful little midsummer night's dream, though. Or, for that matter, if Wade remembers. I would love to hear their respective versions of that night's events.

KELLY, DARREN, AND LIVY

This is probably the most embarrassing of my "developing sexuality" episodes. Everyone has them, I'm sure; if I didn't feel confident that this experience will strike a chord with my readers, I certainly wouldn't repeat it because it absolutely mortifies me every time I even think of it.

Kelly was a year younger than myself, and I didn't have much to do with him–but we were in the same Boy Scout troop (together with his older cousin Mike, who was my age), and I saw him around school. He was very athletic, and well-developed for his age, though not tall. In fact, in high school, he became the star runner on the track team and the star baseball player. But we're talking about grade school here; I was in fifth grade, he was in fourth, and we had only recently been subjected to a new gym teacher, who was a firm disciplinarian (or so it seemed at the time). Among other innovations, he decreed that all students in fourth through sixth grades should "suit up" for gym, instead of wearing street clothes, as we had been doing. I found this immensely titillating: going into the boys' bathroom with twenty other boys and changing. My eyeballs practically dropped out, on a daily basis. But bear in mind that everyone is still wearing underwear–no jockstraps required, yet. Then, one day, Kelly forgot to wear underwear.

He advertised the fact, before pulling his pants down. I was practically salivating, and he didn't seem particularly ashamed. Maybe his family didn't have the nudity taboo that mine did. The social situation made it a whole new experience. I was wildly turned on, in my pubescent way, and somehow I thought the occasion deserved commemoration: I danced a sort of maypole dance–or perhaps the imagery had more to do with Indians, dancing around a cowboy who they'd caught and stripped–around poor Kelly, who handled my behavior quite well, I believe. The other boys may have thought I had gone mad, or they may have been wanting to join in; I'm not sure. All I'm clear on is that Kelly ultimately got the upper hand, by calmly acting as though I weren't there. He may have made a scornful comment, such as "Haven't you ever seen a dick before?" (Yes, I had. Two, maybe three times, in my entire sex-starved childhood.) I felt positively sex-obsessed (which I clearly was), and very stupid. The following year, when we all began taking showers after gym, we were all suddenly on equal footing–and nudity lost the uniqueness that it had previously had. Oh, I enjoyed the showers–I remember once getting a hard-on in the shower, but not especially minding; the other boys were obviously in awe of it, so what could possibly be the matter?–but it wasn't quite the same as the forbidden thrill of seeing just one boy naked amidst a crowd of semiclothed boys.

Okay, I may as well go on to the sixth-grade shower-room episode. This time spent in the showers was always put to good use: I began to catalog the various types of cocks. For instance, there was Scott Johnson, who was by far the tallest of any of us–I think he had failed a couple of grades–and who had a full pubic bush. And, needless to say, the biggest dick. There was my best friend Darren, whose dick . . . well, unfortunately, I can't remember at this point what it looked like. I know that I tested out my artistic skills by making up a chart, with everyone's names on it, and trying to draw their cocks. (I wanted to get a miniature camera, and take it into the showers with me, but never actually bought one.) The chart was labeled (who was I trying to fool?) "Noses," and I believe Darren was the only person I ever showed it to. He may even have contributed a drawing or two, but I don't think he was nearly as obsessed with the subject as I was.

In fact, I know he wasn't. Sometime during that period, I tried seducing him into my newly invented game of Bad Dog, the only serious goal of which was to pull the other guy's pants down and spank him. Now, I wouldn't have minded in the least if he'd won, but instead of cooperating, he just ran home and told his mother I'd been trying to pull his pants down. His mother, when I straggled in a few minutes later, gave me a scolding and sent me home. From then on, I somehow felt that something had gone out of our friendship. Pity; it could've been so swell . . .

There was only one other notable episode in my pubescent cock search: Livy and Ivan. Livy was my other best friend, all through grade school, and Ivan was his older brother–two or three years older, not a big difference. I spent the night at their place several times; one time, I know I tried to start something with them. I don't remember how I went about it; I know I was, again, rebuffed. Don't recall ever seeing either of their dicks.

Simultaneously, but secretively, during this period, I was learning to jerk off. It was in fifth grade, late in the year, that I started to seriously beat my meat; that is, *goal-oriented* jerking off, hoping for that payoff: ejaculation. I'd been given that little pamphlet on "becoming a man" put out by the Soroptimists (whoever the hell they are) sometime in fourth grade, and some months later by my parents (although they had an older edition of the booklet, which was not quite as informative on some of the subjects that interested me most). Just in time! From that point on, I was determined to reach orgasm ASAP. It took nearly a year of practice, however. In May, I experienced my first (dry) orgasm. In early September (in the bathtub, Sunday morning before going to church), I ejaculated for the first time. In the intervening summer, between fifth and sixth grades, while my older sister was away at summer school, I used to sneak into her room and pore over *Everything You Always Wanted To Know About Sex* . . . Okay, laugh if you must; I know it contained a lot of fallacies, but for me, at that age, it also contained much that was useful and comforting. I never believed for a minute that I was destined to become one of the "pitiful queens" described by Dr. Rubin. Lightbulbs up my butt? Puh-leez! I didn't even have much interest in men's butts at that age, and didn't really understand why anyone would; I was just intensely interested in dicks, and what they felt like, smelled like, tasted like. I did, however, find lots of other scenarios to jerk off over: descriptions of voyeurism, exhibitionism, fetishism, and many other possibilities. I don't believe I ever paid any attention whatsoever to Dr. Rubin's legendary judgmental attitude; after all, I heard the same sort of thing from my mother continuously, so I was inoculated.

My sister also had *The Naked Ape*, by Desmond Morris, which has a very stimulating clinical description of the sex act–hot stuff. I still get hot nuts for precise, dry descriptions of hot'n'steamy sex. The words "penis," "coitus," "meatus," or "semen"–oh, boy! In fact, I even compiled a dictionary of all the sexual words I could find–typed it up and everything. I kept it with some Charles Atlas brochures, Sears catalog underwear ads, some handwritten pornographic limericks I'd picked up at school, a used jockstrap that I'd found somewhere, and an old, tattered, paperback copy of *The Strumpet Wind*, a slightly pornographic novel from the 1950s by–are you ready?–Gordon Merrick. One day, yes indeed, my mother found them–and burned the lot in front of me, telling me that it was evil trash, the tools of Satan. If you need a reason, I think this is the reason I'll never grow to love my mother. I know–and I believe I knew even then–that I had a healthy, normal libido, and my mother was the freak. Nothing that I have experienced since then has caused me to doubt that, even for a second. "Sex-obsessed?" Hell, no. I was sex-*deprived* during those years; my life since then is the only rational form of compensation.

WILBUR

My uncle Wilbur–my father's elder brother–was, I regret to say, a slightly forbidding figure to me. This stemmed mostly from the time when our joint families went hiking together, and I slipped on a patch of loose rock and fell smack into him, knocking him down. I was eight years old at the time, not large enough to seriously damage him, but his temper was aroused, and he read me a shortened but emphatic version of the riot act. Profanity was simply not used in my family, so I was terrified. I always stood somewhat apart from him thereafter. Our family visited with him almost every summer, at the old family homestead in Placentia, California. My most vivid memory of those visits is finding one of Wilbur's used jockstraps lying around, and spending an inordinate amount of time trying to decide whether or not to add it to my collection. (I don't believe I did–my fear of his wrath won out over my adolescent libido. Besides, I didn't find a fifty-inch waistband very stimulating.)

My next encounter with Wilbur that stands out in memory was when I was a junior in high school. Perhaps at my parents' urging (I was becoming excessively rebellious, and they might have thought this would calm me down), he invited me on a whale-watching trip to Baja California, in February. I was excited, and couldn't wait to go. The trip was organized by Orange Coast College, which specializes in faux academics, and was in fact a credit course, if you were inclined to take it seriously. Maybe Wilbur did, I don't know. I kept a journal, and took several rolls of slides–mostly of the Mexican sailors who manned our fishing boat. I did everything I could to "get friendly with them," to no avail. The whales? Oh yes, we saw whales. Big whales. I won't say they were boring, but they weren't my main reason for the trip.

After we got back to L.A., on the day before I was to fly home, Wilbur suggested we go to Disneyland. I wasn't all that thrilled with the idea, but then I realized that if I didn't get excited about it, I'd have to come up with an alternative–and how in hell was I going to invent an activity to occupy an entire day with a sixty-two-year-old man who was a complete stranger to me?–so we went. Again, I don't recall any of the rides or amusements–they didn't amuse me– but I do recall the "serious talk" (which may have been the motivation for the entire trip) which Wilbur initiated while we sat with dishes of ice cream. He wanted to know what plans I'd made for college. I told him of my hopes of going to Northwestern, and my parents' objections; he talked about scholarships, but reminded me that I probably couldn't count on other financial aid, since my parents were relatively wealthy. Therefore, I really needed to reach some mutually satisfactory agreement with my parents. There was some other seriousness–nothing much, but I wasn't used to being treated as an adult by adults, and it made an impression on me. Is it possible that he had to take me to Disneyland just to relax himself enough to initiate it? I suppose so.

My uncle Wilbur, you see, was something of an anomaly in my family: he was divorced. Oh, the family was friendly all-round, but he'd lived by himself since before I was born. He had four kids, the youngest being ten years older than I am, and all of them idolized him; but he never showed the slightest interest in remarrying. His primary interest, according to my father, was in a local YMCA men's charitable/discussion group, called The Wise Men. (If he used the Y for working out, it didn't show.) No one ever talked much about him, but I always assumed his closet was rife with skeletons.

So, one last vignette of Wilbur, and we'll let him fade gracefully to black. I'm twenty-five this time, and living in San Francisco, in the full flush of my porno career; and Wilbur calls me up to say that he's going to be in town for a stockholder's meeting (Chevron, I think–did I mention that Wilbur was also a stock market wizard, probably worth a couple million?), and would I care to meet him there. Naturally, I did–and then spent the day trying to tour him around the City. How does one entertain a man of seventy? I'll probably know the answer someday, but it baffled me at the time. We took a bus out to Treasure Island, and up to Coit Tower and North Beach; I presume we had lunch somewhere; then I put him on the bus to the airport. (Yes, rich though he was, Wilbur was always the sort of man to take public transit to the airport. Why take a $25 taxi when there's a $1.25 bus? Which is, I guess, how you get to be a millionaire . . .)

All in all, it was a pretty bland day. Just one snatch of conversation stands out. We were taking the bus through Chinatown, he was asking about my activities; I told him I was into photography, both as photographer and model (which was the truth, if not the whole truth). In a joking tone, he said, "Well, just as long as you're not doing any pornography." I hesitated, and said, "Actually, that is what I'm doing." Without missing a beat, he came back with, "Well, just as long as you're not doing child pornography."–and launched into a cautionary tale about the McMartin preschool scandal, which had recently been invented. From his tone, I got the distinct impression that he didn't exactly *disapprove* of child pornography–he just understood that it could get a person in major hot water, and was worried about me.

Needless to say, I was in shock. The rest of my family treated my profession as if it were akin to mass murder, and I didn't know Wilbur well enough to suspect that he might have differing views. A few minutes later, he even admitted to me that he occasionally went to peep shows himself, and added that he was glad I was doing something that I enjoyed. Wow. Validation from a relative. I was sorta glowing by the time I put him on that airport bus.

Nevertheless, I never saw him again. I thought of him every time I was in L.A., but he lived way out in Orange County, not convenient to West Hollywood, and I wasn't even sure where in O.C. he lived–he'd sold the quaint old house that my grandfather built (there are apartment buildings on that block now) and moved into a condo somewhere. So when I heard that he'd died, this June, I couldn't get very emotional. He'd lived to a ripe old age, had a family, made a fortune, traveled the world–in short, done everything he wanted to do. I hope. No, mostly I felt sorry for my father. Surely, he must now feel a heavy sense of his own age, being the eldest surviving member of the family–and even more, a sureness that he's done everything meaningful he's going to do. He may even feel envy for his brother the black sheep, who did so much more.

I don't imagine that's a very pleasant feeling.

FATHER LEO

I don't flatter myself with the notion that my transition to college life was any easier or more difficult than the norm. I enjoyed myself, on the whole, and the academics of it weren't too strenuous for me; what proved my downfall, ultimately, was the increased liberty that

I found myself enjoying–sometimes to excess. As I got in the habit of going out barhopping, school became less and less important to me, and sex assumed greater and greater importance–until I ended up dropping out before my second semester was over, thus ending my college career. Still, I learned a helluva lot during that year . . .

One of the social opportunities I immediately took advantage of was a Bible study group. Oh, I was as brazenly agnostic/atheist then as I am today, but I liked the company, and the debates could be intense. The other members of the group also appreciated my presence; perhaps they cherished the illusion that they were leading the little lost lamb to the light. I enjoyed myself, and it wasn't until much later that I realized that of the nine "regulars" at the study group, five turned out to be queer–quite a nice average.

One of the guys who was emphatically not queer was Roy. Roy had some real problems with me. He found my attitude sacrilegious, my comments blasphemous, and my behavior completely immoral. I, on the other hand, found Roy irresistibly attractive. He was even the subject of one of my rare wet dreams. I've always been a sucker for redheads (and brunets, and bald men, and the occasional blond), and he was a stunner. Also, he had his wits about him–he could argue sophistry with the best (when he so chose). Perhaps I was a little too free with my compliments on his physique; anyhow, toward the end of the first term, he decided I was already damned, and ejected me from his life. He wouldn't even speak to me. Now, I wasn't completely crushed (this wasn't the first time I'd been "disfellowshipped"), but I wasn't pleased, either. So I went to see Father Leo, the campus chaplain and Roy's counselor.

Father Leo–well, he stands out in my memory. He was one of the gentlest men I'd ever encountered. Not religious at all, in the objectionable sense. He didn't give me lots of advice, but he agreed to act as intermediary; eventually, Roy started speaking to me again. I was impressed. For the first time, I'd seen a religious person who seemed sane and humane, and who lived in the real world.

(I should add that, before the reconciliation came about, Roy had already been to see the Dean of Men, complaining about my "immorality." As a result, I was called in to see the Dean, and warned that if they ever caught me engaging in "immoral behavior" on campus, they'd kick me out. Ah, Catholic universities!)

The term ended. I had no plans for the holidays; my roommate's family had invited me to spend some time with them, but I'd declined, hoping to find someone with whom I could be a little more intimate. So . . . December twenty-fourth, 10 p.m., I was home alone, when a guy knocks at my door. Says there's a call for me in the administrative office. I run across campus with him–it's obviously urgent–and find out that my sister Claudia, the only member of my family with whom I'm on friendly terms, has killed herself. My brother Jim is perhaps not the perfect person to break such news: he has all the sensitivity of stainless steel. I'm stunned. In shock. The guy at the switchboard, who'd come to get me–he's alone in the office–sees the look on my face, offers me a swig of whiskey (or maybe it was brandy). I take it, say "thanks," and stumble back toward the dorm.

I'm almost there when I pass the chapel. Even as an atheist, I'm perfectly willing to take comfort where it can be found; and there is something about the physical presence of churches (especially Catholic churches, with their omnipresent paraphernalia) that is comforting. I go in and sit down (kneel? are you kidding?) and try to cry. No luck. Still in shock. So I leave. On my way out, I run right into Father Leo. Maybe he was on his way to do a midnight mass or something, I don't know. I guess I managed to convey some sense of grief to him, because he asked what was wrong. That's when it happened: with someone present to witness it, I could finally cry. He didn't say much; he just took me in his arms and hugged me. Tightly. For several minutes. Eventually, I stopped, and he got the story out of me; still, I don't think he said anything beyond asking me what he could do to help. I ended up feeling slightly embarrassed, and going back to the dorm to sleep a peaceful night's sleep. The next day, I set out for the funeral, with various and sundry adventures along the way; but that's a whole other story. This story belongs to Father Leo, because I have never known a priest–or even a person–who I admired more. I felt a love from him, in those minutes, that I had never felt from any member of my family. And yes, it was in his job description, but I don't think that diminishes the value.

As a footnote: I heard several years later, from one of the gay members of that Bible study group, that Father Leo had left the university and was acting as pastor to the Dallas chapter of Dignity . . . presumably without episcopal approval. I don't know if he would remember me–I didn't exactly have a lot of contact with him–but whenever I'm tempted by a vision of a monolithically evil Church that believes in suppressing humanity and individuality wherever it appears, I think of Father Leo, and know that somewhere, down at the base of the Catholic Church, there is still warmth and life.

RALPH

Ralph was one of the family fictions: the weather god. When I was growing up, I assumed this had a deeper history than just our family's idiosyncrasies, and that eventually I would find out all about the mythology of Ralph in some abstruse text in college. This has turned out not to be the case . . . my family is more inventive than I ever suspected. I guess they came up with the name simply because it is a null: who, these days, is named Ralph? No one I knew. (They also made reference to another mythical character named "Yoohootee." Or perhaps it was "Yehudi." His area of responsibility was a little more difficult to pin down: the god of lost things, I guess.)

When I moved away from home, I tucked Ralph away in a back corner of my mind; by that time, I'd discovered that people looked at me funny if I called on Ralph to stop the rain. I didn't think about him for two years, while I traveled through Dallas, Chicago, Memphis, and San Francisco. Then I landed in Honolulu.

I wasn't really intending on staying in Hawaii; I'd stopped there on my way to Australia. But Hawaii is an insidious addiction: once you land there, it's difficult to disentangle yourself. Most people who visit have jobs, houses, families back on the mainland, so they reluctantly leave in two weeks. I'd cut all my ties before leaving San Francisco–I intended on being away six months–so I stayed. A week after arriving, I found an apartment; a week later, I found a job, as a janitor at the local bathhouse. A month later, I met Ralph.

Now, you might say that living in Hawaii is much the same as knowing Ralph. After all, the weather is seldom less than perfect–not to mention predictable. Ralph (the person) was the perfect embodiment of the laid-back Hawaiian lifestyle. One of my favorite afternoon activities was going down to Queen's Surf Beach—yes, it's what passes for the gay beach. It's a lawn, really, studded with palm trees, with a narrow strip of sand, low surf, and a snack bar that will sell you huge cups of ice and guava nectar for a dollar. The scenery changes daily; most of the guys there are from the mainland. Every afternoon, around 3:30, a rain squall comes in off the ocean, drenches everything in sight, and moves on inland. It was tremendously amusing, watching all the tourists run for their lives when the rain started. Locals just lay there; the rain wasn't cold, and we all knew that it would be over in five minutes, and we'd be dry in another five. Then, one by one, the sunbirds would hesitantly come back.

I swear, nothing makes you feel quite so omniscient as being able to forecast the weather with certainty.

But I digress. As I was about to tell you, I met Ralph in the back room at the baths, in the dark; I didn't know a lot about him for a long time, though I did find out his name on that first encounter. A name like that sticks with you. I wonder if he appreciates the advantages of having an unusual name? I hope so. What did we do? Oh, the usual: sucking and fucking. Lots of kissing. His cock? Average-sized, but more important to me, it was uncut, and it fit down my throat perfectly when we were 69ing—and his throat did wonders for my cock, too. This was before anyone had even considered the possibility of gay men using condoms (and yet I consider it quite possible, now, that I was actually HIV positive at the time) so our fucking was wild, uninhibited, and very sensual. When Ralph kissed you, you stayed kissed. It's an attitude: when he started in to kiss, you got the impression that he never wanted to do anything else, that he could reach orgasm with no other contact than that between your lips. What a feeling.

Eventually, yes, I saw Ralph in the light, and learned his last name, and his phone number, and where he worked. You learn these things about almost everyone in Waikiki; the resident population isn't large enough to harbor hermits, nor is there room enough for them. What drove me wild about Ralph, what made me obsess over him, was his "scroungy" appearance. He seldom seemed to worry about his hair, which was usually in a mess; he frequently missed shaving, and his beard didn't even grow in evenly, so he didn't get an "unshaven" look; he got a scraggly look. He had several tattoos, not exceptionally exotic ones, but indicative of a life lived far from the place I grew up in, maybe on a freighter; he had a crooked smile, which seemed to invite all sorts of mischief (and how in the world could he suck cock so well with those teeth sticking out every which way?); he even had a little bit of a pot belly, though it wasn't enough to make a difference when we were cuddled in bed together. And oh, his smell! I don't know quite what it was–I'm sure it was all natural, no perfumes or deodorants there–but it was one of the sexiest body odors I've ever encountered. It got so I could recognize him by his smell when I ran into him in that dark backroom. He worked at Hamburger Mary's as a fry cook, and I used to think that part of the smell was fried onions. But none of the other cooks smelled half as heavenly as he did. Part of it, I think, was his marijuana use; I've found that there's a certain sweetish smell to be found in the armpits of heavy pot smokers that's very arousing to me. The rest was probably just his natural smell. I could have spent all night nuzzling in his hairy pits.

In short–no, he wasn't Adonis. He was real, and he grew to Herculean proportions in my fantasies. I was at his apartment exactly once; I don't think he was ever at mine. Most times, I ran into him accidentally at the baths, and we would have very spontaneous, very combustible sex. We never talked, beyond the bare basics of sextalk or sidewalk chitchat. Sometimes we'd sleep together in the bunk-room. Maybe he was a philosopher or a poet, but you wouldn't know it by me. What he was to me was the essence of all things sensual: *Querelle* come to life; a sudden, tropical rainstorm on a blazing hot beach; the smell of freshly spaded earth and new-mown hay, pakalolo smoked during a hurricane. And oh, how I wish I could see him, taste him, feel him, SMELL him again.

"Is That All Real?"

I don't like big dicks. I know you're all going, "Sure, sure, tell us another one." I think a whopper is a nuisance, whether on one's self or on one's sex partners. Yeah, it's impressive to look at, but damn, it takes so much effort to satisfy! I know from experience that even guys with incredibly elastic throats overestimate their abilities when they encounter Supercock. Every time I meet up with Cocksucker Galore, I end up with scrapes and scratches all up and down my dick. Is it any wonder that I don't even enjoy being sucked off anymore? And vice versa: when I'm down on my knees, I like to know that the other guy is having a good time. I can immodestly state that I've got a pretty effective mouth, but if his dick belongs on King Kong, I bet he's just counting the seconds until he can no longer stand it. And no, I don't much enjoy sucking a dick that reminds me of a college fraternity initiation. I prefer a smaller dick, one that gives me the opportunity to treat it as a work of art, to lavish on it all the detail it deserves. When I make a three-inch dick stand up tall and proud, make its owner moan and whimper with his need to cum, it turns me on much more than listening to the stoic silence of a Superbutch He-Man with a ten-inch schlong.

The same applies to getting fucked, obviously. Again, the street wisdom is "It's the little ones that hurt," but I'm not even talking about hurt–I'm talking about my ability to get them in! A little dick (and yes, I mean *little*–two or three inches is plenty, thank you!) slips right into my butt; I don't even need to worry about lube most of the time, and I can get on with the business of making him feel good (and I know that, because of the low esteem in which small dicks are held in our culture, he's probably extremely grateful for my enthusiasm). When I'm trying to accommodate Moby Dick, just relaxing enough to get it in takes all my attention. I don't get much pleasure out of that process, and I doubt that he does either. I know that when I'm fucking someone, if it's clear that he's going through hell just to accommodate me, I lose interest pretty fast. On the other hand, when I meet up with a man whose ass opens up like one of those doors in *Star Trek,* with a big schloooping sound–well, my dick likes that.

So, over the years, I've developed a fondness for small-dicked men. There's only one problem with that: when they see my dick, 90 percent of the men I prefer try to hide their own dicks in shame. Goddamn this culture anyway–can you give me one good reason why a man should be ashamed of the size of his dick? It's a characteristic over which no one has any control, a trait that's obviously genetic; what is there to be ashamed of? Do black men try to hide the fact that they're black? (Well, I'm sure some have, but not lately.) Now, if it were a characteristic that was influenced by personal habits–like bad breath, for instance, or an untidy bedroom–I can see why someone might be ashamed of it. But your dick is *part* of you, guy! It's not something you can change by going to the gym every day, or flossing carefully, or earning a million dollars. Being ashamed of it just doesn't make sense.

Now that I've gone off on modern culture (and ancient culture too? I have no idea), let's get back to the subject of this piece: my dick.

Yes, it's big. I generally call it nine inches (though I think a more strictly accurate measurement is eight and seven-eighths, if it matters). The judge in the Biggest Dick in San Francisco contest, back in September 1983, pretended to measure it at eleven, I think . . . but only the easily deluded believed him, given the sloppy way he was holding the tape measure. More accurately, using the Kinsey technique of measuring along the topside of the shaft, I suspect it comes in at under eight inches. And yes, I have certainly met men who have more dick than I have. One of them (let's reinforce some racial stereotypes here: yes, a black man) even fucked me once, and I haven't felt the same since.

I first started measuring my dick when I was eleven years old, and obsessed with absolutely anything sexual (and so much has changed since then, *n'est-ce pas?*); for a number of years, I kept a chart showing the measurements of all my muscles (chest, bicep, wrist, thigh, calf, neck, waist, dick length and circumference [both hard and soft], ball size and length). Of course, I now know those measurements to be completely fraudulent (I was probably measuring along the underside of my dick), because by the time I was fifteen, I had measured my dick at ten inches. As you can tell, given my obsessive attention to such things, at that age my dick size *did* matter to me. I hadn't had any sexual contacts yet, but I was busily comparing myself to the clinical models—was I muscular enough? Was my dick big enough? Did I masturbate enough? This was not a healthy obsession, I now believe, but not surprising, either, given that I was deprived of the normal sexual outlets that most twelve-year-olds presumably have.

The first real sex I had with another man was when I was fifteen, when I seduced a twenty-eight-year-old. Maybe the proper word is "raped." I certainly didn't give him a chance to say no. I knew he was gay, and I knew I wanted it; therefore surely it followed that he should want me . . . ? I cringe, today, at my youthful certainty, just as I marvel at his tact and gentility. He also marveled at the size of my dick, leading me to assume that this was standard gayspeak during sex (which is, I've found, the case): "God you've got a big dick!" "Fuck me with that big dick!" etc. The second man who I had sex with, some two weeks later, may have made similar comments; I don't remember. I remember the fourth man (not long after), who I met at the county library. He took me back to his apartment and asked me to piss on him, in his bathtub. Today, I'd be delighted to oblige; at age fifteen, I was terminally pee-shy, and completely unable to comply. I was mortified, and surprisingly turned off. He talked a lot about how big my dick was, but I discounted everything he said because he spent the rest of my visit trying to fuck me, which I didn't want him to do. He literally had me pinned down on his bed at one point, while I was struggling to get loose. I'm not especially proud of the fact that I resorted to reminding him that I was a minor, and I could get him in a lot of trouble . . . he did let me up then, and I promptly put on my clothes and fled. It's experiences like this that make me so skeptical of so many stories of "boy rape"–most men are perfectly well aware that the boy has all the power in any sexual encounter, and most boys are equally cocksure, so the "intimidation" argument doesn't cut much ice with me.

There were other men over the succeeding months. By the time I graduated from high school, I was beginning to be aware that yes, I probably did have a bigger-than-average dick . . . but it hadn't sunk in yet that this was a major asset in the gay world. (Just like I hadn't quite figured out yet why a man's ass should be a turn-on. I don't know how long it took me to begin to understand this fetish–years, anyhow.) I'm not sure when, if ever, it really hit home. Maybe if it had, I would've ended up in a gutter somewhere, wasted on too many drugs. As it was, anytime a trick started going on about my big dick, I tuned him out . . . and probably didn't see him again. Even at age seventeen, there were other things I'd rather be remembered for.

Fast forward now to the beginning of my film career, when I'm hanging around Savages–a dirty movie/jackoff show theatre in San Francisco's Tenderloin district–all the time. Labor Day weekend was coming up, and they had two contests scheduled: one to choose their "Mr. Savages," the other to find "The Biggest Dick in San Francisco." Now, I was really interested in winning the Mr. Savages title–I thought that would be amusing; I had a passing masturbatory acquaintance with the *Doc Savage* books, and the notion of going by that name got me going. The theme of the other contest bored me. On contest night, they needed entrants, so after they'd raised the prize money to $100, I volunteered. I think there were four other men up there, and of the five of us, I was clearly the biggest. Not quite a representative sample of San Francisco–all of us, I should point out, were Caucasian–but it satisfied the masses.

A title like that gets attention. It got me a film contract with Falcon (see the story of that elsewhere), and a lot of roles in other videos for other companies. Without a big dick, I wouldn't have had much bargaining power in videos: oh, sure, my face and body and ass are all attractive, but none of them are outstanding. No one ever hired me for my butt (Alas . . .).

So why should I complain? Because I still don't think it's a healthy criterion on which to judge a person. It can reduce me to hopeless tears of frustration to hear a guy talking about someone in a disparaging tone, just because the guy's got a small cock. I feel like breaking in on the conversation and saying, "Send him my way!" Of course, I seldom do. However, when a size-queen friend of mine was recently planning an orgy in my honor, I asked him, with some trepidation, "Now, are you inviting at least one man of moderate dick-size, who I can get to fuck me?" He may have thought I was joking, but he complied with my wishes, and yes, there was one small-dicked man there, with whom I had a fabulous time. The memory still makes my butt quiver.

There was a time, many long years ago, when I was very much into fisting. I spent a truly obsessive year during which there was almost nothing else that interested me. Then I got a case of anal warts, and the process of having them burned off kinda froze my asshole up permanently. I've gone through phases since then, various degrees of looseness or tightness, but I've never opened all the way up again. Occasionally a cucumber, sure; once or twice I've been double-fucked, which is a psychological thrill second to none in my mental library of scenarios, but is physically difficult; and I have a large collection of dildos, mostly on the small side, but including one monster that I've only tried to use maybe half a dozen times over the thirteen years that I've owned it. I don't even know why I bother. Small dildos are more pleasurable. I guess it's just the challenge that is exciting. Some people climb Mt. Everest, some people jump hurdles. Some people sit on progressively larger dildos. But that, as I keep telling myself, is quite different from a real live cock. A dildo is used when you feel a specific itch in your butt. Being fucked by a man–at least, for me–fills a very different need. A man can hold me, can show me that I'm giving him pleasure, can move against me in a way quite unlike anything rubber can ever do. Being fucked, contrary to what most porn videos try to tell you, is not about being fucked. I suspect I could be fucked quite satisfyingly by a man who had no dick at all, if he were truly into it. It's a psychological sense of possession that is important, of surrender and . . . well, all right, love. On those occasions (long ago and far away, now, alas) when I was bent over the bench in the orgy room at Manscountry, being fucked by one man after another, I do think there was more love involved than most people would be willing to admit. Love is very intimately involved with the giving of pleasure; sex is simply one of the easiest ways to give pleasure to strangers. There have been times when I've had sex with men who I didn't care about. Generally I fucked them, rather than vice versa; usually, we did it for the camera. They're not among my favorite memories.

I don't dress deliberately to show off my dick, as some people might suppose. Neither do I dress to hide it. I would go nude 24 hours a day, 365 days a year, if the weather and social mores would permit, without shame or any outrageous sense of pride in my body. Yes, I like my body, yes it turns me on, as do many other men's bodies, but I don't see a big dick as any greater cause for celebration than big ears. Maybe both are survival-oriented characteristics, but I doubt it. Try to imagine a society, will you, where Prince Charles is the most scandalously attractive man on the planet, because of his ears. Defies imagination, what?

That Sandwiched Feeling

I've occasionally made reference to some couple I know or knew. No big deal, right? Everyone knows couples. Graham and David, David and Glen, Juan and Brian, Galen and Greg, Galen and Jim, Marc and Joe . . . there was a period of time when I seriously thought that I was addicted to couples. And why not? For someone like me, an incurable romantic without the ability to maintain romantic feelings, being a third wheel in a couple is the ideal situation: it allows me all the pleasurable feelings of being in a relationship, the warm snuggles of sleeping with a "lover," without the difficulties of having to live with him. I maintained that I got as much "good energy" from a night spent between Juan and Brian as I ever did from any of my more long-term lovers.

This didn't develop consciously, however. I just came to realize that my life was filled with these men, and that some of my best times were being spent with them. Usually in bed.

It was with Juan and Brian that I finally began to see some of the drawbacks of this setup. I was genuinely in love with them; I wrote long journal entries about how wonderful it was to have two lovers. They seemed to feel the same way about me. I was moving out of San Francisco at the time, spending more and more time with them in Seattle while I prospected for land in the area. By summer's end, I'd moved in with them. I'd also learned their domestic habits: espresso in the morning; walking the dog in the afternoon; quiet evenings reading, painting, or listening to music. I could very happily have lived with this. It was on those rare occasions when one or the other of them wanted to go out that we clashed. I had no objections to their going out, but they wanted me to go with them, and, well, even though I knew better, I usually went. Seeing them socializing freely, enjoying themselves, dancing, I became acutely aware of how unsociable a creature I really was, and I was reminded that this was probably a contributing factor to my fondness for couples.

By evening's end, I was usually in a thoroughly sulky mood. You can call it jealousy if you like. If I'd had the good sense to say, "No, YOU go out, I'll stay at home and read," I probably wouldn't have felt that way. But then I would've felt guilty for being "unfriendly"—a no-win situation.

My relationship with Juan and Brian came to an end, however, not over such trivial things as that, but over space issues. They began to feel crowded, in their lovely little one-bedroom house, and I suspect I was actually causing friction between them. I tried to be absent more, but it didn't help. By summer's end, they politely but firmly asked me to not spend any more nights there. I still saw them on the odd social occasion, and we were friendly, but suddenly we didn't have anything in common anymore.

My attitude toward coupledom is, well, to put it bluntly, cynical. Anyone who uses the phrase "till death do us part," and actually means it, has got to be out of his/her fucking mind. No one can say "forever" with any sense of certainty. There are no guarantees. People change; and if they're smart, they allow that change, encourage it even, rather than trying to maintain a persona and a relationship that has ceased to provide them with pleasure. When a marriage ends its useful life, take the damn thing out and shoot it, like an old horse. Nope, guess I'm just not a very sentimental type.

There are other couples I've known in the years since then, couples with whom I didn't get involved sexually (though that's not to say that I necessarily refrained from sex with them altogether). Some of them are among my best friends. The couples that I think work the best—the couples who I actually admire for their complicity in coupledom—are the ones who know the meaning of letting go. Galen and Jim are a marvelous example: they spend a lot of time together, but they also play extensively on the side. What's even more amazing is that they've attached themselves to another couple (who I've not met) who seem to share many of their kinky sexual tastes, and the four of them are now behaving like newlyweds. May it go on forever, I say . . . as long as forever remains a relative term. Forever, as long as it's good for all of them. But "forever for the sake of forever"—now that's sick.

Then there's Dwayne and Carlos. Dwayne is one of my oldest friends, and might once have been my lover, if our communication had been better. He's gone through several lovers in the years since then (and so have I, for that matter), but his current, Carlos, is the first one who I find sexually attractive. "Irresistible" is more like it. Fortunately, as Dwayne said to me on the afternoon when he first introduced the two of us, "Carlos is insatiable. Maybe you can wear him out so I won't have to." I did my best. Oh, I haven't spent a lot of time with him over the subsequent months, but I've spent several afternoons/evenings squeezing the cum out of his balls. On a couple of occasions, Dwayne has joined us; on a couple of others, he's said, "I'm going to see my chiropractor/do laundry/get some ice cream/ whatever now," and would return in an hour or so, bouncing and cheery, and we'd both be snoozing on the couch, and he'd say, "What kind of ice cream do you want, Rocky Road or Vanilla Almond?" This is tasteful, civilized behavior; everyone is made happier, and the relationship is made more tolerable. "In marriage, three is company and two is none," as Algernon says in *The Importance of Being Earnest*. Menages á trois are really nothing new; it's just that with the current mania for domestic partnerships and gay marriage, too many queers seem to be forgetting that they're taking on the many deficiencies of heterosexual marriage, along with their alleged advantages.

Pardon me while I (carefully, carefully) step down off my soapbox.

I do not want a lover. I've had them, and they've proven unsatisfactory for me. I can't imagine how anyone can find the same person satisfying, or even tolerable, for years on end. Still, I know lots of guys who do it, so there are obviously differing points of view. I just have to believe that they're working at it. (All the marriage counselors say that relationships don't just happen, that you have to "work at them," don't they?) I believe that if they didn't have to put that energy into that relationship, there's no telling what great gardens, what cultural achievements, what stunning new poems or paintings might be produced–things that could, in short, be appreciated by the world at large, instead of just the two principals. I think back to all the great geniuses of history, and wonder what they might have achieved if they hadn't been saddled with a spouse and children, and I find it, frankly, shocking. Especially when you compare it with the genealogical record. How many of Beethoven's children grew up to be geniuses, after all? Whereas, if he hadn't taken the time and energy to produce them all, we might have twenty-seven symphonies instead of nine.

But this really didn't start out to be a vicious attack on matrimony. Remember, I appreciate some of the aspects of a well-tuned couple. Being double-fucked can be a real thrill. (It takes a considerable amount of coordination and comfort with your partner; if there's the least amount of uncertainty or doubt, one hard-on or the other will inevitably wilt.) When I lived in Honolulu, I got together on a regular basis with a couple who were into double-fucking, except it was me and partner "A" fucking partner "B." An extreme turn-on, I have to say. I've tried that scenario a couple of times since, and occasionally it's worked. Being in the center of the sandwich, however, is more naturally my style.

Just one more anecdote, and then I'll let you go. I met a man, a couple of years ago, in New York; we hit it off in a big way, and saw each other several times over the next six months. The major thing we had in common was rimming. I was just beginning to realize/admit that life without butt-munching was not a life I was interested in living, and therefore I was ready, again, to discount the various warnings that doctors had been throwing at us for years. (After two years of avid ass-eating, those bogeymen have yet to materialize. Yeah, I get diarrhea now and then—small price to pay.) I met this man at a sexclub, and somehow it was communicated to me (presumably I don't have to tell you how; if you've had anonymous sex with anyone, ever, you know how these things go) that he would welcome my tongue up his butt, and I dove right in. This was a New York sexclub, without beds or privacy; we were in the middle of a squirming (but standing) mass of flesh. I was down on my knees, with my head tilted back, and he was sitting on my face while, I'm sure, five other men did other things to other parts of his body. We kept this up for at least half an hour; I loved the way he moaned and groaned, and I guess he loved the dexterity of my tongue, because he gave me his phone number and we did it again and again and again, over four subsequent visits to New York. And each time, though I did eventually fuck him, it was the rimming that drove him (and me) crazy.

Six months later, he fell in love.

On my next trip to New York, he introduced me to his new boyfriend (who was not yet living with him). The method of introduction was auspicious, I thought: he invited me over, then called bf and invited him over. When bf arrived, my dick was deep up his lover's ass. Bf wasn't appalled or outraged; he was envious, if anything, but when it came to actually taking it up his butt (which was a butt, I have to say, that would've aroused a stone saint), he chickened out. Was it really a fear of my size, as he said, or some romantic notion about only wanting to be fucked by the Beloved? I don't know. We did play, and I think he fucked me; he was very good sex. I felt well and truly "sandwiched." But that was the last time I played with either one. They developed, I'm sorry to say, promiscuity issues. I'm sure the boy is charming and sexy and he obviously adores my friend, but this is a relationship that I frankly wish would come to a peaceful conclusion, so I can get back to sticking my tongue up my friend's butt and making him jabber and moan till he cums.

I give relationships a grade of D+. They aren't actually all bad; they're just used in unhealthy ways most of the time. They're used to stunt people's growth, instead of encouraging it. They're used to douse the flames of lust, rather than fanning them. They're used to close off a person's imagination and inspiration. None of this is necessary. I've seen the proof. There are relationships that don't stifle, that don't starve the participants. One of the prime indicators of this sort of relationship is that they aren't afraid to put a little filling in their sandwich.

Venice Beach: Memorial Day

Lying on the beach with Sir, tightly handcuffed
to the stakes he's driven at my hands and feet
people strolling by, all unaware;
I can turn, rotisserate myself, but nothing more.
He relaxes, unconcerned, only attending me
to replace my beer each quarter-hour
—I suck them through a straw. "Please Sir"—I say,
on finishing my third—"I need to piss . . ."
He looks at me, and at the crowded beach.
"Turn on your back," he says, and I obey—
even bladder-bloated, hard-on still won't go away,
tents my baggy running shorts—he smiles.
"So piss," he says.
The shorts are quickly soaked; the towel takes
a few more beers. Each time I ask—"Sir?" He nods,
and piss leaps up, bubbles through thin material,
puddles on my belly, as he watches.
Sir uses the men's room, but returns with a warm beer.
Later, as I start to put the towel in the washer,
he corrects me. "Save it.
You can sleep with it tonight."

Porn

People are born with the inherent desire for porn. This is a basic element of my philosophy: the idea that watching other people have sex, watching people enjoy themselves, is an essential human pleasure. Voyeurism is the most natural of perversions, the most universal. Translating that to a video screen, or the four-color page, or to a written or spoken fantasy, does nothing to change the basic character of porn: it still stimulates our central nervous systems in the same way, the vicarious joy of being a participant in an act that is giving the participants pleasure. It's equally natural to imagine one's self in the middle of the action, but, like the voyeur at the window, most consumers of pornography are clearly aware that there is a window there, a line that can't be crossed: *this* is fantasy, *that* is reality, and the two don't necessarily have anything in common. Those who have difficulty separating fantasy and reality are often disparaged as "pornography addicts," and other vile names; in fact, they are merely schizophrenic. The abuse of pornography by these people (and I grant that pornography, like anything else in life, can be overused, to the point where it becomes damaging) is a symptom, rather than a cause.

In delving through my memory banks, the first association I have with pornography comes at age ten, when I would "borrow" my mother's *Reader's Digests, Redbooks,* and other magazines, searching through them for any vaguely sex-related articles ("I Am Joe's Testicle," "Secrets for Holding a Man," and one of my favorites, "What Do You Say to a Naked Man?"); I would take them to school, hide them, and then spend the half hour after school out in the football field, behind the fence, reading them over and over, while fierce erotic tingles raced through my body. I tried sharing them with my buddy Darren, but he didn't understand my arousal.

I've described elsewhere in this book my early masturbatory efforts. From age eleven onward, I was obsessed with the printed word, almost any printed word that could even be imbued with sexual meaning. I remember jerking off frantically over several dark and moody passages in Calder Willingham's *End As a Man* (something about a military academy, I think); of course all the *Tarzan* books provided a good deal of fodder for my imagination too, as well as certain science fiction authors. Even westerns aroused me. Sex didn't really need to be mentioned; any scene in a western where the cowboy takes off his clothes to go swimming in the creek would have me shooting a load on my stomach. I frequently read such books after the lights were out, by flashlight, in my sleeping bag; once my mother caught me, when I was reading a *Tarzan* book, and demanded to see what I was reading. Terrified (*Tarzan* was pure pornography in her eyes, I was sure), I refused. I'm rather proud of that: the first time I remember standing up to her, and winning. In retrospect, I suppose she gave up because she was afraid of what she'd find—but I'm sure she never forgave me that rebellion. Fine; I'd long since stopped being interested in her forgiveness. If she couldn't appreciate Tarzan's pecs, what good was she?

If we're deprived of the normal dose of pornography that every child deserves, we make up our own. I bought a men's magazine of some type (nonerotic) and discovered an ad for the *PARR of Arizona* catalog; when I ordered it, I was absolutely agog at the number of gorgeous men wearing virtually nothing. I cut them all out, creating collages, drawing dicks on all the figures. Their dicks, I'm proud to be able to point out, were in reasonable proportion to their bodies, given my limited experience. I never had a Tom of Finland tendency, though I do remember a fantasy I had of being kidnapped and "kept" by a giant, who would let me slide up and down his hard-on as if it were a fireman's pole, sticking my arm down into his urethra, and being drowned by his eventual climax . . . I was charmed to discover, years later, that the artist Etienne had illustrated just that fantasy, in the context of an x-rated *Star Trek* episode. Fantasies aren't really so unique, after all; we all have (more or less) the same equipment.

The first commercial pornography of any sort that I remember seeing was during the summer between my junior and senior years in high school. I was out bicycling, and had stopped by the side of a quiet rural road to take a piss—and I discovered, some ways back from the road, a "nest" where some high school kids hung out: beer bottles, cigarettes, etc. There was a *Penthouse* (or some such) there, quite weather-worn, and even though I did not turn on to the women depicted, the pages were obviously cumstained, so I jerked off also, imagining the circle-jerk that must have taken place over the mag. I refrained from actually licking the pages, though, and I left the magazine there when I finished, hoping that some other boy would find my fresh cum and do something with it.

It was about this time that I discovered the guys at *RFD*. A magazine for rural faggots, it was then being produced at a faerie commune about thirty-five miles north of where I lived. Well, it's a long bike ride, but it seemed worth it. I rode up there a number of times during my last two years in high school; several times I managed to seduce whoever was hanging around. (The only two whose names I remember, Candor and Jamal, are now dead, so I'm not concerned about incriminating anyone.) Some of those occasions were quite special. Memorable, also, is the afternoon when I failed to interest any of the residents in a roll in the hay, and spent the afternoon and evening perusing their gay bookshelf, instead. I looked at *RFD*s, of course, and lots of gay political books that I'd already read at the county library, but also a copy of *Men Loving Men*, an early sex manual with photos, which the Josephine County Library was not likely to stock. Oh, the photos were sadly soft-core, emphasizing the "romantic" side of sex rather than the passionate side, but they were still beautiful. I kind of hoped, as I lingered into the evening, spellbound by those lovely photos, that someone would suggest that I borrow it. No one did, and now I understand why: I'm sure they were picturing my parents finding it, asking how I got it, and coming up to Wolf Creek with torches. (That building was, in fact, torched by local rednecks a year or so later; I hope I wasn't the cause.) I don't think I left there until 10 p.m., and didn't get home until well after midnight. My parents were positively furious, and grounded me for a week. Who cared? I was learning my lessons in life, and how it should be lived.

Another year went by; I was at college when one of my tricks, a wealthy middle-aged man, showed me some porn movies. He had a secret setup wherein he pulled back a sliding panel in the headboard of his bed, and *voilà*, a movie projector, all ready to roll. I think he may have regretted doing so; I'd been real turned on to him prior to that point, but once I saw the movies, nothing else mattered. I spent the rest of the night beating off. I don't know what he did, but he never invited me back. He did come out to the college once, and we had lunch.

In May, at the end of my first (and only) year of college, I stopped in at the Roman Sauna (now called the Rochester Spa & Body Club). I don't remember much about the facility or crowd, despite the fact that it was only the third bathhouse I'd ever been in, because they had a porn corner, with comfortable seating. Once again, I think I spent all night sitting there, beating off. I was learning quickly just how addictive these things can be. It was a video setup, I believe, one of the first such I'd ever seen; and no, I have no idea what videos I saw. I'd be fascinated to know, actually, since I'm sure if I saw them today, I'd have a positively primal response to them, just from the fact that they entered my libido's library at such a formative stage.

For the next two years, bathhouses were my primary venue for watching porn. Despite having worked there for four months, I can't remember whether the Club Baths San Francisco had a porn room; I know that the Steamworks in Honolulu did, and I spent many a night there. I watched *Inches*, *Wanted*, and *Games* more times than I can count, but most vividly etched in my memory is a preview film from Falcon, which they showed over and over. It included previews of their first thirty or so films. Notably, the Steamworks didn't switch over to video until sometime after I'd left Hawaii. I may be the youngest person in the world, therefore, to retain an erotic response to the sound of a super-8 movie projector.

Sometime during this period, I also remember seeing *These Bases Are Loaded* at some trick's house. It stuck with me; even today, it's one of my favorite movies. It also struck me recently that I ended up having sex with three of the stars of that movie–only one of them on-screen. (All dead, now, alas.) The one I was always most obsessed with, however, J. W. King, eluded me. I was told, after he died, that I probably wouldn't have enjoyed meeting him, that he was yet another bottom-forced-into-top-roles, that we'd end up "bumping pussies." Worse things could've happened.

I was in Hawaii from September, 1981, through February, 1983. On my 1983 New Year's list of resolutions, I recall writing three things in particular: (1) move out of Waikiki, probably to Manoa Valley; (2) go back to college, and (3) become a pornstar. What these three had in common remains to be seen. How seriously did I take any of these goals? Not very. I certainly didn't lay any plans for them. In fact, I gave up my apartment in February , put my things in storage, and flew to New Orleans. There, I hopped a Greyhound™ to Andalusia, Alabama, where one of my best friends was living in a trailer his grandmother had left him. I moved in with him for six weeks; we drove back down to New Orleans for Mardi Gras; then I went to Atlanta for the weekend, bought an old Ford van, and drove it across country, stopping in Memphis, Chicago, Oskaloosa (Kansas), Dallas, and Salt Lake City—arriving in San Francisco in early June.

One of the first things I saw, upon arriving in San Francisco and picking up a copy of the *Bay Area Reporter*, was an ad for Savages, a porn theater in the Tenderloin. I don't think I'd ever quite realized that such places existed; they had *live jackoff shows*! I was thrilled beyond words. This was all my fantasies come to life, all those high school circle-jerks that had never come true. I hightailed it down there. Yes, it was a sleazy dive: dark, dirty, broken seats, the usual. But the staff was friendly; the movies were projected on a full-sized cinema screen; and the shows! When that first dancer got up onstage and jerked off, I thought I'd go crazy. I was right up there in the front row—an unpopular position, believe it or not—so the guy onstage played directly to me, and yes I had my dick out, pumping it. I think I stayed until the place closed.

A few nights later, I was back. The next week, when I showed up again, the guy at the door said, with a wink, "You know, it's Amateur Night—you could do a show, if you wanted to . . ." That got my pulse racing, but I don't think I would have had the courage to do it if the first performer, after he'd come down off the stage, hadn't come up to me, stroked my dick, and said pretty much the same thing. He added, "You saw where the light switch is, didn't you?" Yeah, I'd been watching. So I got up there. They turned off the movie, I turned on the lights, and did a show. I don't remember a thing about it—it's obscured by all the hundreds of similar shows I did over the next five years—but I must have liked it, and they must have liked me, because as I was leaving, the manager came up to me and asked if I'd like to work there full-time. "YES!"

Did I have an inferiority complex? I wouldn't phrase it that way, but I certainly found it amazing that I could get paid to jerk off onstage. Well, I mean, that sort of thing was for Superstar Pornstars like Jack Wrangler, right? I was just a boy from the country. Oh, I knew I had a lot of the right fantasy elements about me: a big dick, a leather jacket, blond hair (usually), a sort of "wild" look, and youth. I still didn't (and still don't, for that matter) quite understand my appeal.

I worked all summer at Savages. Sometimes as many as eight shows a week; often it was just three or four. They started off paying me $25 per show, it quickly went to $30, and eventually moved up to $75, once I'd achieved notoriety. Many of the dancers got tips from the audience, but in order to do that, you had to go down into the audience and "lap-dance"–something I didn't feel comfortable doing, so I got no tips. (It didn't even occur to me until years later that I was "supposed" to be doing it.) Do you suppose that inaccessibility was the key to my success? It's a thought. Sometime in July, the manager of the theater approached me about doing a pornflick. He'd never produced one before, but, he reasoned, he had the talent at Savages, and surely he could do as well as most of the producers out there. I got all breathless and wide-eyed again: "Gee, Mr. Producer, can I be in your movie?"

In all honesty, it wasn't quite the first time I'd been on a movie set: while I was living in Honolulu, a grad student at UH had approached me about being in his graduate project, called *Street Kings and the Mutant Child*. (In answer to everybody's question, no, I was not the Mutant Child–and it was not a pornflick.) With my radical punk haircut and incongruously innocent look, I'd been just the perfect character for that effort; I regret that I never got to see the finished product. When I revisited Honolulu that September, I contacted the director, and told him about my new ventures; he seemed intrigued, though not as excited as I'd been.

But, back to Savages, and my budding career. The screenplay was all written; it was called *California Blue*, and it was cast by the middle of August. The next six weeks were spent waiting for the weather to cooperate, since Walt was determined to shoot it all outdoors. One scene was to be shot in the redwood forests north of San Francisco; the rest of the scenes were shot down near Santa Cruz, either on the nude beach or in a barn near the beach. There were several days when everyone gathered at Walt's apartment, listened anxiously to the weather reports (which generally told us nothing about the weather at the beach), traipsed all the way down to Santa Cruz . . . only to discover that the beach was fogged in. After the third time, Walt had the brilliant idea of calling the general store near the beach before leaving; after that, we had no more weather problems.

Being involved with porn was a sheer delight from the word go; it took a year or so for it to sink in, however, that it was more than that. I will probably never be a famous Shakespearean actor (as was my ambition in high school); my voice does not project, and my face does not naturally express emotion in the exaggerated manner necessary for stage acting. Even my Carol Channing imitation is completely unrecognizable, so female impersonation is out of the question. But performing in porn, I came to realize, is an inherently more valuable service. Hey, the world is full of unemployed actors, many of them good. They can handle all the productions of *Othello* and *Hello Dolly* that the world needs to see. The world is, on the other hand, sorely lacking people who are eager to perform in sex films, who consider it a privilege and a pleasure to provide others with orgasmic enjoyment. Most people, for reasons quite foreign to me, are ashamed of that part of their life, and don't wish it to be seen by anyone. Very well: I will teach by example, I decided. I became The Pornstar Who Smiles, the one who tried in every movie I made to let the audience know that I was doing it because I got a big kick out of it and I hoped they would too. Godnose I wouldn't have been doing it for the money–it was never enough to keep a church mouse alive. I did it as a tribute to those pioneers who put out the *PARR of Arizona* catalogs all those many long years ago, and *RFD*, and that early sex manual, *Men Loving Men*, that gave me the positive reinforcement I needed at that age. I have the good fortune to know that my performances have, in at least a few instances, done the same for other young gay men, and I can't imagine another bit of knowledge that could make me feel better.

The Videos: Easy to Work With

Every video has its own story. Here they are:

CALIFORNIA BLUE, *SEPTEMBER 1983*

When the manager of Savages asked me if I'd like to be in a porn flick, I said, "Sure, I'd love to." I mean, it wasn't something I'd spent a lot of time thinking about, but who hasn't fantasized about being in a porn video? I'd bought myself a video camera when they were still a novelty, back in 1981, and I'd taken a lot of home videos of myself jerking off, shaving my pubes, shaving my head—even a couple of surreptitious videos of men having sex with me. I'd always been a ham, so I liked the idea of being put on film by professionals.

Except, these weren't really professionals. None of the guys had done porno before; the cameraman was the most experienced of all of us, and he proved completely unreliable (I don't know, maybe he wasn't getting paid). I can't speak for the other performers, but I wasn't doing it for the money; I was doing it because I liked sex, and I liked the idea of being on film. That, and two of my costars, John and Tony, turned me on in a big way. Tony played the mean farmer who abuses trespassers; John played the cop he calls to help him out. Personally, I couldn't care less what the fantasy scenario was; I liked the reality: Tony's dark, curly hair and bushy eyebrows, John's big, pouty lips and the way his butt seemed to float about an inch behind and above where it should've been . . . So I put up with the long hours and rude treatment that comes with being a sex star, and frankly, I had a blast. The most memorable part of the movie isn't the scene with John and Tony in the brussels sprout field, however, where they "rape" me with a cucumber and then double-fuck me; it's the later scene, up at the barn, where John and Tony get it on with each other. I had to stand by and watch that scene . . . and greater frustration hath no man ever experienced. I knelt on the sidelines, mouth open, eager for a chance to "fluff" either one of them. One time when John went outside to take a piss, I drank that, too, and then sucked him up hard again. He had a fabulous, leisurely manner of fucking a face that really got me worked up; pity it isn't documented better in the movie.

The "finished" product ended up sitting on the shelf for almost two years; the producer/director ran out of money. Finally, in desperation (hey, I really wanted to see this film on video store shelves!), I approached him and asked how much money he needed for postproduction. "$10,000," he said. Fine. I loaned it to him, and just for good measure, we decided to shoot another scene: a scene, in which I describe the action in the other scenes, and end the video with a truly impressive cumshot, and a pan into a still photo that strongly implies that the cop eventually became my lover and "reformed" me. Hey, it's a cliché, but it works . . . especially since I'm obviously a couple years older in the narrative scenes. I wrote the monologue, too. (Should I be proud of this, I wonder?) So we did the postproduction, and got a distributor, and . . . well, other difficulties arose. I don't think Walt ever sold more than 500 copies of the video–definitely not enough to make a profit, much less pay back my loan. For the last ten years, it's been sitting on warehouse shelves gathering dust, although Walt claims his distributor is still selling copies without sending him his cut. For all of you amateur producers out there who are sure you can make a bundle with a pornflick: this is, I'm sorry to say, the grim reality of making porn.

"WATER SPORTS," A LOOP OF WINNER TAKES ALL, *OCTOBER 1983*

Before we'd even finished shooting *California Blue*, I had an offer from Falcon's talent scout, Dennis Forbes, to do a video for them. He met me at Savages, over Labor Day weekend. He'd been commissioned by *Playboy*, of all magazines, to photograph the "Biggest Dick in San Francisco" contest. Well, yes, yours truly was the winner, and so naturally, he gave me his card, saying, "Let's do a video, little boy." I was as enthusiastic as always. (The folks at

Playboy, incidentally, when they saw the photos, were horrified. "You know we can't print shots of penises!" they told him.) So Dennis test-shot me (making me look about fourteen years old, everyone claims–Falcon was too nervous about those photos to ever use them in publicity), and sometime in October or November, I was flown down to L.A. for the one-day shoot. We spent the night in some cheesy Sunset Boulevard motel, and bright and early Saturday morning, we were ferried up to the location: a house up in the hills with a view of a smog-filled basin (with a pool, of course). That's where I met Randy (now this is one occasion where I genuinely have no memory of his real name, and don't care) Page. My initial impression: spoiled little empty-headed blond preppie gold digger. Godnose what his impression of me was. If I'd had a few more movies under my belt, I might have bowed out at that point, telling the director, "Hey, I just can't work with someone like that." Fortunately for my career, that didn't occur to me as an option (and, realistically, it wasn't). So we spent the day lying around, sunbathing, waiting to have sex. The first item on the agenda was the setup shots. I think we got around to them at about 2 p.m. I was then told to give Randy an enema with a garden hose–the single most disgusting thing I've ever done on camera, I have to say. Enemas are not meant to be given with garden hoses. I mean, those brass fittings on the end are not smooth, okay? And this is COLD water we're talking about. If I'd been on his end of the hose, I'd have walked out right then and there. After that experience, I'm not surprised he disliked me. He put up a brave front, though, and I fucked him for much of the rest of the afternoon, while cameramen changed positions, rearranged the reflectors, and so forth. Shortly before sunset, when the director realized he was losing the light, he told us, "Okay, time for your cumshots!" And about time, too. I eagerly shot all over Randy; Randy required a dick in his mouth to work himself up to climax, so I obliged. Afterward, when the cameras had stopped rolling, he spat my dick out as if it tasted bad. Maybe it did. I don't think we spoke another word to each other. Minutes later, cash in hand, I was being ferried back to the airport. I don't want this to sound like it was a horrible experience. It wasn't. I had fun. It just wasn't very sexy.

"HARD-PRESSED," A LOOP OF RAMCHARGER, FEBRUARY 1984

This was a strange little loop, designed to go with two other film pieces that had been hanging around for a year or more–and since Falcon had just switched to video, they needed another film loop to finish up this movie. (There's some technical reason why they didn't want to mix analog and digital on the same tape.) For some reason, they decided that these loops weren't up to their usual standards, and they should be marketed under a new brand name, "Jocks," so as not to sully the fine Falcon reputation–the beginning of my B-movie career.

The premise of the loop was especially loopy: two leathermen are slouching along a country lane somewhere (actually someone's backyard, of course) when we find a naked boy (Brian Hawks) handcuffed to a cyclone fence. Well, of course we let him go, right? Um . . . you obviously don't have the Falcon formula engraved in your brain yet. That's right, we molest him unmercifully, and at the end we leave him handcuffed to the fence again. It's not my fantasy, but hey, I'm not the owner of a million-dollar video studio, either.

I need to go back, before telling this story, to Monday, when I'd met Peter James O'Brien, my co-leatherman. He was part Greek, part Turkish, part Irish–what a combination! He had black hair, dark eyes, full, sensuous lips, and the juiciest-looking foreskin I think I'd ever seen. He also mentioned that he'd recently been in jail, but he didn't say why. We were at the Saharan Motel, changing for dinner. Dennis Forbes was staying with us, as chaperone–a good thing, too, or I'd have been all over Peter at the first opportunity. This man was the stuff of which my fantasies had always been made. We went out to dinner (Italian; I had a cannoli, imagining it was you know who), and then to a garage, where Dennis was all set to shoot stills of Peter. I said, "Excuse me, do you need a fluffer?"–and he agreed, so I got to at least taste that heavenly cock. But it wasn't working, and after awhile Dennis asked me to leave, so I didn't see the rest of the shoot. It didn't go well. Peter maintained, that night, that he was straight, and just couldn't get excited with all these guys around. Not a good omen for the shoot.

On Tuesday, Dennis spent all day trying to get a decent set of stills of Peter. I went shopping. At day's end, Dennis admitted failure. Not good. I spent another night tossing and turning, wondering if I stood any chance with Peter once the shoot was over.

On location, Wednesday, the same problems popped up (or didn't pop up). Admittedly, it was unusually cold for L.A., and outdoor shooting in fifty-degree weather is not very good for erections. No matter what stimulus we used, Peter's fabulous dick stayed limp. It didn't really bother me; just a lick or two on it, and *my* dick was harder than it had ever been. Sort of like fluffing, only in reverse. (Which, come to think of it, is how "fluffing" has always worked for me. Having someone else suck on my dick makes me self-conscious; sucking on someone else's dick releases all my animal instincts, and usually makes me stiff.) So I did all of the plowing of Mr. Hawks, and Peter got his dick sucked a lot. Eventually, the director called a halt to the shoot, saying that maybe the weather would be better the next day, and we all went home–another sleepless night.

The weather didn't improve. We didn't get any better footage. Then, as the afternoon was wearing on, with no sign of a cumshot, emergency measures were called for: a local boy named Gregg who had been in several earlier Falcon videos was surreptitiously called up. He came over, ostensibly to deliver something, and did an emergency stunt performance. He was very professional; I just sucked him a little bit, and he produced a masterful erection and impressive moneyshot. Since his dick, though beautiful, was circumcised, that meant that all shots of Peter's dick had to be cut from the film. I was depressed when I saw the final product; I think they wasted a lot of footage that foreskin lovers would've paid good money to see, hard-on or no. Fortunately, as I said, I had one of the better "performance days" of my career: Peter's dick inspired me as few others before or since. There might actually be some connection to the fact that he was soft the whole time. I mean, a soft dick, especially given my foreskin fetish, is relatively nonthreatening, but retains most of the erotic potential of a hard dick. If he'd just managed to piss down my throat, I'd probably have had a spontaneous orgasm.

That night at the motel, I was frantic. I wanted to get into Peter's bed so bad I could taste it. Instead, he went out on the town, looking for pussy. I don't know if he found it. In the morning, he gave me his address, and said I should let him know if I was back down in L.A.; but when I wrote, my letter was returned. I did hear from him once more: he wrote me a letter from prison, a month or two later–he told me it was due to a parole violation. There was no response when I wrote back. I pined for months.

SLAVES FOR SALE, *JUNE 1984*

The genesis of this rather horrible little video was when I innocently shaved one side of my head, in March or April of 1984. I was intending on leaving it that way–very punk, you know–but then I wandered through the leather store on Folsom Street that just happened to be the storefront for *Drummer* magazine, and John Embry (the publisher) saw me, and said, "Hey kid, ya wanna get the rest of that shaved on film?" Having heard the magic word–film–I batted my eyelashes at him and agreed. He grabbed Patrick Toner, who was tending the front counter, and we went upstairs and took some photos of Patrick shaving my head. The photos looked quite impressive–it isn't obvious that I was half-shaved to begin with, and one of the shots was used on the cover of the next issue of *Drummer*–and two months later, John Embry called me up again. "Hey kid"–always his term for me, and maybe for all his stable of boys–"how's your hair?" He wanted to reenact the scene, on video.

I am nothing, if not willing. I've been told that's what doomed my video career: I didn't know how to say no to those inevitable "B" grade producers. (And, ten years later, have I learned how to say No? Well, let me think. Surely I've said No to *someone* in the past year . . . ?) So John paired me up with Ken Bergstrom, a Top From Hell who had recently moved to San Francisco from Florida. I can't say I liked the man, but that was kind of irrelevant under the circumstances; in an S/M video, you're not *supposed* to "like" your partner, you're just supposed to play your role adequately. Since my "role" was to hang from the ceiling like a piece of meat, in shackles and restraints, while he shaved my head and body (and applied various other indignities), that was easy. He also clearly wanted to fuck me, but I hadn't agreed to that; he pretended to do so, anyway. No climaxes. Hey, it wasn't much fun to shoot, and I've only watched the thing once. If your thing is v-e-r-y s-l-o-w videos, this one's for you.

THE OTHER SIDE OF ASPEN, PART II, *APRIL 1985*

It takes a certain amount of chutzpah to take an acknowledged classic of the genre, like *The Other Side of Aspen*, and try to make a Part II–ten years later. Several of the original performers were still alive and still available, but Falcon chose an entirely new cast. (Or was Jeff Turk in the original? I can't remember.) I found the thought titillating–being connected to one of the original gay pornflicks, by whatever tenuous connection there was–so I was more than eager. When I arrived in Tahoe (no, it wasn't filmed at Aspen–and neither was the original), I was even more glad that I'd agreed to do it: that's when I met Tony Bravo.

Oh, okay, his name was Michael. That's the name we used on set, too. "Noms de porn" are generally ridiculed by the very people who insist on using them. I've never cared for the institution. Oh, I've used pseudonyms for various purposes throughout my life (mainly for mailing lists), but never to separate my sex life from my "real life." I would consider that an unhealthy psychological attitude toward sex. I was proud to be in these movies. Most other men are not, for whatever reason. Some will say, "But what if my boss found out?"; some mention their parents; some have lovers; some have wives. Some really do anticipate meteoric political careers. (And yes, the discovery of a past life in pornflicks would truly make a politician's career "meteoric," in the sense that a meteor is only notable when it's crashing and burning.) Curiously, most of the porn performers I've stayed in touch with over the years have eventually come out to their parents–and their parents have generally been quite intrigued by the idea of having a pornstar son.

What was Michael's reason? I have no idea. I never asked. He was one of the sexiest men I'd ever met, and it's difficult to ask serious questions (beyond: "Wanna fuck?") of someone who sets your blood boiling. There was also a fellow on set named Maurizio (known to the world as Giorgio Canalli, and familiar to me from several William Higgins and Nova films), who similarly made my knees weak. He and Michael had met, coincidentally, a couple of weeks earlier, at a Big Dick Contest in L.A. Maurizio had won; Michael had come in second and won a special prize for having the "sexiest" dick (and it was!). The three of us, together with about six other young porn-bunnies, were shut up in a good-sized chalet for the weekend. Oh, what torture!

Actually, all joking aside, it really was. As mentioned heretofore, Falcon keeps a close watch on its stars to make sure they're not having fun offscreen, wasting precious juices. There was always a chaperone present. On Saturday morning, when we were supposed to begin shooting, we were all sitting around waiting for the van to take us up to the location (another chalet up on the mountainside, not materially different from the one on the lake). After two hours of waiting, I got a headache and retired to a bedroom to lie down. Not too long afterwards, Maurizio wandered back that way, too. Or maybe I followed him back; who remembers? Before we knew what was going on, our hormones were at work: we were locked in a vigorous sixty-nine. He had a very tasty piece of Italian sausage, oversized but not so huge that it wouldn't fit down my throat (which, when I'm really turned on, doesn't acknowledge much in the way of limitations), and he had an amazingly deep throat, too. He came pretty damn close to bringing me off. He then spewed down my throat, a load that seemed at the time to be the most perfect cumload I'd ever swallowed; and moments later we heard the van drive up outside, and someone got out and called, "All aboard!"—and we quickly got dressed and ran outside. It all happened so quickly, I don't think anyone even suspected . . . but I felt guilty all that afternoon, as Maurizio's angle of erection consistently failed to measure up to what we all knew it was capable of doing. I knew that I had his best load of the day percolating in my stomach. Guilty—but smug and turned on.

Up on the mountainside, it was another case of hurry-up-and-wait. It was another four hours before any shooting got done; some of that time was spent outside, shooting stills in the snow (I'd brought along my own new Nikon, and shot a few stills of Michael and Maurizio which I treasure), but most of it was just sitting on the couches, watching TV, talking, snacking. (Not too many of those donuts, boys . . .)

When we finally got around to shooting, it was nearly sunset.

The "plot" of this scene–a group of skiers repairing to their cabin at the end of the day for group sex–had me, the brazen hussy of the group, doing a striptease up on a table, in an effort to get the orgy going. Okay, I did my part. I was looking forward to the orgy myself. I hadn't had nearly enough of Maurizio's meat, and I hadn't even tasted Michael's. But then, Falcon choreography stepped in. "Scott, you work with Chris and these other three blonds. Michael and Maurizio, you work together, over in that corner, with Jeff." God, talk about frustration! I mean, blonds are really not my cup of tea. For the next three hours, I kept trying to sneak over to the Italian corner. No success. I found out later that the plot of the film called for those two to be sort of in love–and I was just a casual acquaintance. At any rate, during one of the breaks, while the cameramen were having coffee, Michael and I were relaxing by ourselves on the set–and I noticed his toenails needed trimming. Ever ready with my clippers and file (once a fister, always prepared!), I set to work . . . and then started massaging his feet . . . and then sucking his toes . . . and when the cameraman happened to glance into the room, a few minutes later, I had half his foot crammed into my mouth, and we were both intensely turned on. They quietly started filming, and the scene gradually built up around us. I got several of his toes up my ass, which Michael seemed to enjoy and I certainly did. Before long, though, we were directed to separate, again–yanked apart by cruel, unfeeling video-Nazis–and I had to go back to fucking the blonds. Maurizio did get it up enough to get into at least one of them, but basically the fucking was my responsibility. How ironic. No one in my private life has ever accused me of being a top, but when you have a big dick, porn directors want you for one thing and one thing only: your ability to fuck. And yes, this film does stand out as one of the more brilliant documentaries of my scimitar-like dick. When it's really, really hard, my dick curves upward rather beautifully (it's been years since I've seen it that hard), and I don't remember having any hard-on problems on this particular set. Ah, the vigor of youth.

When I saw the finished product, I was furious to learn that they'd edited the footage in such a way as to make it seem that the foot-in-ass scene (all ten seconds of it) was my foot in one of the blonds' asses. So the most genuine moments of that entire day's shooting (if you discount the private session with Maurizio) got hacked to pieces, and most people probably don't even realize how it relates to the rest of the video. Pity. Michael did give me his phone number in L.A., though (so did Maurizio, but unfortunately I never used it, being thoroughly besotted with Michael at the time). A couple weeks later, I made a special trip down to L.A. just to see him, and we spent a fabulous night together; it wasn't until nearly a year later that I discovered he was really in love with a man he'd met the week before *Aspen*, and therefore wasn't really devoting his whole attention to me. But a man like Michael can get away with dividing his attention since he was at least twice as sexy as anyone else I knew at the time.

And the video? Oh, I think I look pretty silly, up on the coffee table doing a striptease, but others have disagreed, telling me it's a hot scene.

SIGHS, *APRIL 1985*

The major draw on this set–shot just one weekend after *The Other Side of Aspen II*–was Craig Lovorn, aka "Joel Curry." A "new discovery," fresh from Ohio, I think everyone was gaga over him. Ron Pearson, our fearless writer/director/star, certainly was. So was I; he was innocent and fresh-faced in a way that few porn-bunnies manage to maintain much after their first film–that's an irresistible quality. Hey, that's why he was such a valued commodity for the brief duration of his career in porn. But I wasn't scheduled to play with him; I was to be manhandled by Eric Ryan, an old-time performer who I'd never met. For once, I was told about this casting a week before the shoot date, giving me time to psych myself up for it. I watched *Screenplay* over and over–it's one of my favorite videos, and while I'd never especially turned on to Eric before, I began to see how I could eroticize him. He had a certain animal magnetism; he clearly got Jon King's hormones raging. By the Thursday of the shoot, I was rarin' to go.

I arrived on set early, having offered to act as "second still photographer." I got acquainted with all the performers, and knew right away there was a problem. Not a physical problem; Eric looked just as beefy and appealing in person as he did on film. Just . . . his personality grated on me. Maybe it was all due to drugs; I think there was more drug activity on this set than on any of the Falcon films I'd done. He was loud and obnoxious, telling offensive jokes and laughing his head off . . . after a couple of hours, I collared Steve Scott (our "assistant" director, who did most of the work–don't ask me why a director of Steve Scott's caliber had been reduced to doing grunt work on someone else's films) and told him, "This won't work." I understand Eric expressed some doubts, too. He probably called me "Miss Priss," for having declined his offer of drugs. That evening, we shot two scenes that didn't directly involve me; by the next morning, the script had been rewritten, and I was recast with Craig. Eric was put in a three-way with Ron and Gary. Naturally, I couldn't have been more delighted.

The scene with Craig–shot at ShapeUp, a formerly trendy San Francisco bodywork emporium–began in a weight room, proceeded to the locker room, and ended in the Jacuzzi. By way of preparation for this film, I had gone out three weeks prior and enrolled myself at the gym on a one-month trial membership, just so I'd know the ropes around there; it was the one time in my life when I've worked out regularly in a gym. I can honestly say I never saw even the most discreet sex going on there during business hours. (Ron had hired the place at night for shooting the two relevant scenes. Did the owners know what was going on? I presume so. And who, in San Francisco, would care?) I still wasn't very happy with the way my physique measured up–let's just say that I don't think I looked very convincing while I was sweating away on the weights–but once we got into the Jacuzzi, I think most viewers' thoughts were far away on some other tangent. I confess to having a weak spot in my heart for that scene (and my ex-lover Bill certainly left the videotape at that particular spot often enough . . .): I fucked him of course, on the locker room bench and then in the Jacuzzi, but Craig ended up with his tongue halfway up my ass, while I sucked my own dick and shot cum on my face–a most satisfactory climax.

None of us "got" Craig; he lived just opposite Dolores Park, on Church Street, and I developed a habit of sunbathing in Dolores Park in hopes that I'd run into him. He did invite me up to his apartment once, and I went out to dinner with him once. He then moved to L.A., to be in more pornflicks and to cohabit with one of the reigning pimps of the industry. He did come back north one time for a brief visit, and stayed with me–no sex, but very friendly. Some months later, I was shocked to hear that Craig had gone back to Ohio–and killed himself. So far as I know, no one ever established a reason. I think everyone who ever met him was distraught. I don't think he ever made a bad impression on anybody.

In my darker moments, it occurs to me that learning that he had AIDS could have been the impetus for his suicide . . . and that, conceivably, I could have been the person who gave it to him. If . . . if . . . if. I don't have answers, or solutions. I can agree that from a health maintenance viewpoint, what we were doing in those movies was not beneficial; I also know that in 1985, we did not have the option of wearing condoms in films. Video producers would not have allowed it, because "It's not sexy. It reminds people too much of the epidemic." We knew the realities of the situation; we knew the risks, and the rewards. I wanted to be in porno, more than anything else. I guess Craig did, too. I'm only sorry his career had to end so soon. There was a man who deserved to be a superstar.

SGT. SWANN'S PRIVATE FILES, *JUNE 1985*

Why do producers get into the business of making porn? In some cases, it seems obvious: because they obsess over the medium, because they think there's a lot of money to be made in it, because they genuinely want to improve the product, or just because they know lots of guys who they think would be hot on-screen. These are a few of the motivations I've seen. I've spent a lot of time puzzling over why Dirk Yates does porno. He obviously isn't hurting for cash; he has a successful series of businesses, including several adult bookstores and a theater. As near as I can tell, he does it because he wants the fame and glamour, and he's too old to actually be in the videos himself. He surrounds his stars with all the paraphernalia of Hollywood: airport limos, reasonably classy hotels, even "Gala Premieres." At least he did for *Sgt. Swann's Private Files.*

SSPF starts with me jerking off in a tent–a fantasy sequence, beautifully lit in silhouette. When I go down on myself, and you see my shadow on the tent wall, it's about as breathtaking as any scene I've ever done. Glenn Swann comes in–slowly, ominously–dressed in a bizarre eighteenth-century Foreign Legion-type outfit; I undress him, and lick his body all over. It takes a long time. I'm his slave. Then I rim and ream him. A very tasty and thoroughly enjoyable process, as I recall.

Now, Glenn Swann is a curious creation. At the time of filming, he was happily married, described himself as straight, and was recently out of the Marines. He loved to get fucked. Oh, I don't think there's anything unusual about that; many straight men love to get fucked. Many others would if they could bring themselves to try it. Marines, especially, have a reputation for loving to get fucked (though this may be more sour grapes than reality). Getting fucked is inherently pleasurable for anyone with a prostate; it's only societal conditioning that makes us unable to appreciate it. (And don't think I underestimate the power of that conditioning! Even lots of gay men haven't beaten it back all the way.) So I'm really just expressing admiration for Mr. Swann; he knows what he likes (pussy and getting fucked) and he's willing to go out and get it. All of it. Would that more men were so open and aboveboard about their desires.

Anyhow, I enjoyed my time with Glenn. We got on well, and our scene climaxed quite satisfactorily. I spent the rest of the day resting and recuperating, while other scenes were shot. Then, in the evening, we shot the orgy scene–barracks, of course–me and three (four? five? I forget) other guys. Most notable was an acrobatic maneuver involving holding someone upside down off the edge of the top bunk . . . it wasn't very successful. At the end, we all shot our loads on Glenn's hat. Okay, it was hokey, and for someone like me with no military fantasies whatsoever, it was all sort of silly. But the guys were cute, I had a generally good time, and as I said, Dirk treated us royally.

Come the release date, however, I was in for a surprise. As I said, there was a Gala Premiere at one of the adult theaters in San Diego. I was flown back down and put up at the Balboa Park Inn, a very gay establishment with theme rooms. In the "Tara Suite," I felt slightly ridiculous, but excited, too. And the limo that delivered us to the theater . . . and the hors d'oeuvres (need I add that they were all phallic-shaped?) . . . and the 8 × 10 glossies that Dirk had for us to sign! I'd never seen a pornflick get this sort of treatment, and I have to say it was gratifying. Yes, it was all a bit excessive (Hollywood IS excessive), but it was also the real-world recognition that what we were doing was valuable and important. With ten years of perspective, I appreciate that acknowledgment; it's one of the messages that I've spent my subsequent career pushing. Thank you, Dirk.

OVERSIZE LOAD, *SEPTEMBER 1985*

I first met Al Parker–Drew, to his friends–in August, when he was up in San Francisco to act as a judge at the Greasy Jockstrap Contest, held at the Powerhouse Bar on Folsom Street. I didn't go in for these contests as a general rule, especially in bars–it didn't seem like my arena. I mean, you can't show your dick in a bar, and godnose my chest is nothing special to look at. I don't have rippling abs or dazzling deltoids. But hey, a jockstrap contest is crotch-oriented enough that I figured I could win it. I also wanted to meet Drew, and hopefully be in one of his videos. (He'd already established a reputation as a foreskin lover, even before his own foreskin restoration; I figured that if I were in an Al Parker video, I could count on some uncut dick, at the very least.) As the Saturday night approached, I realized I needed that $100 prize to buy groceries for the weekend, having dreadfully mismanaged my checking account the previous week. So I showed up, still somewhat uncertain about actually entering; no one else wanted to enter, either, so they upped the prize to $150 and got (I think) three contestants. Maybe it was four. I think two of the contestants were twins. Mr. Marcus, the perpetual emcee at these events, poured motor oil all over our jockstraps, and we got to be as lewd and lascivious as we felt comfortable with, which meant that my dick did get exposed (surprise, surprise), and yes, I won. Drew and I made the connection, he made the inevitable offer, and we scheduled the shoot for early September. He even hinted that I might be paired with Jon King–which made my dick jump to attention right away. I'd never met Mr. King, at that point, but I'd always wanted to. Unfortunately, it didn't happen: Jon got arrested, or disappeared, or something.

The week before the shoot, Drew and his lover invited me down to spend the weekend at their house in Hermosa Beach. Oh, it was an official audition, too, I suppose, but I was just enjoying myself. It's the only real "casting couch" interview I've ever had: I spent the night sandwiched between the two of them. I've always liked sandwiches. I fucked Steve, Drew did his pretzel number with his dick and my dick, and eventually fucked me. A good time was had by all. And I was officially hired.

The next weekend, it was frantic and laid-back, simultaneously. Drew, having been a performer himself, knew how to make performers perform: don't tell them how to do their job, just turn them loose on each other and let them go to town. I was in three scenes in that video, all shot over the course of the weekend. Only one of them was really difficult for me, partly because I was asked to fuck someone standing up. That's never been an easy position for me to work from—and my partner, a lovely blond, although quite turned on and enthusiastic, with a wonderfully muscular bubble-butt, just didn't inspire me the way one of the Italian boys in the other scenes might have. Still, I think all the scenes worked out adequately. I have only one complaint, and I can't decide if it was deliberate sadism or accidental bad luck.

Drew, in his original interview, had asked me what sort of partner I'd be most turned on by. I had a pretty good stock description of my ideal type: dark-haired, dark-skinned, foreskinned, with a last name like Lopez or Rodriguez or Alfaro or Dal Porto. He got the picture. He and I shared similar tastes, in fact, and he assured me that he had several such men on line for the production.

So he did. Two of 'em. He even put them in a scene with me: the final scene, when I was supposed to be standing at a washbasin shaving, watching this scene unfolding in the showers. I got to jerk off, watching—but never joining in. To this day, when I watch that scene, I get hungry...and angry. A foreskin I was *that* close to . . . but never tasted. A set of tattoos I saw, but never licked. A pair of hairy calves that I would've loved to worship, but didn't get the chance. God that man knew how to tease.

THE JOYS OF SELF-ABUSE, *SEPTEMBER 1985*

There's not much to say about this one; it's another *Drummer* masterpiece, a jackoff video—nicely done, I think, and I enjoyed several of the other performers, but I don't remember watching it more than a couple of times. The process of shooting it left no indelible marks on my memory. A fake stage was set up in the *Drummer* offices, with rows of chairs that were occupied by the office staff, so they could include shots of the backs of the audience's heads. I think John Rowberry is one of them. I did my usual masterful masturbation routine, but my mind was elsewhere. Maybe just because it was shot three days before my big feature of the year: *Below the Belt*.

BELOW THE BELT, *SEPTEMBER 1985*

If I meet a fan who starts waxing rhapsodic about one of my scenes, at least half the time it's a scene from this film. If I show up at a bathhouse and one of the attendants realizes I'm there and puts on one of my videos, chances are he'll choose this one. It's the closest I ever got to being in the L.A. big time porno circuit: the Matt Sterling crowd. Surprisingly, I enjoyed myself immensely.

The director, Philip, was a rather fussy little queen who was nevertheless quite endearing . . . except for his extremely tightfisted attitude toward money. I don't remember how he contacted me originally, but he had a list of credits that included several grade B mainstream Hollywood movies, which I found impressive at the time. He also had done one pornflick, the year before, which had gotten a lot of attention . . . so I was eager. Yippee! I'm about to break into the Big Time!

The locations Phil had chosen for shooting: a suburban house in the San Fernando Valley, a nearby bathhouse, and a warehouse next door to the bathhouse where most of the karate class sequences were filmed. Actually, I don't think we did any shooting *at* the bathhouse, but it was where we all cleaned up before and after filming. It was also where Chris and I did most of our extracurricular fooling around while we were waiting for scenes to get underway.

Chris Burns, old friend and pornstar extraordinaire, provided the technical expertise that made the karate sequences in the film possible. I don't know his training background, but he was capable of some very impressive moves, and he taught Chad Douglas how to appear dangerous. He also filled in for one of our more delicate cast members when the boy proved unable to accommodate everything Phil wanted him to take in his virginal butthole. Chris was known for his capacity, which he just loved to demonstrate–anywhere, anytime.

I think we shot three scenes indoors on Saturday. They kind of fade together. There was the dream sequence, where a bunch of phantoms move in on a helplessly bound Asian boy and shoot their loads all over him (very spooky and surreal, and still quite sexy–and I produced one of the best cumshots of my career); then the locker room scene, which sandwiches the dream sequence; then the orgy grand finale, in which I had the dubious honor of deepthroating Chad Douglas (who has all the delicacy and finesse of a jackhammer). So that was my second orgasm of the day, and then we all got to hang around while we waited for the last scene to finish (the romantic conclusion to the orgy, between Chad and Jim Steele). I got turned on again, and actually moved in on the scene and shot another load all over Jim's tits. Don't know whether it improves the video or not, but it did move him to finally cum. (Can we go home now?)

On Sunday, we moved on to the Valley Ranchette for two more scenes. One was the straight boy seduction scene, which I, thank god, did not have any part in. The other was the infamous Wussie (sometimes spelled "woosie," sometimes "woozy," in the hilarious script) Scene, in which David Ashfield and I double-dick (a faintly protesting) Michael Cummings. This was Chris Burns' opportunity to jump into the action as a stunt-butt. I was given the chance, for once in my career, to essay Real Acting, heaping verbal abuse upon the "wussie" bottom; for this reason alone, it's the movie I have the most difficulty watching. To whatever extent I was successful, I find it unsexy: I don't like watching scenes of brutal meanies taking out their frustration on wussies. I was a wussie when I was in high school, and lots of brutal meanies took out their frustrations on me (never sexually, alas), and it was never any fun. But hey–I wasn't writing the script, and I don't dictate the fantasies of Gay America. My fans tell me it's a hot scene. It's the one time I've double-dicked someone on film, which gives it a certain status in my mind, since that's one of my all-time most effective sexual fantasies. (The reality never lives up to the fantasy. I had, I'm sorry to say, difficulty keeping a hard-on. Fortunately, David had no such problems. He never does.) Aside from the stress of working for a Just-One-More-Shot-Please director, the afternoon was enjoyable. And hey, I won't complain about Phil's perfectionism. At least he put those shots together into something of which I can be proud. That's more than I can say about some other projects, such as . . .

HUNG & HORNY, *JANUARY 1986*

This was the nadir of my career. I don't remember how Ms. R. Stilskin found me, but god I wish she hadn't. She's a short, hyperactive woman who talks a mile a minute, insisting on telling you in great detail about her latest obsession and how it's bound to be the greatest porn film since *Deep Throat*. She'll also tell you about her long-standing relationship with porn legend Alex de Renzy (some straight porn magnate), and gush over her latest dumb blond stud boyfriend (who's going to be the biggest gay porn star ever). I don't remember, frankly, whether or not I had suspicions about her expertise from the start; if I did, the fact that she paid remarkably well silenced them. Woe is me. It was the most chaotic, unprofessional shoot I've ever been on. The "star," a straight boy who Ms. Stilskin was apparently trying to fuck (and who supposedly had a foot-long dick), continually raised objections that he didn't know he was gonna have to work around fags . . . and he didn't know he was gonna have to show his dick on camera . . . and he'd better be getting paid extra for this . . . and no way was he gonna touch another guy's dick . . . etc. This was boring enough, but when they shot the box cover, they shoved a huge dildo into his pants because he couldn't raise a real erection. At this point, I lost all hope for the production. I just wanted it to be over.

I don't remember what the plot of the movie was; there may not have been one. I remember sucking a variety of dicks that were stuck through a series of gloryholes, which would have been erotic if the gloryholes hadn't been in aluminum-foil-covered cardboard. (Someone thought she was a designer.) They probably had a fog machine, too. Hey, why not? The climax is indelibly branded on my memory: I was lying on the floor while the six or seven other guys jerked off on me. Hot, right? Well, it might have been, if the warehouse had been heated and/or I'd been lying on something other than a concrete slab. I felt like a stone-cold corpse by the time the last guy had shot. Then, just as I thought I could move, Ms. Stilskin cries out: "Stay there! we have to get another camera angle on that!"–and she brought out some milk, fresh from the refrigerator, which she proceeded to drip all over me, trying to simulate cum-shots, while the cameras shot me from above. And again, and again . . . after the third time, when she was saying, "Wait! I think we need to get that one more time!" I was finished; I said "No!" and got up and walked away, trembling with equal parts frostbite and fury. I've always had the reputation of being "easy to work with"–but this woman was the devil incarnate.

THE GUY NEXT DOOR, *FEBRUARY 1986*

For years, I'd been jerking off to Old Reliable videotapes: solo scenes of street hustlers, mostly, talking to the camera, boasting, stripping, flexing their muscles, shadowboxing, and jerking off. Some of these tapes featured wrestling or boxing between two or more of his models–home video, long before home video became a commercial subgenre of porno. I never thought of being in one of Old Reliable's videos, though–I mean, I've never been much of a street hustler. I'm not his type.

Then, in late 1985, I ordered one of his tapes–and who should be the first model on the tape but Peter, my incredibly sexy costar from *Hard-Pressed,* two years earlier. I hemmed and hawed, but eventually I sent David (the producer of Old Reliable) a letter, asking him to forward the enclosed note to Peter if he should see him again . . . lust makes us desperate, sometimes. Of course, you see, I was on David's mailing list under a pseudonym, to avoid getting unwanted fan mail; so I was surprised when I got a letter from him addressed to Scott O'Hara. He'd opened my letter to Peter, obviously–since, as he wrote, Peter hadn't been seen around his place since the video had been shot, many months previous. Upon finding out that M. Schroner was Scott O'Hara, he immediately wanted to know if I'd appear in one of his videos.

Well, hell, I never say "No."

Besides, I reasoned: Old Reliable videotapes reach an audience that none of my other videos were ever likely to reach. I'd be introducing myself to hundreds, possibly thousands, of new men. Let's face it, by this time in my career I was starting to seriously worry about how much longer I could keep it up. I wanted to get as many performances recorded on film as I possibly could. So the next time I was down in L.A., I dropped in and did a jackoff sequence for him. It went well—hey, what could be easier?—and I was happy with the way my body looked at the time. He even managed to sell some photos of me to one of the gay magazines, which gave me a tasteful eight-page spread. I appreciated publicity; I always have. After the video shoot was finished, I managed to play a little joke on David. He's a very shy, self-effacing fellow, who is always very careful to avoid putting himself in any of his videos. (Despite the fact that his apartment is *filled* with mirrors, I've only once caught a glimpse of him in one of them; maybe he's a vampire.) So I was fiddling around with my own camera—still nude, of course—while he was seated at the kitchen table doing the model-release paperwork. I walked over to stand behind him, and started rubbing his shoulders. A few seconds later, the flash went off. He was terribly embarrassed. I told him I'd keep that picture, oh, just in case.

Now, I'm just not a blackmailing type (and besides, David is much too open about what he does to ever be blackmailed). I just like to record people, all sorts of people, on film. I've got similar unpublishable photos of dozens of my costars and producers—unpublishable because I never bothered to get model releases. Nevertheless, it tickles my sense of irony that for once I'm in the position to be more controling than controlable in the producer/performer relationship.

SEX-HUNT, *OR,* YOU GET WHAT YOU PAY FOR, *APRIL 1986*

I don't remember how I got this job; I just remember being on the set, doing numerous takes on all the dialogue (although I had only one sex scene, according to the script I'm the major character, the owner of the phone-sex line), and then doing an extremely long evening of shooting. I was with David Ashfield (one can always count on David for a consistent hard-on, bless him) and a brutish, tattooed, ostensibly straight Latino; they both got to fuck me, in turn. Maybe they tried to double-fuck me, I'm not sure. I got a little wild; watching that scene embarrasses me a bit (but turns me on intensely) because I sound like I'm trying to act. I wasn't; I was just squealing like a stuck pig, which is a good description of how I felt. Personally, I have no interest in the particular fetish documented in that scene–I'm dressed up, initially, as a state trooper, and so is the Latino–but it's nice to know that I can render a moderately effective imitation. Maybe there's hope for my acting career yet.

At the same time, since it's one of only three films in my entire career where I get porked, I'm also especially fond of this one. Jim West put a lot of care into his videos: it's got some class. Regardless of whether or not any of the fantasies portrayed are personally arousing (they aren't), I can get off on the sight of a *cholo* fucking me. Personally, I think I got a lot more than I paid for in this video.

STICK SHIFT, *APRIL 1986*

This is one of very few videos where I knew who my partner would be beforehand. I don't remember how I found out, but I did, and I practically burst into flames on the spot. I never can remember his name–it was so clearly fake, modeled after Jan Michael Vincent, and there was a certain similarity in their faces–but I'd been jerking off to one of his previous bisexual videos for most of the past year. He made a very convincing show of acting like he was a virgin when he was being dildo-fucked, then turning around and fucking a couple of women–a major turn-on. I was looking forward to plumbing the depths of that spectacular ass, and finding out whether it was easier for him to take the dildo, or get excited over cunt.

It turned out that in person he was, well, less than totally agreeable. He didn't actually claim to be straight, but he was a bit freaked out by having to take my dick. He claimed he'd never had anything that big up his butt and didn't really want to. Oh, once it was in him, he seemed to adjust (though his hard-on went away), but he was never enthusiastic. Hey, that would've been fine with me–I'd have been perfectly happy to let *him* fuck *me*–but that was contrary to our director's script.

(Strangely enough, I discovered when I saw the finished product, the final scene has "Mr. Vincent" paired with Rick "Humongous" Donovan, cast as his character's "dream man." Once more, we have a case of a director not listening to his talent, I fear.)

The upshot of all this is one of the stranger lessons I ever learned on a set: you really shouldn't be *too* turned on by your partner. A moderate amount of attraction is good, but I was overexcited in this instance: I don't think I'd been fucking him for more than five minutes when I lost it, and shot my load. Oh, I pulled out, and the camera got a good close-up of my cumshot, as required; then, quickly, before I lost my hard-on, I shoved it back in and did another five minutes or so of fucking while everyone else did their cumshots. The video version seems hot enough–but I wasn't happy with my performance. I've done better with lots of other performers who didn't turn me on nearly as intensely.

ADVOCATE MEN LIVE!, *SEPTEMBER 1986*

What's to say? Another jackoff movie. The *Advocate* was always pretty tame; they didn't want to get into anything hard-core, they just wanted to do a video version of the magazine. So I recreated the Spunk character that I'd done for a photo spread the year before, rented a skateboard from a shop on Haight Street, and Dennis filmed me being as truculent and foul-mouthed as I was capable of; it was a lot of fun. I like it when I'm given the opportunity to be creative, and this was one of those times. No, being a nasty punk does not come naturally to me. I'm a pussycat by nature, but I do enjoy acting. Just as long as I'm not forced to keep up the charade too long. I'm liable to burst out laughing if there's anyone around who takes me seriously.

IN YOUR WILDEST DREAMS, *MARCH 1987*

Problem time. We're coming down to the end of my career, now. I'm starting to be real concerned about the lack of condoms on set. I almost asked about them before this shoot; I wish I had. I was paired with Joe Cade, a very hunky bodybuilder with a tasty uncut dick, and Bosch Wagner, a tattooed, slightly vacant boy with an asshole that he claimed could accommodate three fists. That was the plan: two of Joe's, one of mine. Or vice versa. It didn't work out. The scenario, improbably, was a doctor's office–mostly because the producer had recently acquired a medical examining table, and wanted to use it (I'm sure it cost a small fortune, and he needed proof that it was a business expense). I was the assistant, Joe was the vaguely Nazi-like doctor. I came in on the scene halfway through, feeling like a third wheel. Bosch's asshole proved to be less elastic than he had thought; I forget how much we managed to stuff up his hole, but my services were definitely not needed. I'm sure I fucked him, but I wasn't much into the scene; I never got a really convincing hard-on. I spent most of my time wishing that I was wearing a condom, but knowing that you have to have a real hard-on in order to put one on, and therefore I was in no position to make such a demand. I was very much into Joe, but the official scenario had no place in it for me to suck Joe's dick. That's the trouble with scripts: they don't generally leave room for improvisation. Oh, eventually it all worked out: I came, I guess everyone else came, and the producer expressed satisfaction with the result. Then, with the whole affair safely out of the way, I finally summoned up courage enough to say to him, "Look, you know I like working for you, but I really wish you would let us use condoms." I was ready for him to blow up in my face, to say, "Not on my sets you don't," or some such.

Instead, he looked me in the face, all wide-eyed innocence, and said, "Well, geez, guy, you should've said something! I had condoms and lube in the bag, right there!"

I've seldom felt so low as I did at that moment. My chance to make video history—the first Falcon video with condoms!—and I'd blown it, through lack of forcefulness.

SWITCH HITTERS II, *MAY 1987*

The only film I ever made that was shot on a real, live commercial soundstage. It was produced by a straight big-bucks porn producer; I guess they used a couple of gay industry talent scouts, because the talent was mostly from gay videos—an interesting mix. They used real, type-written scripts (and the performers were expected to deliver lines convincingly!); they spent a lot of time on makeup, hair, and costuming, and it was unusually heavy on plot. For all these reasons—and the more obvious one that I got to do something on-screen that I'd always wanted to do—it's one of my favorite films. I always recommend it to people who ask "What are some of your films?"–followed by the caveat, "You don't mind seeing some snatch, do you?"

I was cast as a baseball star, modeled after some then-famous hitter; I was to be blackmailed into joining an inferior team by having my sexual peccadilloes captured on film. Naturally, it didn't work out that way, but in the interim I got to suck Jim Bentley's dick, and fuck a very willing woman whose name I'm afraid I don't remember. Yep, that was the novelty, for me: you see, in all my years of ass-pounding, I'd never once gotten into a pussy, and I felt as if this were a serious gap in my sexual education, which needed filling.

She was a truly delightful partner, eager to put me at my ease; she spent an inordinate amount of time telling me how *big* my dick was–which is not the sort of commentary I expect from a woman, especially a woman experienced in the art of porn-making; maybe she had the idea that all men needed that ego boost in order to perform adequately. Maybe in straight porn she's right. Anyway, I had a great time. We used rubbers (making this the first film set on which they were used, in my experience!), for both fucking and sucking–and we were told that if either Jim or I did any cunt-licking, we should use dental dams. The prospect of licking a sheet of latex put us both off our feed, and we declined, even though we both expressed interest in the act. (I've since seen one video in which Jim did get to lick pussy–it's another R. Stilskin masterpiece–and he appeared to enjoy it. I don't know whether it was shot before or after *Switch Hitters II*.) In practice, how'd the scene work? Well, one of us would be fucking Ms. Willing; the other one would be standing up at the head of the bed, waving his dick in the first guy's face, giving him something to stay hard over. I don't think Jim was any more bisexual than I was (i.e., not at all), but he was at least as experimental, and he knew how to maintain a hard-on. I liked working with both of them–and it was a revelation, seeing how a real professional camera crew works. Talk about efficiency! In all my previous films, I'd never seen three scenes shot in such quick succession. Three *good* scenes. No sooner had we finished with the action in one section of the soundstage, than they'd dolly the camera over to another section, where the lights had already been set up, makeup had already been applied, and the performers were ready with their lines. I don't know how many times they shot the scene in the bar where I get "picked up" by Ms. Willing, but when I watch it, I'm kinda proud. Hey, I look *butch*!

ADVOCATE MEN LIVE! #4, *SEPTEMBER 1987*

An amusing event... no, my face isn't featured in this video, and I can't remember whether or not they ended up even using my dick. (The film is not in my collection, so I can't even verify this rather crucial detail.) I was originally supposed to pick up the *Advocate MEN* magazine that the mailman had just delivered, open it up, and have a good long jerk-off session over each of the models (each one, of course, coming to life from the photo spread). Corny but effective. I remember the director, however, worrying about my presence becoming too intrusive: that after all, they were trying to indicate that my perspective was the viewer's perspective, and therefore using my dick, or face, or even my hands would intrude onto the viewer's fantasy. In other words, a black man couldn't watch the video realistically if he's trying to imagine *his* hands are *my* hands. Where do these directors get off with their high-flown filmic devices? Do they think they're modern-day Eisensteins? Get real. In any case, my section of the filming–flipping through the magazine–was soon over. The major portion of my work was yet to come, however, and it's what makes this video special to me. You see, for once, I was credited in the technical credits–as "Technical Support," I believe. Translation? I did fluffing duties for one of the models, a delightful little daddy-boy from Honolulu. Never-say-no O'Hara, that's me. It was the one time I crossed over from being "just talent" to being a techie. It may seem strange to many of you that a glamorous porn-star should dream of being a lowly cameraman, but that's the job that gives you the chance to be creative. I was proud.

DOUBLE STANDARDS, *NOVEMBER 1987*

This was the second film I did for Ms. Stilskin. How did she convince me to work for her again, following the previous debacle? Frankly, I don't remember. I recall her enthusiasm being a factor; I recall rationalizing to myself, "Hey, she's made umpteen movies in the past year; surely she's learned something about how to deal with the talent."–well, she hadn't. It wasn't as annoying as the first project, though, mostly due to the presence of Cory Monroe. We hit it off in a fairly big way: he's an enthusiastic sex pig, with a fondness for big dicks, so he spent a lot of the time with a look of sheer ecstasy on his face. I always like seeing that look, and so few filmic bottoms actually seem to love their work. We got along just fine, despite the fact that his cocksucking enthusiasm outstripped his abilities; I had bleeding scratches along the length of my dick by the time I finally slipped into a condom and into his butt. (He was bleeding from that end by the time we finished.)

What can I say? It's another Stilskin movie. Maybe she lured me by telling me it would be a bisexual flick–that's always been a weakness of mine, and my previous experience was so positive that I probably thought it would work again. Alas, no. It was another nightmarish day on the set (the Le Salon warehouse in the low-rent southern district of San Francisco), relieved only by my attempt at minor industrial/political sabotage: I put a Libertarian bumper sticker on one of the filing cabinets that I was sure would appear in the video. I think they ended up editing it out, but I don't really feel like watching the damn thing to find out. The heterosexual scenes (in which I did not participate) were only mildly amusing, but to my surprise and pleasure, Cory and I got along famously. We both decided to ignore the cameras and have a good time, with tolerable results. Like I say, I still wouldn't watch this one for fun, but there's a certain amount of nostalgia associated with it. Cory and I keep running into each other in unlikely places over the years, and he keeps saying that we should get together. I'm tempted every time–he looks better than ever, in my opinion–but then I remember that he's a smoker, and come to my senses. One of these days, he says, he'll quit.

NEW RECRUITS, *NOVEMBER 1987*

Someone recently showed this one to me–I'd completely forgotten about it. Filmed on the same weekend as the preceding video (possibly on the same day, I frankly forget), I was paired up with Vladimir Correia, and despite all my lascivious comments about

Latin men, you can keep Vlad the Impaler. A truly obnoxious heterosexual boor, he loved to boast about his straight video career in Brazil. Personally, I've never seen his charm, but he's been in a lot of videos; maybe just because he's always available. He fucked me (that's virtually all he does, though he did comment in an offhand way that, sure, he'd get fucked, if a producer would pay him $10,000–fat chance); he was rough, dull, and had too much machismo, but at least he knew how to use a condom. Since my role in this video was as a photographer (something with which I had a more-than-passing familiarity), I was able to take a roll of photos of him, which I still have. Of course, I can't use them for anything, not having a model release, but I'm a photo packrat. I've got gazillions of photos that I can't ever use. Just having these men recorded on film, in all their naked glory, is good enough for me.

THE MASSAGE BOYS, *FEBRUARY 1988*

This one is memorable to me for two reasons: seeing retired legend Will Seagers come back from retirement (looking a little bit worse for wear, I admit, but still pretty sexy), and a long and amorous return encounter with the vampiric Cory Monroe. Cory was every bit as good as before; we did it in an indoor pool at a tacky 1960s house in Marin, this time, two rent-boys on their time off exchanging stories of the filthy things that the clients were always trying to do to us. Okay, the plot line wasn't quite Dostoyevskian. Get over it. It's an R. Stilskin video.

The major problem, actually, was that we were just getting into it too much, especially in the grotto/hot tub: we'd be getting smoochy and romantic, and start ignoring the director's imperious orders. Bad, bad, *bad* boys! Anyhow, I don't think the ultimate product is anything worth buying, but at least I had more fun on-set than I had with *Hung & Horny*.

HEAD OVER HEELS: THE COMPLETE GUIDE TO AUTOFELLATIO, *APRIL 1988*

My last video was also, fortunately, one of my safest–except from a chiropractic standpoint. It was a self-sucking "dickumentary," with just three performers. One of them introduced himself to me by saying, with awe in his voice, "You know, you're the first person I ever jerked off over, back when I was fifteen." Gee thanks, sonny, you sure know how to make a guy feel his years. Oh, don't think I didn't feel a surge of pride. I like being an icon. I also suddenly wondered if my back was going to be able to straighten out after that afternoon.

It did, but I also developed a serious backache for the next week. I'm really not as flexible as I used to be. I did like the format of the video, though: each of us was "interviewed." We talked a little bit about how we learned that we could do ourselves, why we liked it, and so forth; then we did it. Then, after all three of us had gone through our paces individually, he brought us all out together–this is the bizarre part–and had us all perform separately but together–three men having sex, each one ignoring the others. Oh, not "ignoring," exactly–I, for one, was turning onto the others–but not interacting, either. It was a weird feeling. But the video has been very popular, I'm told, so who am I to judge?

About sucking my own dick: it's not a big turn-on to me. It's painful, and not really satisfying. Still, it does give me that irreplaceable feeling of a dickhead between my lips, on those long, lonely winter nights when there aren't any other options, so I'm grateful for that, at least. It's a lot better than having to keep a lover around.

There was, in fact, one more video that I did. I showed up at a friend's house in L.A. the weekend he was directing his first video; he asked me if I'd come down and do background in a sex-party scene. This was in 1992 when I'd been officially retired for quite some time; I didn't really have any intention of participating. But hey, put me in a room with a bunch of naked guys, and whaddya expect? I had a good time, and I'm told I produced a great cumshot. I wasn't included in the credits, by my own request; it just seemed a bit of an anticlimactic end to my video career. Only devoted O'Haraphiles will even be aware of this appearance, and most of them will tastefully avert their eyes.

Then again, perhaps it's not the end. Cory Monroe has been talking, lately, about producing a video with an all-HIV-positive (all-singing! all-dancing!) cast. Now that sounds like a really intriguing possibility. I just wonder if my dick could be persuaded to respond. It's been in retirement a long, long time.

AIDS

When I moved to Hawaii in September 1981, after a summer of unrestrained sex in San Francisco (ah, the memories from that summer!), I had never heard of AIDS. Well, no one had heard that term yet, but I don't believe I'd even heard about the "new gay cancer." I think it first started making headlines, at least in the gay papers, that fall.

The last person with whom I had sex before leaving The City was a man I'd met at a garage sale, a benefit for the victims of the Folsom Fire; his last name was Cox. He was a big bear of a man, whose furry chest felt very good against my back, and I liked him a lot. He also ran a mail-forwarding service, to which I subscribed, so I heard from him regularly for the next year. Then . . . something happened. I stopped hearing from him. On my next visit back to San Francisco, in glancing through the *Bay Area Reporter*, which had recently started running obituaries, his name was one of the first ones I saw. I don't remember exactly when that was, but his was the first name that brought home to me that yes, men who I knew were now dying of this disease.

All during my time in Hawaii, I could ignore the growing epidemic. In 1981 and 1982, it was still a San Francisco/New York thing, unrelated to reality. With the death of Cox, I realized that I'd had sex with someone who probably had been infected. It scared me. This disease was still a mysterious, unknown quantity; men were dying, without any rational explanation. My sex life began tapering off.

By the time I moved back to San Francisco in June of 1983, I was heavily into jerking off. I drove down to L.A. one weekend, to attend a "seminar" on masturbation. Yes, we spent the morning listening to boring lectures, but then the afternoon got down to what really mattered: getting our rocks off in a group setting–lots of fun. And yes, I was soon performing at Savages; I also checked out all the other jerk-off palaces in The City. The Nob Hill Theatre, the Circle J, the SF Jacks, and a multitude of others. The bathhouses were already under attack, and though I was as active as anyone in defending them, I had begun to phase out my bathhouse attendance. For the next year, even as I was beginning my porn career, my private sex life ground to a halt. I don't think I had sex with more than twenty men in that period—including professional work. While that's a number that would undoubtedly shock my parents, it would probably shock many of my previous boyfriend/tricks, for exactly the opposite reason. I'd been in the habit, up till then, of having a different man every night, or nearly.

So . . . 1984 proved to be the Long Dark Night of the Libido. Sometime in 1985, I snapped out of it. Not exactly with a bang, but I remember telling the curious that I considered sex to be "an occupational hazard" for someone in my profession. Because that was the point at which I began to think of it as my profession, the point at which I began viewing myself as a professional, with the various perks and drawbacks of professional life. (No unemployment insurance, but no time clock, either.) It was sometime late in 1984 when I started using rubbers regularly in my personal life, on those rare occasions when I fucked; my affair with Bob lasted from August to mid-October, and I recorded in my sex journal an occasion on October fifth: "frustrated, 'safe' sex." (An earlier entry records that he fucked me "dry," and that it was a thoroughly ecstatic, if brutal, event. Had I persuaded him that it didn't matter with us? I don't know. Memory is not the perfect record keeper that I'd like it to be.)

Bob cut off contact with me in October, for reasons that even at the time were unclear to me; I kept trying to get together with him, but he never returned my calls. A year later, I heard that he was sick, and went over to visit him. He'd lost a lot of weight, and looked incredibly haggard; I'd begun to get used to seeing the PWA (People With AIDS) look around town, but this was the first time I'd seen it on someone I remembered as a vital, healthy person; I was shocked, and a little bit freaked. We did have some variety of sex, but it wasn't quite up to our previous standard. We didn't fuck. I kept meaning to get back over to see him again, but I never did. A few months later, I read his obituary.

During this period, late 1984 to early 1985, since I wasn't having a lot of sex with other guys, I began to be meticulous about recording the sex that I was having with myself. My sex journal is rather monotonous: myself, myself, myself. I recorded the time, place, what fantasy I was using, what visual or chemical aids I was employing, the intensity of the orgasm, etc. Many days have as many as three or four entries. Now, that makes me think that I must not have had much else to do. Today, even if I had the energy, I couldn't find time to jerk off three times a day even if I were paid.

I also regularly visited SF Jacks, or other jackoff parties, and I would record the names of as many guys as I knew at these events. Some of them I met later, privately. One man who I met at a jackoff party in February of 1985 turned into a long-term fuck-buddy–or, more precisely, suck-buddy. Rob didn't like fucking. He said he'd been fucked once in his life, by his soon-to-be-ex-lover, and he hated it. Hey, I don't believe in pushing limits; I like doing what the other guy likes doing. Rob was so incredibly good at sucking cock that it seemed insane to quibble. We'd get into a 69 position and it felt like interlocking pieces of a jigsaw puzzle: our dicks seemed to fit down each others' throats perfectly, and we'd usually stay there until we blew our loads, simultaneously. Every time with Rob was a religious experience. But there weren't that many; we only got together maybe five or six times over the course of the next eight months. I'll never forget the last one: we'd started to get to know each other on a social and intellectual level, and the subject of politics, as it always will, came up. Well . . . Rob was, to put it mildly, a Leftist. He was very clearly of the camp that thought that anyone who wasn't, was a traitor to the cause. Now, I've always landed on the very conservative end of the political spectrum, at least economically, and when I started voicing objections to some of the things Rob was saying, he blew up at me. I think that was the occasion when I made a mental note (still prominently displayed in my cerebrum) never to discuss politics with tricks. Rob stormed out of my apartment, and I never saw him again. I talked with him on the phone once, a month or so later, when he was in the hospital; he was weak, but cheerful. He'd only received his diagnosis days earlier, when he came down with PCP (Pneumocystis pneumonia, at that time, the main killer of PWAs). He was convinced that he'd gotten infected from his ex-lover's fuck, and of course I can't contradict him. His illness had robbed him of some of his vitriol; he was downright conciliatory. He told me eagerly of a new drug he was on that was certain to cure him.

A few days later, I heard from a mutual friend. That new drug had lowered his blood pressure to the point that when he fell out of bed, being too weak to get up, the blood rushed to his head and killed him.

This was still pretty early in the plague. Men were not living very long after their diagnoses. If the HIV test had been introduced yet, it was still very controversial. I was thinking seriously about emigrating to Australia. Remember, if you will: the U.S. electorate had just reelected, the previous November, a beloved actor who couldn't seem to say the word AIDS. I was thinking, quite seriously, "concentration camps." It didn't seem the least bit far-fetched to me. When the HIV test came out, I knew quite definitely that I didn't want to be tested because I have never trusted the government about anything. Why should I trust them when they promise me, with that oh-so-sincere tone in their voice, "But of course it's confidential! We would never, ever, release these results!" I began making plans for emigration, with regrets that it would probably mean the end of my porn career. (To the best of my knowledge, they still don't have a porn industry Down Under. Pity.)

February 29, 1984, 1 a.m. entry in my journal: "Is insomnia another warning symptom of AIDS?" That's the first mention of my concern. Does it seem odd that it should take so long for me to write about? Well . . . oddly enough, AIDS just didn't seem to concern me. It was an annoyance, but since I had more-or-less eliminated fucking from my life, I felt relatively immune. And my journals, I blush to admit, were 99 percent concerned with agonized discussions of whether I was truly in love with X, and if so, whether X might possibly be in love with me. I also had some discussions of my goals, priorities, and activities; a certain amount of discussion of the daily events (including, of course, all video projects); but AIDS had not yet become a subject of major concern.

In February of 1984, my journal reveals that I was fucked by someone who used a rubber; I described it as "kinky" and "hot." By January of 1986, I thought it worth recording that someone tried to fuck me "bare," and described him, furthermore, as a "lout" for doing so; a month later, when I met a Mexican man named Hector at the baths in L.A., who was only interested in fucking, I refused him, and would only jerk off. I don't mention either of these incidents because I'm especially proud of them, merely as an indication of how quickly my rules were changing. (Today, of course, I would do just about anything to have another Hector, someone who would fuck me uninhibitedly.)

In late 1985, I met a boyfriend. We saw each other steadily throughout 1986, sleeping together, typically, one or two nights per week—usually at his house, since he was the older and more established of the two of us. Our sex was quite safe. We never fucked; I'm not sure either of us ever swallowed. The sex did not remain very exciting, for me, but the companionship was welcome, and the safety and security of the relationship helped me to forget what I wasn't getting. Still . . . when I met Bill, it didn't take me more than about two days to forget all about the boyfriend.

Bill and I fucked with rubbers every time. His ex had recently been diagnosed; he even came to live with us for a time, the next year, when Bill and I were a firmly established couple. Brooks was pretty bad off, not entirely in the real world; he didn't live long. This was 1987, and I had a list of dead friends and boyfriends as long as my arm; the only unsafe sex I was having was on camera (and I was growing more and more concerned about that) and with Michael Pietri (as described in a later chapter). I don't remember when or if Bill got tested. He must've done so at some point, but I still refused. No one that I recall ever asked me if I'd been tested. It wasn't a very polite question.

Finally, in May of 1987, I used a condom for the first time in a video. It worked out okay; in fact, it seemed reasonably natural. Oh, I still don't believe it's possible to make a pornflick with condoms and make it look like the actors are enjoying themselves, but we at least made a decent simulation. Subsequent videos also used condoms; the industry standard seemed to have suddenly changed overnight. Prior to that, the prevailing wisdom had been "no one will buy a video with condoms." Now, suddenly, producers had realized the disadvantages of producing a video and having the star drop dead before the product arrived in video stores. Maybe it was the death of J.W. King that made the difference. Economics of the marketplace, as usual, rule.

All this time, what was I doing about my own health? Nothing. Hey, there was nothing wrong with me. Well, I vividly recall one memorable night, probably in 1986, when I noticed a strange-looking brown patch on my arm. I didn't remember doing anything to myself, and it had mysteriously appeared overnight... I spent an entire night panicking, pacing around the apartment, and going to pieces. By morning, I had convinced myself that it was from an unnoticed spatter of the paint stripper I'd been using a couple of days previously, and indeed, about three days later, the brown patch flaked off, an ordinary scab, and I was able to laugh at my all-night terror. But it's no laughing matter when it's happening. Death was sitting on my shoulder, grinning at me.

In 1987, I did finally make it to Australia for a month; the next year, I went back for five months. It was in the middle of that five-month stay that I noticed a purple spot on my calf. I went to a doctor, who looked at it and assured me it wasn't melanoma—which, since I'd spent the last couple of months lying in the sun, was my primary concern. So I forgot about it (convincing myself that it was a scar from a motorcycle exhaust pipe burn, which had somehow gone unnoticed for three months), and it wasn't until September of 1989 that it hit home, with the weight of a sledge hammer, that this was KS (Kaposi's Sarcoma). I was modelling for the Gay Men's Sketch Group, something I loved doing, and I'd struck a rather difficult pose in which I was sitting down with my left foot twisted up; so I spent the next twenty minutes staring at the sole of my foot as it went totally numb. Somewhere in there, I became aware of what I was staring at. Not just one purple spot: two. Three. Four. Five. . . . I stopped counting. Plus the one on my calf, which had never gone away. By the time the pose was over, I had mentally accepted that this was undoubtedly KS, and so what? Things had changed significantly by now on the AIDS front. Michael Callen was talking, loudly (did he ever talk otherwise?) about the possibilities of living with AIDS. There were lots of long-term survivors. I didn't much like the term "survivor," but I also no longer freaked out at the thought of being one of them. It took me all of twenty minutes to realize what was next for me. Since my porn career—

which I had, up to that point, regarded as my raison d'être–was obviously over, and even my personal sex life seemed in doubt, I needed to go someplace quiet and isolated; I needed to find a rural retreat where I could write and garden, because writing and gardening were the two things that immediately came to mind when I asked myself that all-important question: "What do you want to do with the rest of your life, however long it might be?" As it happened, I'd just recently ridden my motorcycle through Wisconsin, and been awed by the rural beauty of the state. I'd picked up a real estate catalog, and been amazed by the low prices.

So, that September evening, I laid out a schedule that strikes me, today, as being one of the most perfectly realized plans I've ever made: I would go down to Southern California for the winter, because I really didn't want to try moving to Wisconsin with winter approaching. I would spend the winter investigating alternative therapies (still being heavily distrustful of doctors). Then, come spring, I would ride east and find myself a few acres in the country, and learn to relax and write...and give up sex.

I ended up spending that winter in a beachside cottage in Oceanside–truly idyllic. Walking on that deserted beach on cold, stormy days was the best possible medicine for my soul. I spent a lot of time in solitary contemplation of whatever one contemplates when one is solitary. I also had a lot of visitors. Once I let the word out that I had AIDS, all my friends were determined to see me one last time. A friend of mine in L.A. turned me on to an alternative treatment that was at least as bizarre as anything I'd heard of previously. There was this cancer drug, you see, produced in the 1950s, which the FDA had never licensed because of a conspiracy to keep it a secret, because the drug companies were afraid it would put them out of business. There was a limited stock of this drug available, from a warehouse in Bermuda or somewhere. The "doctor" who was dealing in it couldn't prescribe it in the United States, so I had to go with him across the border to Tijuana, where we picked up the drug and the sharps with which to inject it, and drove back north to Oceanside, where he sat and watched me give myself my first dose. I'd warned him previously about my severe aichmophobia; the mere thought of giving myself an injection has always made me sick to my stomach, which had made me certain that I could never be a heroin addict. But somehow, with my life at stake, and with this doctor sitting there watching me . . . I was able to do it.

I injected myself daily for the next month, with this yellowish liquid. And lest you misunderstand: I don't think I held any serious belief that it was a cure, or even a treatment, for AIDS. No. I understood that a cure wasn't available, and wasn't necessary. What was essential was the knowledge that I was doing something–taking action, not sitting helplessly in a doctor's office, saying, "Help me, Doc." I'd watched too many of my friends go through that; the ones who survived were the ones who rebelled, who asked questions, who were downright belligerent, who sought out their own experimental treatments. The ones who died were the ones who meekly took AZT "because the doctors recommended it." I'm not saying that doctors are actively evil; of course they're not, they want a cure as much as we do. But this disease has them stymied–and most of them don't know how to respond to that. Doctors are used to being omnipotent; it takes a lot of retraining to swallow their pride and admit that they don't have the answers. In the process of retraining themselves, they've managed to kill a lot of trusting patients.

I don't believe that those daily doses of Reticulose did me any good whatsoever, medically. But the fact that I was doing something, and that it was such a dramatic step for me–overcoming my fear of needles!–was a major psychological boost. By winter's end, when the doc had disappeared into whatever third world country he inhabited between miracle cures, my self-confidence was pretty solid. I knew I wasn't a survivor; I was ALIVE. I was planning on staying that way.

Oh yes: I only fainted twice while injecting myself. I didn't throw up even once, not even when I accidentally hit a vein and bled all over the place.

The next two years don't really have a lot of relevance to an AIDS story. I hibernated in Wisconsin, writing, building rock walls, and gardening. Muscles sprouted in places where I'd never had muscles before; I got lean and tan and healthier than I'd ever been in my life. I had very little sex, but I produced quite a lot of writing. When Beowulf, editor of *Diseased Pariah News*, asked me to write something for him, I produced an eight-part serial called "How I Got AIDS," about eight episodes from my life that might have had something to do with my getting the virus–all quite tongue-in-cheek, of course; *DPN* was not a victim-oriented magazine. All my friends wrote me worried letters, and many of them came to visit; they were all sure that I was holed up dying, and they were probably looking forward to giving me comfort and sustenance in my last days. I had the distinct pleasure of disappointing them.

And yes, I did decide to check in with an AIDS doc in Madison; I figured there might come a day when I would actually need one, and it would go easier if he already knew who I was. Ditto with the Madison AIDS organization. I saw the doc three times over the next six months; after the third visit, which went exactly the same as the other two ("Let's see, your name is . . . Scott O'Hara. And how're you doing? What? You're all right? Are you sure? Really? Nonsense, we'll find something wrong with you. And of course you need to be taking AZT . . . "), I wrote a rather tart letter casting some aspersions on the doctor's morals and parentage, and told him in no uncertain terms that I thought I could handle my medical care better than he could. That's what I did for the next thirty months. Seldom even remembering, I might add, that I was supposed to be dying.

In December of 1992, I recorded in my journal that I'd read about Lamar VanDyke, a tattoo artist in Seattle, tattooing "HIV+" on certain radical queers' thighs. Wow! I was thrilled. The advantages were immediately apparent to me: I was, after all, the person who had so much difficulty raising the subject of AIDS with potential sex partners that I'd essentially given up sex rather than learn to discuss it. A tattoo would make it visible. Besides, it would be the ultimate out-of-the-closet gesture: I thought of showing it off to all my rural Wisconsin neighbors, people who probably thought they'd never met a PWA, and a thrill ran through my body. Maturity has diminished, but not entirely destroyed, my need to shock. So I said to myself, "Think about it. If you still want it in four months, then get it."

But four months later, at the March on Washington, my health again became an issue. That's when I began having pains in my left leg. By May, it was severe enough to keep me in bed most of the time, and force me to take painkillers (which, fortunately, I had on hand); June, July, and August all passed in a haze of drugs and continual, unbearable pain. I still refused to see a doctor, though I went to quite a number of quacks: an orthobionomist, a therapist (who encouraged me to visualize my leg as a crumpled piece of aluminum foil, and picture myself smoothing it out with my hands), an acupuncturist, and finally a chiropractor, who sensibly suggested that I needed to have an MRI done on my lower back, which I did. The lymphoma was quickly diagnosed, and willy-nilly, there I was in the Medical System. After five months of pain, I was glad to be there.

Now, the fact is, lymphoma is not exclusive to HIVers. People have been getting it for years and continue to do so. But if you're HIV positive, suddenly it becomes "an AIDS condition." Humbug. One more way of classifying us: these are the ones who won't survive anyway; we can do anything we want to them. They treated me, and I guess I shouldn't bitch too loudly, because the tumors went away. I spent the next six months in chemotherapy, every three weeks; I gave myself daily injections of a miracle drug to keep my white blood cells going (and if it hadn't been for that winter spent self-injecting Reticulose, I might not have had the fortitude to do it); all my hair fell out, right down to my eyelashes, for which I was very grateful (never having much liked having hair); and in general, I enjoyed being mobile again. In June, I was declared "in remission," and I've stayed that way ever since. There is no such thing as a "cure" from lymphoma, I gather, but it's quite possible to be in remission for sixty years.

Once the lymphoma was behind me, thoughts of that HIV+ tattoo surfaced again (I'd kind of forgotten about it while I was busy dying). In April of 1994, on a trip to New York, I got it done–not on my thigh, where only sex partners would see it, but on my left bicep, visible to almost anyone. (I promptly started tearing the sleeves off all my T-shirts, and many of my long-sleeved shirts too.) I added a tasteful little circlet of swimming spermatozoa. As I phrased it to myself, these are the two most important things in my life: sperm and HIV. They've both changed my life. And no, the tattoo has not ended up doing all the things I'd hoped it would; it's not nearly prominent enough, for one thing. I kind of wish I could have it emblazoned on my forehead in glow-in-the-dark letters. I want absolutely everyone to know. As I keep telling everyone: a closet, even the slightest of closets, is the most high-maintenance structure there is, and I just don't have the energy for it anymore. I don't want any secrets. I don't have the patience to deal with AIDS-phobes. I'm not primarily an educator, but I think this tattoo may have opened a few people's eyes.

Since 1994, I've had no life-threatening HIV-related illnesses. An unsightly fungus of the toenails; occasional diarrhea that certainly makes me feel as if I'm dying, but is unlikely to finish the job; yes, of course the traditional nightsweats; molluscum, those little white bumps on the face that freaked me out back in 1989, when I got back from Australia and saw them all over Bill's face; a touch of thrush. All very minor. No, I'm not as rabidly healthy today as I was when I was living in Wisconsin, but neither am I lying in bed, waiting for the sound of angel wings. My libido has recovered nicely, thank you; all it took was the realization that there were other HIVers out there with whom I didn't need to worry about transmission; men who didn't worry about isolating bodily fluids.

I've become somewhat notorious, over the past year, for my positions on HIV. To put it as briefly as possible: I can't quite believe it's a curse. I'm not trying to out-Louise Ms. Hay, but in my life, AIDS has been an undeniable blessing. It woke me up to what was important; it let me know that NOW was the time to do it. And–this is the part that upsets people–it also gives me the freedom to behave "irresponsibly." I look at the HIV-negative people around me, and I pity them. They live their lives in constant fear of infection: mustn't do this, mustn't do that, mustn't take risks. They can't see past that simple "avoidance of infection," which has come to be their ultimate goal. They believe that AIDS=death sentence. Well, I'm sorry, but I was quite possibly infected in 1981, and I'm in pretty good health fifteen years later. If that's a death sentence, I guess life in a prison of negativity sounds a lot worse. My life is so much more carefree than theirs, so much more "considered," that I shake my head and count myself lucky to have been infected. Risk taking is the essence of life, and people who spend their entire lives trying to eliminate risk from their lives are . . . well, they're not my kind of people. I know a couple of people who have consciously made the decision to seroconvert; I admire them tremendously, because it takes a considerable amount of self-confidence and self-knowledge to make a decision that flies in the face of every medical and journalistic opinion in the world. I applaud this sort of independence. These men are, I might add, some of the most inventive sex partners I've ever been with. No surprise.

I don't necessarily think that everyone should rush out and get themselves their very own dose of HIV. It isn't for everyone, obviously. But for those of us who are more interested in adventure than security . . . it's *the* fashion accessory of the 1990s. I wouldn't be caught dead without it.

Foreskin

Keeping a sex diary wasn't an idea that required much thought; it came naturally to me. It's only natural to want to remember "the good times," and vacation and sex are the two things that best fit that description. When you're visiting the Grand Canyon, you take photos (or videos); when you're sucking dick in Griffith Park late at night, you write about it the next day. It's one of the things that people have become reluctant to admit to–after all, in the 1990s we're supposed to be, if not monogamous, at least carefully promiscuous, and it's no longer PC to need an aide-memoire of how much sex one had in a night at the baths. It's true, I no longer have much need for such a record, since sex has become scarce enough to warrant a place in my regular journal. But yes, for more than a decade I did keep a detailed list of all my sexual encounters: who, what, where, how big. For several years, I even extended it to include all orgasms–i.e., every time I jerked off. There's quite a stack of these journals, and I expect that someday the Kinsey Institute will use them to determine the sexual proclivities of gay male pornstars in the 1980s. In the meantime, they make great jack-off material for me, and some of the entries even find their way into fictional accounts.

They also serve a rather clinical purpose: they remind me of the ways in which my tastes have changed over the years. For instance, flipping through 1982, I notice a period when every significant sexual encounter included lots of heavy-duty rimming. Back in 1979 and 1980, I hardly bothered recording any sexual encounters that didn't include fisting and/or hallucinogens. There is even a period in 1985 when I wrote down a number of entries with extensive comments about the shape, texture, taste, and sensitivity of each trick's feet. There was a six-month period when I had sex several times each day–with myself.

I consider it all to be valuable information. The development of my libido is a subject to which I devote a lot of time and energy. I view it as an integrated part of my personality, quite as important as any other part of my brain, and since it was cruelly deprived of developmental stimuli during the first decade or so of my life, I try to compensate by giving it extra attention today. Besides, it feels good.

All this having been said: I find it fascinating to watch the way in which my turn-ons have changed over the years. They certainly have changed. Why? I'll let the Kinseys field that question. I can only chronicle their development. For instance, the development of my primary fetish: foreskin. I have one vivid memory of a foreskin from my adolescent years–an older boy in the locker room (as it happened, we were both drama students, and I admired him for his thespian abilities as well), whose penis was the most perfect torpedo shape I have ever seen, before or since. I only saw it once, but the memory is branded on my brain cells. The fact that he was one year older undoubtedly made it even more memorable. And yes, even at age fourteen, I knew without a moment's hesitation that I wanted to fall down and worship that hunk of meat (no, it wasn't huge–just very pretty).

Next vivid memory: the third man I had sex with, a dark, hairy man named Jamal, had a marvelous foreskin. The previous two sexual encounters seemed, from the perspective of being skewered on his dick (and for the first time, being fucked felt *good*, not painful), like practice runs. I was fifteen. Unfortunately, it was a one-time event–though very leisurely and loving. I never encountered him again. I understand he's dead now.

On to age eighteen–away from home, living in the big city of Chicago, going to the Gold Coast or Manscountry every night I could. It was definitely a time in my life when I needed to keep a sex journal. So let's refer to it. For instance: "Lew, 25, 5'10", 7", Chicago. Fucked me, in 'disco', Manscountry. Uncut–beauty! *Eight*." Or: "Tim Q., 22, 5'11", 8", *thick, uncut, dark*. Security guard; real rough trade. Jerked off, sucked inexpertly. He came in my mouth, I in his hand. *Ten*, for what it was. Boiler room on the fourth floor of parking garage behind YMCA." The point being, though, that already I was very aware of foreskin when it came my way, and made a point of noting it in my journal. The men who carried it also seemed to have a certain something extra in the sexiness department, whether because of taste, smell, or some indefinable ethnic characteristic. I'm not sure that I ever tasted smegma, on all the cocks I sucked; at least, I never tasted one that offended me. Maybe smegma simply tasted natural to me (as it indubitably is!) and therefore I couldn't identify it, anymore than distilled water is identifiable. I began to develop a major case of foreskin envy and downright hatred of my parents for allowing mine to be shorn off; watching the way the skin slides back and forth, feeling that delicious "slurp" under my fingers, elicits a sympathetic frisson of pleasure in my own dick, making me sure that the genuine experience must be a hundred times better . . . but of course, I'll never know. I've got to content myself with manipulating that marvelous skin on other guys' dicks. I just wish there were more of them out there for me to play with (as good a reason as any to move to Mexico).

In twelve years, the fetish has certainly grown and refined itself: for instance, my preference for darker-skinned (and darker-haired) men has come about mostly, I suspect, because they are more likely to be intact. I now can get a hard-on aurally, just from hearing a name like Egidio or Basilio or Fabio. Foreskin seems to open up my throat, or my ass, in a way that nothing else can match. But I think I can state that the fascination and fetish was well-established even before the first time I tasted an unclipped cock. Maybe even before I tasted cock, period. This seems contrary to all the laws of developmental psychology, I know. How do I explain it? With the same answer I give when people ask how I got into pornography as a career:

"Why, it seemed perfectly *natural* to me."

The Noose

Aunt Jeanne (who was not a blood relation, but who lived next door to my family when I was very young) let me sit on her lap—something I don't recall my parents ever doing. She was a very tall, masculine-appearing woman, who had never had children; she was in her seventies or eighties at the time, and her living room always had a strong Victorian scent about it, with a ticking grandmother clock, a parakeet, old, old Persian rugs, and antimacassars. One time, when I was sitting on her lap, she chucked me under the chin and crowed, "A mole in the center of your neck! That means you're going to die by hanging!" Aunt Jeanne was an amazing woman—not afraid to say something like that to a six-year-old. I'm sure a psychologist would have a field day with comments like that; me, I just grew up to be fascinated by the idea. Of course, I think I'd already gotten a miniature preadolescent hard-on over *Zorro* (the book, not the series—no television, remember), especially the scene where Benito Avila is almost hanged. Zorro, of course, cuts the rope and saves him just before the evil Commandante gives the signal—but a secret part in all of us, I think, wanted to see those next few seconds that were averted. Connecting this scene with the rest of the book, I suspect, had a great deal to do with the formation of my formative libido. Those illustrations of Zorro in his skin-tight black clothes! The picture of him with his hands bound at his sides! And the one of Benito (in Zorro drag) being dragged by his heels down from the tiled roof of the jail! Come to think of it, my fetish for names that end in -o or -a may also be traceable to that book. My interest in leather boots, tights, masks, and black clothing certainly originated then, unless you believe that such things are genetic and innate. Then there's my fascination with hanging...

Just what exactly is it about a noose that is so erotic? Hard to say. The rope itself has a certain appeal: just being tied with old, rough, farm-type rope is erotic in and of itself. The notion of being out of control–as in other forms of bondage–is very sexy, and what could be more out-of-control than being about to be killed? Death itself has erotic associations for most people, whether or not they're willing to talk about it. The asphyxiation brought about by hanging is a particularly slow and vivid method of death (to both hanger and hangers-on): it gives the subject time to contemplate approaching (but not yet inevitable) death, unlike most other methods. (Poison is the only other delayed-reaction death I can think of, and unfortunately it's pretty inevitable once administered–and therefore not erotic.) Then, there's the legend associated with hanging: the mandrake, the plant that springs up where a hanged man's semen strikes the ground. I don't know whether or not to believe this legend (the hanged man having an orgasm, not the plant itself), but it's extremely titillating. Physiologists have explained it as an autonomic nervous system response to the breaking of the spinal cord; okay, fine, if that's how you want to describe it. I call it a desperate, last rush of pleasure, a body-wide orgasm that probably exceeds all other orgasms by an order of magnitude, just by virtue of the fact that it's necessarily the final one. Finality is such an aphrodisiac.

Be that as it may, as adolescence approached, I left behind my hanging fantasies for quite some time. When I discovered men, it no longer required internal fantasies and fetishes to get my dick hard: almost any man would do, and did. The next time I recall being led down that particular dark alleyway of the soul was when I was nineteen, visiting San Francisco, and met a charming young man who was 5' 3", 120 pounds, and who loved to be fucked by the largest fists he could find. Since I have fairly large hands, and was gaining some expertise in the art, we hit it off quite well in bed–he was so light, I could actually lift him up on my fist, a truly novel and sensual sight–and the second or third time we made it, he told me to tie a bandanna around his neck as he was approaching orgasm. With one hand buried far up his butt, the other twisting this red noose, my dick was harder than it had been in years, I think, and his was spurting like he'd just been *really* hanged. As his asshole spasmed around my wrist, and he blacked out, I shoved my dick in there with my hand and shot a gusher–then loosened the noose and watched, nervously, as he gradually came back to consciousness.

Other times, dareK (yes, that's how he spelled his name) asked me to use my hands to choke him, instead of a bandanna. Incredible! I'd never actually tried to make someone pass out that way; I found it an amazing turn-on to watch. He'd time it carefully, tell me when he was about to cum–then go down on my dick as far as he could, and I'd start choking him with both dick and hands. I could even feel the pressure from my thumbs on my dickhead. A sure fire way to get off in seconds, even if watching him squirm about in orgasm weren't enough. That boy was about as noisy a cummer as any I've encountered–and feeling the grunts and groans and yells vibrating and squeezing my dick, and for once not having to worry about whether I was allowing him any air . . . well, sex with him was probably the best I've ever had. He certainly had the best fists I've ever felt. I regret having lost track of him.

After two or three sessions, I hesitantly implied to dareK that I'd like to feel some of those sensations myself. He was agreeable, but it clearly didn't turn him on as much; he liked having things done to him, rather than doing unto others. We did it, and I remember having a very sore throat the next day; the actual physical experience, though, was anticlimactic. Like most sex for me, it's the fantasy, the suspense and the build-up, and especially the excitement it generates in my partner. Watching dareK squirm in orgasm with my hands around his neck was far more erotic, for me, than telling him to do the same to me. I don't like having to tell people what to do. Now, if he were to approach me with that same feral glint in his eye, and tell me he was going to practice hanging me . . . well, I'd undoubtedly be scared shitless, but I'm damned sure I'd have a stone hard-on, too.

As the years have passed and my sexual exploits have grown much more tame, I've put away this fantasy. It only gets taken out and dusted off every couple of years, when I encounter a stroke story themed around hangings (rare, in today's censorious and fearful climate). It still gets me stiff as reliably as anything else I can name. Hell, just getting out my old copy of *Zorro* to check Benito's name for this article distracted me for most of an afternoon and two orgasms. That's better than nine-tenths of the stories that appear in *Honcho* with the stated intent of getting me off. What *were* those Disney creative geniuses thinking of, when they turned a whole generation of kids on to capes and swords, boots–and ropes?

Open Wide

The baths are a playground for me, but more important, they're a place to relax. I can get fucked at the baths, without worrying about the mundane niceties of home-type sex: Is my butt douched thoroughly? Are there towels and lube handy by the bedside? Do I have enough eggs for french toast in the morning? That's what they're charging admission for: a respite from the cares and worries of the outside world. That's why there aren't any clocks or windows in most bathhouses. This freedom from worry is what allows my asshole to open up, to welcome in a dick, in a way that it can't even in the privacy of my own home.

Nevertheless, there are times—probably half the time, in fact—when I go to the baths and don't get fucked. I don't have sex at all, in fact. Some nights, I sit in the hot tub and watch the passing parade. I usually won't even bother to get a room, knowing that it would go unused for the larger part of the evening. Those are the nights when I find that I'm most attractive: when men who would normally ignore me seem to be falling at my feet. Fortunately, my policy of worry-free time at the baths prevents me from agonizing over this irony. I just accept. I leave myself wide open, and whatever comes, comes.

I was getting ready to leave, one Sunday afternoon, after a quiet but friendly day, when I found myself flanked in the locker room by a pair of cute little gym studs. Oh, not Colt models or anything, but clearly they'd been lifting some iron. One of them had a very cute blond buzzcut—that always gets my engine going, that bristly short hair look—and the other was lean and tall and sexy, and both of them were in a wonderfully playful mood . . . and I didn't get out of the locker room. One of them had gotten a room, too, so after they'd made sure I was firmly in tow (they freely admitted, later, that they'd followed me into the locker room after seeing me swinging my big dick around), we scuttled into it. We didn't come out for a couple of hours.

One of the first things to come out of Jerry's bag, after the door closed, was a can of Crisco. Talk about icons! Oh, it had been over a decade since the last time I seriously handballed anyone; Crisco has been seriously out of fashion as a sexual lubricant since condoms and gloves became *de rigueur*. But I've never lost my response to it. The unique reek that pervades a room where Crisco's been used for years—there's nothing like it. Some people like poppers; I'll take that pheromone-drenched greasy-kitchen smell any day. What followed the Crisco was a veritable parade of symbols: towels, dildos, a couple of red hankies (just in case symbolism needed to be taken to its most extreme), and poppers. I wondered: did they really expect to come to the baths and meet people as uninhibited as they were? I asked, because I need to be open about my doubts and fantasies, lest they overwhelm my erectile capability. Greg replied, confidently, "Oh, we're infamous around this place. We always run into another positive or two who's eager to dick us. And if we don't find any other fisters, we can always do that to each other."

I was positive, and more than happy to practice my fisting. My dick got pretty hard at the notion of fucking fist again, too. That's something I hadn't done in even more years than I'd been without fisting: sticking my fist up someone's butt and then putting my dick inside also, and jacking off inside of him. Oh, it's awkward, I admit; mostly, it's a psychological thrill. But then, what part of sex isn't? Fisting itself is mostly psychological overload: "Wow, man, can you believe this? I've got my fuckin' fist up this guy's ass!" Or, conversely: "I've swallowed it all the way up to the fuckin' elbow!" Either way, it's a trip. Adding a dick to it—the idea that an ass is actually capacious enough that you can maneuver your hand enough to jerk off inside it—merely makes the fantasy even more of a mind- and nut-blower.

Greg, Jerry, and I didn't spare any holes. They both fucked me that afternoon, I fucked both of them, and fisted each of them at considerable length, until my fists (both of them) were tired. Greg loved to be punch-fucked: he'd pull his ass off my fist and shove himself back down on it so fast and violently that I was actually freaked out, it seemed inevitable that something would tear. But at the same time, it was exciting. It's always exciting when you're aware that someone is this turned-on to you. I'd have my fist up

Greg's ass, he'd be riding it like a drugstore bucking bronco, that glassy-eyed stare plastered all over his face, his asshole wide open around my wrist, and Jerry would slather some more Crisco over my dick and back up against it, and I'd slide right in; then I'd start fingering his butt, shoving in a finger here, a finger there, alongside my dick–and before I knew it, I had one fist up each man's ass and was going from one to the other with my dick, shoving it in alongside one wrist and jerking off a little bit, then jerking it out and shoving it into the other ass. Talk about a flashback to the 1970s! I never knew Crisco could make such a difference. My dick hadn't been that hard in years.

Like I said, we kept it up for well over an hour that afternoon, and when I got ready to leave this time, I really was exhausted. None of us had ever reached an orgasm–who wants to call a halt to such sensations?–but we'd made firm plans to get together again, in the privacy of Greg and Jerry's home playroom, and get even more inventive. What this meant, for me, was that yes, I wanted to fist and fuck both of them again (and again, and again), and maybe double-fuck Jerry, and get fucked repeatedly by both of them–but it also meant that I was seriously intending that my own ass was finally gonna reopen its gates to the five fingers of bliss–something that hadn't happened in the thirteen years since AIDS began, since, in fact, the case of anal warts that closed my ass down in the first place.

It was another three weeks before we were able to get together (after all, I lived several hours away from them, and only came into the city on my regular sex jaunts), but I put the time to good use: I jerked off dozens of times remembering fucking their asses, and practiced opening up my own ass with the largest dildos I owned. By Memorial Day weekend, I was crazed: I just had to have it. And they gave it to me. Oh, I spent my share of time on top that weekend; but this time, the action went about equally both ways. They each fucked me at least three times (four? five? I lost track) over the course of the weekend, each depositing multiple loads of cum up my ass. I did the same. God it felt good to shoot inside an ass again . . . and then reach inside and feel my cum squishing around in an asshole made fiery hot by the friction of my dick. Did my own asshole succumb to all this urging and sympathetic relaxation? Well, almost. I didn't dare bring it up until the weekend was almost over;

after all, despite our session in the bathhouse, I hardly knew them, and the most essential element for being successfully fisted is trust. But by weekend's end, what with the hours I'd spent talking and relaxing with them, I had gained a considerable degree of trust; so Sunday afternoon, after Greg had gone off to work, I told Jerry that I wanted to try getting his fist up my butt. I cleaned out as best I could, and told him to fuck me senseless first, so my hole would be as relaxed as possible; he did, too, to the point where you'd think that a whole herd of horses could've galloped through my ass without causing a tremor. But when it came to his fist, whoa, boy, those o-rings clamped down again without any command from my conscious brain. Oh, I relaxed, and breathed deep, and tried my damnedest, but it's not something you can "try" to do. You just have to WANT it, more than anything else in the world. I guess my mind was still seriously divided on the subject. I couldn't get myself to go past the thumb-knuckle. Oh, it had felt like it was all the way in, believe me; but that was just my sphincter spasming around those big, bony knuckles. Can't quite get over the thought that once it's in there, and my assring is comfortably settled around the wrist (and I know from experience that it's bliss, at that stage), there will still be the agony of exit. That's why I can't quite understand the joy of punch-fucking; entrance and exit are not, for me, pleasurable experiences. Having him inside me is heaven; getting there can often be hell. I gave up trying, eventually, telling Jerry "next time." Perhaps it will happen next time. Next time for sure I'll bring it up before my ass is fucked raw, but ultimately, it doesn't really matter, because I know my own fists will be in constant use. When I've got two asses in front of me, each wanting my fists more than the other, how could I manage to bitch and moan about not being able to take theirs? I know my dick will be hard and in action most of the weekend, and I know I'll leave their house exhausted, but looking forward to my next holiday.

There's a popular idea in gayporn, taken directly from hetporn I guess: the notion that an asshole needs to be tight to be exciting. The fact is, I've always found it to be just the opposite. I don't want virginity in my partners, or even simulated virginity. I want experience, self-assurance, and the ability to speak to me with their sphincters. Men who are into fisting are usually adept at this kind of communication. When I encounter an asshole that can gape wide open all on its own, so that my dick slides in virtually lubeless; when I can stick my tongue so far into an ass that I'm licking the inside walls of the butthole; when he's taking my dick and my fist and moaning for more–then I know I've found someone who deserves canonization. I dream of the day when I will be so relaxed and talented. If I can't be wide open myself, I guess the next best thing is encountering other men who are.

. . . and Perhaps Some Wine, to Clear the Throat

The stereotype of harps'n'haloes Halleluia heaven
was not expounded to me in so many words–like most
societal norms, it's passed on almost telepathically.
It's widely ridiculed, now–and yet, I have no doubt
there are adherents to the Old School of Hereafter. My
Reward is subtly different: if there truly were a god
who wished me happy in eternity, he would provide
(I use the masculine advisedly: notwithstanding all
respect due women, any deity I'd acknowledge "Omni"
must be male) endless rows and ranks and crowds and hordes
of men with one desire: to sink their cocks into my throat
and plant their seed. Concomitant to this, a thoughtful god
would smooth my teeth (or pull them), strengthen my mandibulars,
and pad my knees. To such a god, yes, I would gladly kneel.

Passion by Mistake

Or, my oddest sexual experience. One sunny day in San Francisco, I went out to Land's End, feeling horny as usual. Unfortunately, as is often the case, by the time I got to the beach, the fog had rolled in, and it was about fifty degrees. I about-faced, and caught the bus back home.

I noticed, on the return trip, another guy who I'd seen on my brief trip down to the beach. Now, I see dozens of attractive men every day when I'm in a city (any city!), and I don't have enough spare libido to even fantasize about them all, but I do remember trying to imagine what this guy was like: what his voice sounded like, what he did in bed, etc. Because, you see, he wasn't merely attractive. He had character, which is another thing altogether.

As the bus got closer to town, and grew more and more crowded, we got crushed closer and closer together, until conversation became inevitable. Suddenly, as soon as he spoke, my entire image of him changed, because he was obviously British, and well-educated—not at all the macho type I'd been imagining him to be.

Yes, we arranged to meet for dinner (I was charmed instantly by his accent, and Alan was at loose ends in a strange city, eager for company), and yes, we ended up having sex. I know we did, though I don't specifically remember it. He didn't excite me very much, in bed—though he appeared to be having the best sex of his life. Regardless, we liked each other, and on my next trip to London, I made a special trip out of the city to visit him. (He lived in Bristol, a couple hours west of London by train.) I even got to meet his lover.

Oh, Peter wasn't the jealous type; in fact, I was told, he wasn't even the sexual type—a major source of incompatibility. Alan took me out to see the local sights, including the local trysting park, where sex could be had late at night. Peter, he said, did not approve of his frequenting such spots. We crept into the bushes, and had a quickie. Again, no bells were set ringing for me—though I always have a soft spot in my heart for sex alfresco.

That night, after dinner: I was shown to the guest bedroom, which happened to also be the room that housed the VCR and TV. I heard Alan and Peter retiring; I continued to read. Twenty minutes later, I heard a small "click," and noticed that the VCR had sprouted a red light, as in "recording." Moments later, I heard noises outside, and then Alan slipped into my room.

Now, I understand, as well as anyone, the excitement that goes with "dangerous" sex—even if the danger is only in your mind. This time, though, was different, because I had suddenly made the connection between the VCR and Alan. Somewhere in the room, there must be a hidden video camera, which he had turned on with the remote control before entering the room. (Do I sound like I've done this before? Well, I have.) Either he or his lover wanted to have a candid tape of us having sex.

Well! Believe me, there is nothing like the knowledge that I have an audience to make me perform. Suddenly, sex with Alan was no longer humdrum; suddenly, I was inspired. The sex was hot, sweaty, and even moderately noisy—as noisy as we felt comfortable being, with his lover "sleeping" (I felt certain that he was not, in fact, asleep) two rooms away. I still don't remember just what it was we did, exactly, but I know we both came, and I vividly recall trying to choreograph it all in my head so that, no matter where the camera was hidden, it would have some good angles.

Afterward, lying there in the afterglow, I began giggling. Alan probed; and, like a fool, I responded by saying "You can turn off the camera now." Alan seemed puzzled; I explained that I'd noticed the light on the VCR . . . but where was the camera? He burst out laughing. Peter, you see, didn't like to stay up late enough to watch *Dallas,* so he programmed the VCR to tape it. Boy, was I pissed. If only I'd kept quiet, I'd have had one of the most perfect sex memories ever. Instead, I had to go and burst the bubble. Typical.

Colm

I just love odd names. "Colm" means "dove" in Gaelic, I was told; even if he hadn't been an adorable ballet dancer with the most beautiful eyes I'd ever seen, I might have fallen in love with him just for his name.

My favorite part of London is Hampstead Heath. Naturally: I am devoted to outdoor sex, and that's the only place I know of in London to get it. Maybe some daring souls can find spots in Kew Gardens or somesuch to suck dick, but the Heath is the accepted trysting place. The first time I went up there, I couldn't even find the right place: I trudged up to the top of the hill, walked around the field, gave up, and went home. It wasn't until the following year, when I was given more explicit instructions (follow the path past the reservoir, down the far side of the hill, to your right, walk about five minutes–and look around you . . .), that I found the action. Even then, I lingered in the "vestibule" for over an hour, watching men coming and going, trying to get them to stop and play, before someone had the kindness to tell me, "you know, the real action's down that trail . . ."

And yes, there is action there. There is a night I remember sucking off six men in quick succession–most of them uncut, most of them smelling like men–yes, I was in heaven. Americans will never learn the seductive power of natural body odors. Or perhaps they know all about it, and are mortally afraid of it. In any case, it's one of the things that thrills me anew every time I visit Europe: the abundance of smells. Nothing strikes me as more appropriate than man-smell in my face, leaf mold and mud smell on my knees.

The concomitant cigarette smoke on the breeze, however, I can do without.

The delightful thing about the Heath is that it's active at all hours of the day and night. Less so, perhaps, today than five years ago; they say that London is only now entering its AIDS-phobic, sex-phobic stage. I wouldn't know, it's been four years since I've been back, and that was in the dead of winter, when no one in their right mind goes to the Heath. (Yes, I did. Sentiment, you know. Not as much action as there once was . . . but I still had a good time.) I recall having sex there at noon and at midnight, and all hours between. It takes a devoted sex pig to stay after midnight, since the Tube closes then, and you have to take a cab home or walk . . . or wait for the night bus, which only goes to Charing Cross. Several times, I've walked–two hours to The City.

Anyhow, it was full daylight when I met Colm. He was nineteen, and a more charming piece of jailbait I've never encountered. We had sex–notable mostly for the fact that we both smiled, and talked, and were generally friendly (not common on the Heath)–and he didn't smoke. I think he felt a bit relieved to run into someone who wasn't English. He told me later that he often felt downright unwelcome in London, that he'd been stopped by the police and searched, just for looking Irish. This had never occurred to me, then, as a problem. I guess I don't have an integral awareness of the difficulty of being Irish in England, despite my surname. Of course, I don't look or sound especially Irish, so Customs agents are the only police liable to know about me, and compared to the vipers employed by U.S. Customs, the Brits are a breeze.

Back to Colm. It being full daylight, we sat on a log and chatted for awhile after sex. We watched the other men hover, laughed over their obvious envy, and eventually, deciding to leave together, walked down the hill to the Tube. It was on the subway car, almost at Charing Cross, when he finally gave me his phone number, and I promised to call. He was staying, it turned out, with a priest; he claimed the relationship was nonsexual. He was a dancer with one of the opera companies. I was smitten.

I was staying with my friend Philip (the person who had given me detailed instructions on how to find the right stuff on the Heath), and when I got back home, Philip knew something was up. There's a certain starry-eyed look that I get–I defy you to meet someone as sweet and innocent-looking as Colm, and then try coming down to earth immediately thereafter. I immediately went out and got tickets to *The Magic Flute*, then playing at the English National, for the following night, and called to see if Colm could make it. Why yes.

Although I went to see some other memorable show in the intervening night, which one it was is completely lost to memory.

The night at the opera was one of those romantic affairs that only rarely works out. He'd had to come almost directly from rehearsal, so we didn't have time for dinner, but the opera itself was stunningly presented, with dancers that made us both breathless, and very sexy costuming. Still, it's the afterward that will always stick in my mind. Both of us were staying on the south side of the river, at least a forty-five minute walk from the theater; we decided to walk along the riverbank in the moonlight, stopping every few yards, or wherever there was a bit of shadow, to suck face. Eventually, around 2 a.m., we reached Philip's flat; Philip was still up (I think he'd just gotten back from a club), and he made tea for the both of us. Then Colm had to leave. There was only one bed in the flat, and it really was not big enough for three.

Let's just say that I felt as if I'd scarfed down seventeen concentrated, dark chocolate Cadbury bars and a cup of espresso.

Two days later, Colm and I went out to Hampton Court Palace, doing the usual sightseeing number, just for something to do together; two days after that, I had to leave. I swore I'd write, and I did. He even wrote back a couple of times. A year later, I was back, and this time he lived in a different flat, with somewhat more accommodating (or at least absent) flatmates. He invited me to spend the night. I can't say much about that night, except that it was the most perfect night in my memory.

What makes one particular night stand out so, from among the hundreds of nights of good sex that I've had? Cynically, I have to say that it's largely due to the fact that I never saw Colm again. We never had a chance to become familiarly contemptible (or is that contemptibly familiar?) toward each other. Oh, nothing violent or unpleasant happened; but the next day, I left for Australia, and the next time I tried calling Colm, his flatmate told me he'd moved to South Africa, no forwarding address available. So–Colm, if you're out there somewhere reading this, I'm not quite sure what to say to you. Do I really want you to contact me again, and possibly end up ruining what is one of my most treasured memories? Even worse, do I want to hear from someone who knew you, who will tell me you're dead? A chill runs down my spine at the thought; some pairs of legs are so perfect, they should never be allowed to decompose. Like, say, Rudolf Nureyev's . . . Let's leave it at this, beloved: since I do not believe in sentimental, empty gestures, just send me a recent photo. Nothing nasty; just something that will reassure me that those jaunty, child-like eyes had a chance to grow up, and did so without learning terror and hatred. Is this unrealistic, or what?

Then, later, when I've gotten used to the idea that you're still alive, maybe you can send me one of your used dance belts.

Philip Core

London has always had a strong sexual mystique for me. I know, the English facade excludes sexuality completely, but I think I instinctively knew (and experience has borne me out) that there was a repressed inferno behind the facade. Nevertheless, it took three visits before I was able to penetrate it.

My first visit was with a tour group, when I was fifteen. No chance. Next time, I was on my own, twenty-four, and staying at the central London Youth Hostel. Naturally, most of the men staying there were young and foreign, and I admired several of them in the showers, but out on the streets during the day, it seemed impossible to break through to anyone. I was growing downright discouraged, when, two days before I was due to leave, I met Philip. He wasn't actually English, so he knew how to connect with Americans, but he'd lived there for fourteen years, so he knew how to manipulate the English, too. I instantly fell in love with his versatility.

I spent the next two days with him, and we didn't have sex, oddly enough: neither of us, for whatever reason, made any overtures. He may have felt that I was too young to be interested in him (he was thirty-eight). I think I was just intimidated. He was a painter, and a good one, and I was somewhat in awe of his formidable talents and forceful persona. We talked. For hours on end. He told me about his fascination with "skinheads," the current manifestation of rebellious youth in Britain (rather different, I should add, from the skinheads of America); about his various fetishes–outdoor sex (especially Hampstead Heath), Dr. Martens boots, "braces" (suspenders), and buzz-cuts, among others–and about his fascination with the tearooms, or "cottages," of London. I became even more awed by the variety of his experience; I thought I'd seen and done it all, but Philip's brazenness had gotten him into situations that I'd never dared hope for. I'd gone up to Hampstead Heath, just a few days previously, but hadn't even been able to find the cruisy area (he gave me more precise directions, and on subsequent trips to London, I generally could count on finding a good time there). He told me about going to Carnaval in Venice, and fucking in an alley (with teeming hordes of celebrants just around the corner) when the temperature was below freezing. He told me about the bicycle messenger who, after delivering a package to Philip, asked him if he could take a piss. Philip said, "Sure," invited him in–and the messenger added, nonchalantly, "On you, if I could . . ." Philip turned around, slightly surprised; the guy was looking at him with just the right mixture of truculence and uncertainty, a trademark of the London skinhead. So he went out onto the tiny patio between his building and the factory next door, and lay down on the cement. The guy unbuttoned his pants, pulled out his dick, pissed all over Philip, put his dick away, and walked out, while Philip was still jerking off.

If it were anyone else but Philip, I would classify this story merely as an extremely good fantasy. But these sorts of adventures happened to Philip–constantly. They even started happening to the men who spent time around him, as I came to realize over my next four visits. One of the most vivid episodes I remember was when he first took me down to his local pub. Strolling around with our pints in hand, he introduced me to a friend of his, who was wearing a latex bodysuit. Philip took my hand, by way of introduction, and placed it on the man's inner thigh–and nodded to his friend. I immediately felt the strangest sensation of warmth and motion–he was pissing in his latex. He stopped after a few moments, but kept my hand there by holding his legs together; and while he and Philip talked (with an occasional word to me), every now and then I would feel another pulse of warmth flowing down his leg.

Does it seem as though piss played a large role in Philip's sex life? I have news for you: it plays a large role in the *English* sex life generally. I don't think I've met one person there (admittedly, my sample is somewhat skewed by having met Philip first) who hasn't had a taste for piss. It goes hand-in-hand with the fondness for latex, which is another national fetish. Philip hypothesized that it dated from WWI and WWII, when rubber gas masks became erotic because they were soldiers' gear, and pissing your pants was something everyone did when an air raid siren went off. I don't go in for theories much, myself; I can't trace the origins of my own fascination with the yellow stuff, much less the tendencies of an entire nation. I just made up my mind to enjoy it.

My most memorable time with Philip was the third time I visited him. Again, he'd taken me down to the pub, to pour lots of liquid down my throat–he had every intention of finally overcoming my pee-shyness. I swilled down four pints (which is really much more alcohol than I can comfortably hold) and in the process, once when I was in the loo, found myself next to a handsome tattooed demonic-looking man who took one look at me, dragged me into a stall (okay, he wasn't really doing much dragging), forced me to my knees and shoved his dick down my throat. He finished pissing, then kept it there, fucking my face, until about two minutes later he shot a load. He pulled me up, kissed me ferociously, and was outta there before I could pull up my pants. He never said a word. I staggered out of the loo with what must have been a truly silly grin on my face; Philip saw me, looked at the quickly departing demonic young man, and just lifted his eyebrows. We went home soon after.

Once home, Philip got out his camera. He made a large pot of tea, and told me to force it down; he then stripped me down to my twenty-hole Dr. Martens. He sat me down on a kitchen chair in his studio (painted entirely black, "to eliminate distraction"), and told me to piss. It took a while. I have strong inhibitions about pissing: I'd never been able to piss on anyone before, no matter how much they begged, though I enjoyed being on the other end of the hose. Eventually, the bladder control gave out, and I produced some truly remarkable shots for him–of me spraying a fountain up and over myself, directly at him (I hit the camera once, accidentally, a six-foot spray), and generally all over the place. After which, he told me to go out into the hallway, close the door, and stick my dick through the gloryhole he'd cut in the door. No, he didn't suck me off (though I think he did lick off a few stray drops of piss); he just told me to keep pissing, and snapped some more photos of an anonymous spurting–rock-hard!–dick.

"Spurting," I say. Yes, it's hard to tell whether I'm talking about pissing or cumming. It's hard to separate the two in my memory and fantasies, too. That night vibrates with some of the most vivid sexual urgency of my entire life, yet I don't think either of us actually shot a load of cum. (Philip, I should add, was pissing in his leather pants the whole time he was shooting me. They were quite soaked by the time we were through–and the floor was positively flooded. Those leather pants are now in my wardrobe, among my choicest souvenirs.)

Two nights later, we were both back at the pub. This time, we were planning something a little more elaborate: Philip had asked one of his long-time playmates, nicknamed "Beautiful Stephen" to come over, later, for more piss'n'boots photo action. So I was getting tanked up again. Who should I run into but my demonic friend from the other night. Told of what was up, he got a glint in his eye, and we invited him back home with us. There has never been anything like that night in my experience: three horny guys, all with bursting bladders, in a twisting mass of flesh lit by flashbulbs, with constantly shifting dynamics–first I had Stephen down on the floor with my boot on his neck, pissing on his jeans; then his jeans came off, the Demon's dick came out, and I was sucking them both off. Then I was on my back, and they were pissing on my chest from both sides while I jerked off; then I was forcing the Demon's mouth onto my cock, while he protested and his dick turned iron-hard. We didn't fuck, though some of the photos look like that's what we were doing. We kept it up for two hours, until Philip ran out of film and we'd all cum two or three times. (Another of Philip's tricks stopped by in the middle of the scene: he joined right in, dropped his load, and then vanished.) The party broke up–and after they both left, Philip kneeled on the floor, in his best naughty-boy pose, began rubbing his crew cut under my balls, and said quietly, "Please, sir–piss on my head." So I somehow mustered up a few dribbles (pee-shyness, at least with Philip, a thing of the past), and he came in buckets.

And that's how I'll always remember Philip. He died a couple of years later–cigarette smoking was really what did him in, complicated by HIV, among other things–and I went over to London for his memorial service, two months later. It was the day that a hurricane hit the city; some of his friends joked nervously that maybe Philip hadn't wanted a memorial service after all. I endured the stodginess of the service–oh, Philip had a formal side, too, dating largely from his days at Harvard and his art criticism for *The Independent*; I just never had much exposure to it–and then I did the only sensible thing: I went out on a pub crawl to all his favorite pubs. Got thoroughly pissed (seven pints), got pissed on in several back rooms, sucked a cock or two, made my winding way up to Hampstead Heath (deserted, in the middle of January), jerked off, and stumbled back to my room as dawn was breaking. And felt that I'd properly memorialized him.

Scott in Love

There are half a dozen times in my life when I've been in love, deeply and thoroughly, for a period of a month or more. Luck, distance, or calculation has sometimes managed to prolong the agony for up to six months. But on every occasion, cohabitation restores my sanity.

My first real Lover was Marc. We met at the Stratford Festival, in Ontario, in June. I was eighteen and he had just turned twenty-one; he was acting as chaperone for a church junior choir, I was tootling around the continent on my Honda CB500. Marc saw me swaggering around the theater grounds, dressed in several cowhides, during the day (there are three theaters there; they do a wide variety of plays, from Shakespeare to *H.M.S. Pinafore*), and then introduced himself a couple of evenings later, when we met at the gay bar in nearby London. We chatted, and gazed soulfully into each others' eyes, and then he had to get back to his adolescent charges before midnight. I forget who I went home with, but I thought of Marc all night.

Two months later, I stopped in Memphis to see Marc en route to New Orleans; we corresponded all that fall and winter, and in March I arrived on his doorstep intending to stay awhile. We stayed there a month, in a small, cheap-rent house in a run-down neighborhood (though he was still officially living with his parents), I bought a 1966 MGB (he'd been driving his parents' car) and we headed west, having removed his possessions from his parents' house in the middle of the night. I never met his parents. He drove the whole way; I still didn't have a driver's license. I got one upon arrival in San Francisco. Memorable stops: the bathhouses in St. Louis, Kansas City, and Denver; sitting by the side of the freeway in Idaho for most of the night with our second flat tire in twenty-four hours; and stopping to visit my parents in southern Oregon. We arrived in San Francisco in late May, and moved in with a friend of mine for the week it took us to find an apartment.

Pretty much from that point on, the affair was over. We spent the next four months pretending to be Lovers (I was working at the Club Baths, he was looking for work), but it drove me crazy. Being young and inexperienced, I had not yet accepted the fact that love need not be concomitant to sexual attraction. I still loved Marc, but my passion for him had faded, and both of us were having a hard time facing that. He was financially dependent on me for the whole summer. With some help from a vicious snake who whispered stories in my ear, the suspicion began to grow that he wasn't seriously looking for work, merely sponging off me. I finally gave up and hopped a plane to Hawaii in September. It was two years later before I contacted him again; he'd moved back to Memphis, found a more stable relationship, and was still as sweet as ever. We'd both matured a bit, too. Separation, I think, has been good for our relationship. I like his current lover immensely; I've even had a couple of three-ways with them. Absence, you know, makes the font grow harder. I like their dogs, too.

The next affair started in Hawaii, and continued all over the country. This time the ages were reversed: I was twenty-one; Jay was seventeen. This was the first time I'd ever been involved with anyone younger than myself, and it freaked me out at first. He also lived with his mother, but a different sort of mother altogether: she approved of his bringing boyfriends home, even overnight guests. It took at least a month before I was invited to spend the night, and by that time, I was head-over-heels. We swam, nude, in the pool the next day, and Jay improvised on the piano–a skill I found perfectly thrilling. For the next six months, I was gaga over Jay, though we saw each other only once a week at most; when he left for college in the fall, he didn't seem particularly distressed at leaving me.

Eighteen months later, I popped in to visit him at college, in Denton, Texas. After a joyful reunion (and a night of ecstatic sex), I was on my way again.

Two years later, he called me up in San Francisco, said "Guess what? I'm living about five minutes away!" We got together a couple of times; I'm not sure whether he disapproved of my new career, or what, but he didn't call back for a long while.

Next time I heard from him, he was living in a cabin up near Lake Tahoe, running a computer software company out of his home.

From all indications, the boy had grown up into a certifiable genius while I wasn't watching. He'd also taken up Scientology, and couldn't shut up about it. I suggested a joint trip to the Oregon Shakespeare Festival, and we had a fabulous time (including more sex than we'd had in our entire relationship; I think I got fucked seven times that weekend, and It Was Good), but the subjects of religion and philosophy clearly had warning flags all over them.

The funny thing about this relationship is that for months at a time, Jay would never cross my mind. He disappeared; I forgot about him. Then he'd turn up again, and suddenly the smoldering coals of passion would ignite. In this fashion, my romance with Jay actually bracketed four of my other major romances.

Finally, a year later, he moved to Wisconsin, about 150 miles away from me. I met him once for breakfast near his new home, and it seemed to me that we'd come to have a great deal in common, so I invited him up to my place, a few weeks later, for a relaxing weekend. At least, I'd thought the purpose was relaxation. He thought it was his duty as an enlightened Scientologist to bring me to the light. After the first four hours, when it became clear to him that I wasn't convertible, he told me he thought he'd better leave–he didn't want to associate with people whose minds were closed to the Truth. I haven't heard from him since. I sometimes wonder if he's still alive. Perhaps I should call his mother.

The next time I fell . . . well, this story is told in bits and pieces elsewhere, but I may as well tie it together. I met Michael on the set of a movie: *The Other Side of Aspen, Part II*. I don't know whether or not he had the same visceral response to me that I had to him. I suspect he didn't. In any love affair, there always has to be the pursuer and the pursued. Michael seldom seemed to realize he was being pursued, which made him all the more charming. He was Italian/Puerto Rican, raised in Puerto Rico; in candid photos, his eyes appear to be a touch too close together, but that's the only physical flaw I ever found in his body. He, of course, couldn't stop criticizing his body: too fat, too short, too pale, too whatever. Beautiful men do that; insecurity is what makes their beauty tolerable. Anyway, there were at least two other men on the set of that movie who were enamored of Michael, and he flirted equally with all of us. During the course of the shooting, I was kept strictly separated from him, so as not to waste any vital juices. I acceded to their demands, with very poor grace. At the end of the shoot, however, we all exchanged phone numbers.

Michael and Maurizio lived in L.A.; Eddie and I lived in San Francisco. I know Michael came north to visit Eddie at least once; I think the romance proved to be off-color, and Michael went home disappointed. I regret to say that I never got around to contacting Maurizio, being obsessed with Michael–and I never really had much interest in Eddie, though I saw him on the street occasionally, and we were friendly. Instead, a few weeks later, I fabricated an excuse to go down south, and invited myself over to Michael's.

He lived, at that point, in a charming little cottage above Sunset, near La Cienega. He had a large dog, a couple of cats, and a Peugeot–one of my favorite cars. (He ended up abandoning it on the street, shortly thereafter, when it refused to start–too expensive to maintain.) I said to myself, "Yes, this man is boyfriend material." We had sex; I would be hard-pressed to name anyone in my life at this period with whom I *didn't* have sex. Sex was my social currency. Some would say it still is, but to a lesser, and more theoretical, extent. I fucked him, and caught his cum in my mouth when he shot–very tasty. Then I pulled out and shot on his stomach.

This was the spring of 1985. We were all well-indoctrinated with the doctrines of safer sex by this time. I was using condoms regularly; I had them in my bag. But with Michael . . . well, I've always fumbled when trying to describe this to people. It just wasn't possible. I was too heavily involved with him, too obsessed with him; it was too important to me that this relationship work. And, more particularly, that my dick get hard. Condoms don't contribute to a hard dick. Asking him if he wants me to wear a condom doesn't contribute to a romantic mood. I just couldn't break the mood. I felt terribly guilty about it, then and later, but I just couldn't do it. Not with Michael. Not with the most beautiful man I'd ever met. So for the next five years, whenever Michael and I fucked, it was without condoms. Having started that way, it seemed silly to "reform." Silly, and impossible.

The sex was . . . good. The best. Once again, I was in love. In retrospect, I think it might have had something to do with my budding career: yes, I was becoming a porn superstar, but I suspect I felt the need for a more personal level of validation. Sex was in danger of becoming totally commodified in my life; I wanted to attach some meaning to it again. This reasoning did not, of course, impinge on my conscious mind, but I have a suspicion that if I hadn't met Michael at that moment, I would've fallen in love with someone else. That's the way love works.

That was all I saw of Michael on that trip. We slept together, but early the next morning he said he needed to go to the gym, and offered to drop me off back in downtown West Hollywood. I learned, later, that he was just starting his affair with Ben (which lasted for the next five years), so he may have had other concerns, such as getting me out of the house before Ben showed up (I make a cynical suggestion like that only because I've been in that situation far too often myself). I went back to San Francisco humming to myself, sure that I was embarking on the love affair of the century. I've seldom felt so blithely optimistic in a romance. My journal entry practically glows in the dark.

When next I spoke to Michael, he'd moved to San Diego. It can't have been that long; I'm sure I tried to arrange another visit ASAP. But there he was, and suddenly I found an excuse to visit San Diego: a theater piece by Miller and Sadownick. I think it was *Buddy Systems*. Yes! So I flew down and called Michael; he gave me his address, I went over there . . . and met Ben. They were living together. It was awkward. I've seldom experienced jealousy, but in this case, yes. I didn't know how to behave. Then Michael suggested that he take me for a ride on his motorcycle, and we went roaring off to Balboa Park, my hands uncertain of where to land on his body (after all, he had a lover . . . was I supposed to be "hands off" now?) until, halfway to the park, he reached down and took my hand that was tentatively resting on his stomach, and shoved it forcefully down into his packed crotch . . . which made me feel much better. Now, we have an understanding. At Balboa Park, he stopped, we got off, and he led me down the hill through the underbrush, till we were standing just across a cyclone fence from a busy freeway. He pulled down his pants, pulled out his dick, and said, "Go ahead. Suck it." He wasn't quite as macho as this sounds; he said it with a smile on his face, more of a dare than a command. And me? I was in love. I realized that it didn't matter in the slightest if

Ben had him full-time, as long as I got occasional episodes like this. Michael had the world's most beautiful dick: fat, spongy, worm-like, with a thin, clinging foreskin that kept the head of his dick always glistening and satiny-smooth. It didn't get really rock hard until he got very close to orgasm, so in spite of its impressive size, it didn't bruise the throat the way some dicks do. I was at least as much in love with Michael's dick as I was in love with the rest of him. I went down on him without hesitation, on my knees on the hillside, and didn't come up for air until he'd shot his load down my throat, five minutes later. I think we both were very satisfied. He always had a very childlike need to satisfy his desires NOW. He didn't believe in postponing pleasure.

As I pulled off his dick, licking the last drippings from it, savoring every drop, beating my own dick furiously, suddenly I saw movement at the top of the hillside: it was a mounted policeman, patrolling the woods. I suspect he saw us, but we were in a pretty inaccessible spot, so I guess he decided to ignore us. Anyway, my hard-on disappeared quickly, and we buttoned up and skedaddled.

Michael dropped me off at the theater, and that was the last I saw of him for a while.

Next time I came down to San Diego (don't know what the pretext was this time; maybe there wasn't one), I had breakfast with Michael and Ben. There was still tension between us, but we coped. It was a friendly, relaxed breakfast. Michael and I didn't have sex.

And again, and again, and again . . . I got to be a frequent flyer (and, occasionally, Amtrakker) between San Francisco and San Diego. On some of these occasions, Michael and I would have sex, sometimes not. Whether I returned north in a state of delirious happiness or black depression depended mostly on whether or not we fucked. One time, I actually got Michael to fuck me (he really wasn't much of a top, but then, neither am I, and I managed); I think that was the highlight, for me, of our sexual connection. At some point, at the end of the fourth or fifth visit, I remember Michael asking Ben to take me to the airport. I was disappointed to miss that time alone with Michael, but determined to try to make friends with Ben. I guess Ben was nervous, but eager. We ended up parking on a side street and sucking each other off in the car; and from that point on, tension in the house eased considerably. Was Ben aware that I'd been having sex with Michael? Officially, no. Michael was very secretive about such things, and every time we had sex, he worried about Ben coming home and finding us. Unofficially, how could he have not known? Wasn't my lovesickness obvious? Anyway, it remained an official secret that Ben and I were having sex, too. Which we did, on a regular basis, every time I came to visit. Officially, I think they were monogamous.

Next phase: I had the use of a cabin at the Russian River for a long weekend. I invited Michael and Ben up to join me. They came; we finally ended up in bed together. Ben confessed that he'd always wanted to try being double-fucked. Well, okay. And now, for some bizarre reason, now that we were all together, doing this legitimately, not "on the side," out came the condoms. I can't claim that this was one of the more successful sexual episodes in my life. It was more experimental than anything else, and the sex was still fraught with tension, but I was glad to at least have it out in the open.

The major result of the weekend, though, was that they fell in love with the Russian River. Inside of a few months, they'd moved. I was thrilled; it meant they were closer. For the next year, I spent a lot of time at their house. They had two big dogs by this time, seven cats, and a parrot–quite a menagerie. Michael kept trying to get more. Every time he saw a kitten, he wanted it. Childlike, as I said. Truly endearing.

I don't think Michael and I had sex much more after this. I still found him as breathtakingly beautiful as ever; but we were friends, now, and it's difficult to initiate sex with friends. (In principle, I've always thought sex with friends was a first-rate idea. In practice, it's often awkward.) I remember sucking him off in the woods at Wohler Beach once (he didn't let me suck him off very often, it didn't seem to really click his trigger, so the few times he allowed, even encouraged, it . . . well, they stick in my memory. The taste and feel of that dick . . .), and I'm sure I fucked him once or twice more. He wasn't big on sleeping cuddled up next to a partner, so I tended to sleep on the couch. Then too, he began having night sweats, and lost a lot of weight, and began to be very tense around "body issues." He didn't feel much like being intimate.

I moved away from the City; and over the next two years, I only saw Michael and Ben perhaps half a dozen times. The last time . . .

well, I admit to being shocked. I'd known he'd been having trouble with weight loss, but I really wasn't prepared for the dramatic change in him: from muscular sex god to wasted stick figure. He was lying on the couch, and he didn't even have the strength to get up. I hope the horror didn't show in my face, but that's what I felt. I just knelt there on the floor beside him and stroked his body for a while. Talked. Tried to stay cheerful.

As much as I loved Michael, I was not the one who tended him during those final months of his life. I was off in Wisconsin, building a new rural life for myself. I felt guilty when Ben wrote to tell me he'd died, just a couple of months later, but like anyone who deals with that process, I also felt relief. I didn't want to have to face him in that debilitated state again. Michael was not the most goal-oriented person I've ever known; aside from his videos, he didn't have great accomplishments to his name (though he had a certain reputation as a stylish hair-burner), and he seldom had daily ambitions beyond going to the beach. But I know that lying on the couch with an IV was not his idea of living.

Fourth on my list of Major Romances was Bill—and with Bill, as with Michael, there's no chance of revival. I met him when he moved from Miami to San Francisco and began working as a clerk at the Libertarian Bookstore, where I occasionally helped out. I took to hanging out there whenever I could, flirting with him, playing *Chess* (my then-favorite musical, and his, too), talking politics. A skinny, short, quiet, intellectual type, who nevertheless had muscles of steel (as I learned one day when we were moving some furniture around the store). It wasn't love at first sight; it took me at least a month to realize that I was mooning around him like a lost puppy. Something about his quietness, his ability to say nothing and say it well, took my breath away. I've known very few men like that, before or since. After I'd known him for about three months, I took the unusually forward step (for me) of inviting him to my apartment for dinner. Dinner was a miserable failure, I'd made all sorts of spicy food that he couldn't eat, but we managed to admit, at some point, our mutual attraction. He spent the night, we fucked like bunnies, and he never left. I don't think I've ever seen such a radical transformation as Bill made in bed: from bookish theoretician to Wild Tiger Unleashed. Kind of like the change in the comic strip tiger Hobbes, when adults leave the room. He took my breath away . . . and he was incredibly good sex, too. He was versatile: we both got well-fucked that night (and many nights thereafter). With condoms. Ironic to me, now, knowing that we were both already HIV positive.

For the first time, with Bill, I began to be aware of my sexual limitations. Time-wise, that is. After two months, nothing had really changed, I still loved him, but I'd lost all interest in sex with him. He thought this was unfair. Me, I just thought it was normal. That's what I told him, and it really did a number on his self-image, I'm sorry to say. For the rest of the time we were "together" (and I use the word in its broadest sense, since much of the time I was out of the country), we had sex rarely, if at all. He also objected to my long absences. Were we Lovers during this three-year period? That's debatable. Neither of us took other Lovers, but we both had a fair amount of sex outside the relationship. I considered him, as I told him repeatedly, "the most important person in my life." Is there a word for this person? No. I suspect he felt like Kate Hepburn in *The Lion in Winter*: locked away as a wife in title only, trotted out for special occasions. I know he had a couple of affairs during this period, but I got the distinct feeling that as long as I was still a possibility, he wasn't interested in anyone else. Which is a flattering feeling, although it may have ensured my continual absence. I would've been much happier if I'd known he was going on with his life. One time I did walk in, after a two-month absence, to find him in bed with someone–I don't know who–and he was terribly embarrassed. Well, so was I, but certainly not offended, or jealous.

In November, 1990, six months after I'd moved to Wisconsin, I finally got to meet his family, at Thanksgiving dinner, in Miami. I'd half-heartedly invited him to come live with me on the farm, but he wasn't enthusiastic about the idea. Instead, he suggested we go to Miami together. Bill had been pretty sick for the past couple of years (a fact that certainly contributed to my guilt over "abandoning" him), but I was horrified by how gaunt and sick he was at that point–all skin and bones. We slept in his old bedroom at his mother's house, on an eggshell foam pad; I tried to hold him, but he was too frail for even that to be comfortable. I fantasized about having sex with him one last time (it was pretty clear that he didn't have much time left), but I didn't know how to approach it. I don't know how he might have reacted. A week after he got back to San Francisco, he died. And yes, I cried. I still dream about him. He's usually going somewhere I can't–as he always seemed to be doing in life, with his chessbooks.

Colm, though the shortest love affair I've ever had (and one of the shortest men), also deserves inclusion in this list. You can read about him elsewhere in this volume, however.

Kosta was a man I met in Sydney, in 1988. He was Greek, a chain-smoker, an IV-drug user, and a doctoral candidate in philosophy–truly a man of contradictions. I met him after seeing his work in an art show, and calling him up; he showed me a number of large textile pieces he'd painted (one of which I bought). He then sat down on the couch, and stretched. The moment he exposed his underarms, I was in lust. I don't think I've ever encountered any sight that reduces me to a quivering mass of hormonal jelly more effectively than Kosta's underarms. Did he know it? Probably not. I think his essential oblivion to his pheromonal effect on me was a large part of the effect. (Is there an interpersonal corollary to the Heisenberg Principle?) Kosta had a lover, I soon learned, but he invited me to a party at their house, and later to a weekend retreat at a rented beach house 100 miles south of Sydney. I rented a car, finally daring (after four months of residence) to try driving on the left, and drove down with my friend Jack. On the Saturday night, a huge electrical storm broke. Kosta immediately suggested running down to the surf naked. Five of us (including one woman) did so. There was an amazing amount of phosphorescence in the water (as we ran through the surf, we appeared to be outlined in green fire), and the lightning was nearly nuclear in its intensity. The rain was pounding on the sea, blood-warm. An experience that I'd previously thought possible only with strong hallucinogenic drugs. We danced and capered and cavorted and shouted, generally behaving like lunatics on holiday. On the way back up to the house, exhausted, Kosta and I lagged behind, embraced, hard-ons jutting, kissed deeply . . . came up for air five minutes later, and walked back up to the house. God, I love frustration. It's the only thing that beats satisfaction.

At about 5' 4", Kosta probably weighs no more than 110 pounds; his body is extremely hairy, which he hates. His dick is decidedly small, and uncut, and I have found that he is more-or-less indifferent to having it sucked (although I certainly love to do it); what he likes to do is fuck, and, occasionally, be fucked. I think he would prefer, on the whole, to be a blond Nordic god, with a 6' 6" hairless body. I don't recall ever hearing him critique his body, but he often makes disparaging comments about his fellow Greeks, or Greek culture in general. As for me, I think his body is as close to my Ideal as makes no difference. I know that I should probably visit Greece; there are probably millions of men just like him there who would happily fuck me until my brain's pleasure center short-circuited, but I'm afraid I would become intoxicated and drown in the Sea of Pheromones.

Before I left Sydney–reluctantly–our affair had progressed beyond the looking and longing stage; we'd spent several nights of violent passion together. I can state definitively that I have *never* felt so well-fucked as when he was finished with me. Big dicks have never been more than a curiosity for me, but it was Kosta who taught me, once and for all, that the size of a dick bears no relation to the amount of pleasure it can give. If it did, his dick would measure fifteen inches, at least.

My ticket was already paid for, and my visa to stay in Australia was expiring, and Bill was getting sicker and sicker; I had to go home. I planned on coming back to Australia the following year.

I didn't. Instead, I spent the next winter in a cottage on the beach in Oceanside, California–and Kosta, sometime in February, came to visit me. He was on his way back from a trip to Greece, and he kept changing his flight; I went to pick him up at LAX twice; both times, he wasn't on the plane. I gave up. A week later, just two days before I was scheduled to go on a winter vacation to Puerto Rico, I woke up at 2 a.m. to see the silhouette of a man standing in the doorway to my bedroom. I very nearly had a heart attack. The light switched on, and it was Kosta, and all that adrenaline turned to pure lust. He'd had to take the bus down from LAX, since I didn't have a phone, and of course I never locked my door, so he just walked in . . . it's a good thing he got the right cottage, several of my neighbors were Marines, and they probably wouldn't have been as thrilled.

I changed my ticket for Puerto Rico. I lied, and got a doctor's excuse and everything. Kosta stayed for five days, and I was in heaven again. I kept telling him, "No, of course I don't mind your smoking indoors . . ." really, seriously, hoping that his cigarette smoke would be enough to finally end my obsession with his body. It had worked with every other smoker I'd ever found attractive. Not with Kosta. Something about his Greekness, I kept telling people, made it seem only natural that he should smoke. (What, had I seen an Attic red vase advertising Kools, or something?) I make no claim of rationality for this argument; I still despised cigarettes as much as ever, but for this one person, I didn't care. Frankly, it put me into a bit of a funk to discover just how malleable my grand Principles proved to be, when they were in conflict with my libido.

For the next three months, my journal entries are monotonously similar: Kosta this, Kosta that, When Will I Get Over Kosta? It didn't help that when he got back to Sydney he discovered that his relationship with Mark was over. He wrote me the most beautiful, lyrical love letters–or perhaps I only interpreted them that way, because they were from Him. Objectivity is so hard to come by when you're obsessed. I freely admit that I still am, five years later. Hey, I've still got a photo of him sitting on my desk. The one in which his arm is raised just enough to see that mouthwatering armpit.

He's visited me once since then, in Wisconsin. Again, he changed his flight three times without telling me. He stayed several days, then we drove around Lake Michigan to Saugatuck, where we spent the night at a gay resort . . . why is it that fucking in a motel room is always more memorable than fucking at home? The way he pinned me down to that particular bed–three times in one night!–can still make me spurt a load, just picturing it. Then we drove over to Grand Rapids, to catch a Flirtations concert; and then home. I dropped him off at the airport in Milwaukee. Two years later, he told me he was coming for a visit, but never showed up. I got a letter some weeks later, from San Francisco, telling me why he'd canceled. I vowed to have nothing further to do with him, that I didn't need that sort of irresponsibility and immaturity in my life; but I have a sneaking suspicion that if I were to see him laid out on a bed, with his arms stretched out over his head, smiling that signature drugged smile at me . . . I don't think my spine would be strong enough to resist. I think every atom of my being would crave him, and if I didn't give in, my body would melt down and flow toward him. There are some attractions that science calls Absolute. This is one of them. Is it love? That's another question, and one I don't feel truly qualified to answer.

I don't dance, I don't handle alcohol well, and I loathe cigarette smoke; this seems like a categorical exclusion of bars as a venue for meeting men. Once or twice a year, I'll have a particular reason to attend a bar event–such as when I'm stranded in some bathless city for the evening, and want to find a place to spend the night. On a particular November night several years ago, when I'd driven into Madison to see a production of *Jerker*, the first snow of the season fell, and, not wishing to drive home in it, I went to Rod's. Almost immediately, my eyes locked with an intense, ascetic-looking man at the other end of the bar. It took awhile for us to meet; first I had to chat with the bartender (who was my prime suspect for going home with) and have a reconnoiter around the premises. Then Stephen came over and introduced himself.

Okay, fine: he's good-looking, warm, and witty. He's also got a pack of cigarettes in his shirt pocket, and he's drinking a beer. Eighty-six this one, huh? But we chatted in a friendly fashion, and he was an actor ("Oh, *that* Stephen! Yeah, I saw you in that Chekhov play last year!"), and he said, "Hey, why don't we have dinner sometime?" "Okay, sure," I said–mentally adding, *But that's all.* We made arrangements–as it happened, I was due to be in town the next week for a doctor's appointment. We had dinner together, and I'd carefully planned how to make it clear to him that I wasn't available for further intimacy, a way that would surely scare him off immediately. "I've got AIDS," I told him. "Oh–so have I," he replied. Oh, *fine.* That response had just never occurred to me. Now what?

The "now what?" as it happened, was perfectly logical: I fell in love with him. This was the first I'd heard of HIV-positive romance; I found that just the knowledge that you don't have to worry about infecting someone gives you a sense of relief from the epidemic. At the same time, the camaraderie that comes of having dealt with the same inhumane medical and insurance industries provides endless material for discussion. Maybe it's a weird basis on which to build a relationship, but my relationships have often had shakier foundations. We also shared a love of acting, of literature, and of decorating–though this last, as many of you know, is a mixed blessing. We never tried living together, fortunately. Putting two decorator queens in one house can be deadly.

There needs to be some other, more basic explanation for this relationship, however. It ended up being the most important relationship of my life to date: a man who taught me more than any other, a man who made me live up to a standard. I guess that last part is the crucial aspect: I respected Stephen, admired his acting abilities and his seriousness, in a way that I hadn't felt toward anyone since Bill died. When I watched him prepare for a role, I was in awe. He researched every role as if he knew it would be preserved on celluloid and judged by Sir John Gielgud. Most impressive of all, to me, was his basic lack of ego. Oh, don't mistake me: he knew he was good, and he had a typical Actor's Vanity; but the fact was, he was good enough to make it big in New York, and he chose not to. He liked living in Wisconsin; he liked working at American Players Theatre; he liked teaching school kids about Shakespeare. He was devoted to Acting, not to building a reputation. I would like to think that I feel the same way about writing, but sometimes I catch myself in a purely Publicity-driven move, and blush with shame.

This relationship dragged on for most of a year–though much of that time, predictably, was nonsexual. Uniquely in my experience, he was the one to tell me that he needed to tone down the level of intimacy, and he seemed to lose his sexual response to me even faster than I lost mine in him. I thought I was the independent one, but Stephen proved to be even more shy of intimacy than I was. Somehow, in my hormonally induced Nesting Phase, I wanted someone who would be a Lover with a capital L, and this was far more commitment than Stephen would accept. He needed his independence; when he was on tour with the Great American Children's Theatre, I think it seriously threatened him to have me show up in Los Angeles for a visit. I kept trying to restrain myself, to hold back, to give him his space; but I was pining for a Partner. So I found one, as it turned out, in midsummer, and began spending less and less time with Stephen. By year's end, the new man had practically moved in with me, and Stephen was out of the picture (temporarily).

The new man proved to be the biggest of my many mistakes. He moved in, and immediately started asking for tokens of real commitment from me. I was hesitant, but I was determined to keep him around, so I acquiesced. Some months later, I developed a mysterious lower-back pain, eventually diagnosed as lymphoma, which kept me in bed for six months, and made me totally dependent on Larry for trips into town, meals, housekeeping (which he didn't do), and all the other practicalities of life. It was somewhere in the haze of pain and drugs when I decided I should transfer the house into joint ownership, since obviously I was at death's door, and that action would avoid probate. And yes, Larry continued to care for me, but when I declined, that November, to transfer the rest of my rather substantial estate into joint ownership, he realized the bloom was off the affair, and began making my life as miserable as possible. "You don't trust me," he said, in that wounded tone of voice. No, Larry, as a matter of fact, I don't. It took me another year and a half to make the final break–I'm a slow learner–and he still isn't completely out of my life, but I'm doing my best to avoid thinking about him.

Now I have to talk a bit more about Stephen. Because as the bloom faded from the rose of my relationship, I began spending more and more time on the phone with Stephen. He'd moved to Milwaukee by this time, for the winter season, and he'd found a lover of his own: Tony, another actor, who'd seen Stephen in *The Recruiting Officer* and fallen instantly in love with him. (I missed that show, somehow.) I got to meet Tony; I liked him immediately. As their relationship deepened, and I saw Stephen agreeing to all the things that he wouldn't do for me, I felt . . . what? Jealousy? No. I could see, very clearly, that Tony was a better lover for Stephen than I could have been. Envy, certainly: the development of their relationship was beautiful to watch, and I couldn't help comparing it to the emotional tar pit in which I was floundering. They had their troubles, true–I spent some hours on the phone listening to Tony cry on my shoulder over Stephen's unthinking cruelties, his resistance to intimacy–but they worked them out. We both were in couple's therapy at the same time, as it turned out, although Stephen and I only admitted it to each other several months later. (I was mortified that I'd allowed myself to be dragged into such a silly process, and I think Stephen felt similarly.)

Stephen's acting continued to develop; his Falstaff at APT was his proudest role. And then . . . he started getting sick. All of the

1995 season was agony for him, as the Chorus in *Henry V*; after each performance he'd collapse. I'd talk to him on the phone every couple of weeks (I was back in San Francisco by now, and unable to drive over to see him at will); some days he'd be bright and chipper as ever, but usually he'd sound totally drained.

As late as March 1996, I thought he was going to get back up on the stage. He'd even given up smoking. I interpreted that as a pretty serious indication of a will to live. But then, one more hospitalization, one more opportunistic infection, one more set of IV medications . . . and he decided it wasn't worth it anymore. I spoke with him the afternoon that he got home from the hospital, when he'd told his doctor he was ready to give up. We talked about other things, too: I asked how Tony was doing in *Falsettos*, and Stephen said he was the best part of the show. "Well," I concluded, "I guess I'll have to come out and see him." I don't think I was aware until that moment (isn't this always the way it is?) just how important Stephen was to my life, and how important it was for me to see him again.

So I flew to Milwaukee, and spent a week with Stephen and Tony, helping them organize the parade of visitors, callers, and nurses; and when I said good-bye on Tuesday, it was with complete finality. That's hard to say. Stephen died on Friday.

I'm grateful to him for that one final favor: giving his friends the opportunity to say good-bye in person, instead of wailing it at a funeral. That's a rare thing, perhaps a little more common in AIDS cases, but still, very few dying people have that much consideration. Other things become more important. Perhaps death can never be "good," but I do think he had the best death available. And, true to form, it was extremely dramatic.

As I write this, in mid-1996, I am again in love. I am in that jumping-through-hoops phase, that He-Hung-the-Moon phase, that Happiest-That-I-Have-Ever-Been phase. Joe and I are not Lovers; we've hashed all that out. We're boyfriends. That is to say, I am one of his boyfriends. This fills me with pride: the knowledge that I can provide him with something enjoyable, but that I don't have to be all things to him. When he wants something else, he spends the night with Kenneth, or Frank, or anyone else he chooses. Therefore, I know that when he chooses to spend the night with me (once a week, max, and I eagerly anticipate each sleepover), it's because he wants what I provide. There is no element of possessiveness here, and no desire to make this into something more than it is. Will it last forever? No. Nothing lasts forever. It will last until it's no longer meeting our mutual needs, and I sincerely hope that we'll both have the good sense to recognize that phase when it arrives.

I hope that I will never have another Lover. In fact, I've been writing in my journal for the past four years all the reasons why I don't want a Lover. The concept of "Lover" (or "Spouse," or "Partner," or whatever) is basically, intrinsically antithetical to what my Philosophy of Life holds up as the ideal. I do not believe in Commitment; I think it is simply insane to promise that your feelings will never change. They will. Feelings, opinions, goals, and ideals are malleable things because we are malleable creatures. As we grow, we learn, and "till death do us part" is a futile attempt to ignore that simple fact. So, no, I do not want a Lover. But I do hope that the rest of my life will be spent engaged in regular bouts of intensely romantic, riotous Love–with a wide variety of partners. One of the classic justifications given by men (and women) who are addicted to relationships is: "So I'll Have Someone To Grow Old With." Actually, it's usually phrased in reverse: they comment, pityingly, that those of us who are devoted to bachelorhood will undoubtedly end up lonely and loveless in our old age. I'm afraid I don't see it like that. I have never been so lonely as during those periods when I was in a relationship gone sour. In my life, Stephen– the Lover Who Wasn't–became my closest and most cherished friend, while Larry has become the bane of my existence. That says it all. I look forward to a vital, busy, love-filled *single* life–however long it lasts–and feel no need of a Partner to stave off loneliness. A man who can't stand his own company can hardly expect that others will wish it; I love solitude and the pleasures it provides, so I am confident that I will never lack for companions when I want them.

Dear Ex-Lover:

We are pleased to inform you that your ex is dead. Since there is now a vacancy in this post, it would behoove you to fill it as rapidly as possible. Please let us know when you have a nominee for the position, and our review board will meet to consider whether he meets the necessary criteria, to wit, being an absolute and irredeemable bitch. At that point, we hope we may be of service in finding a candidate to fill the vacated position of lover.

In the meantime, may we congratulate you on being, however temporarily, without an ex-lover.

Sincerely,

William H. Truvel
Truvel, Truvel, & Treuve, Romance Consultants

---

first published in *LISP*

Pornstars in Private

I've written rather extensively about my off-screen relations with Tony Bravo/Michael Pietri (and his lover Ben–now also, alas, deceased). Michael was the major example of my porn life carrying over into my private life, but there were others. There were lots of pornstars who did scenes with me in private that never made it to the screen. Some of them really should have.

The most stellar of these was Jon King, aka John Gaines. No, I never made an on-screen appearance with him (it might have happened in *Oversize Load*, but didn't). I never even got to meet him until 1986, when I went to see his performance at the Campus Theater–hot stuff. He recognized me in the audience, sought me out afterward, and made sure we got together. Nothing subtle about that boy: when he wanted something, he went for it. I like that in a man. We got together: I vividly remember meeting him at a motorcycle dealership to pick up his bike, which had been in for repairs, and riding home with him on the back of it. Jon enjoyed taking risks. But once home, this changed: it was Rubbertime. I'm not sure, at this point, whether or not to be happy about this. He claimed, at the time, that he was still negative–despite having been fucked, condomless, by a lot of men over the years. Well...I gather that, sometime in the next nine years, his luck ran out. I could take satisfaction in knowing that it wasn't me who infected him; or I could, wistfully, wish that we'd fucked unprotected, since in the long run, it wouldn't have mattered. I guess I have a love/hate relationship with my virus; if someone like Jon King was determined to get himself infected, I kind of wish he'd chosen mine.

Yes, our sex was truly stunning, right up there with the all-time best fucks of my life. That boy knew how to work his butt in a way that no one else could. He was hungry, and demanding. (It's nice to know that even a megabottom like Jon King can occasionally be manipulated into a top role–which he performed with great panache.) He only fucked me once, in all the times we played . . . and I found myself wishing, as he shot inside me, that I could keep his cum up my butt as a souvenir.

I remember a quiet, romantic sushi dinner with Jon in Japantown; and another dinner, somewhat less quiet, that he made at his apartment on Liberty Street. He claimed, at the time, that he was signing up for chef's school. (He may have signed up, but I doubt he attended more than two classes. While he was certainly one of the most charming men I've ever met, he was also one of the most unreliable and capricious.) Then there were the times we ran into each other in New York: he spent a couple of nights with me at the Colonial House Inn, when I was performing at the Black Party. I think he was drugged out of his mind; I know he was impossible to wake. But the most poignant of our encounters—not the last, but certainly the most painful—was at Bill's apartment in San Francisco.

I'd already moved out of the City; I guess this was 1989. I was back visiting, and somehow I got a call from Jon. He sounded very dispirited. Bill wasn't there, so I invited Jon over. We sat on the futon and talked. Jon poured himself out to me; most of what came out was "people only want me for sex." I could sympathize, but at the same time, his body language was sending out a strong "hold me" message. I did; and guess what, before you know it, we were having sex—foreplay, at any rate. I didn't understand, but it seemed like it was what he wanted. Comfort. But after just a few minutes, he got even more depressed, and withdrew, huddled up like a kid who's just been hit. He left soon after, leaving me truly distraught. Somehow I'd failed him: I'd confirmed his worst fears about the animal natures of gay men.

The thing about pornstars, which the general public forgets (and even I forget it, obviously) is that no matter how sexually insatiable the public persona, there are also times in their lives when they'd like to be...nonsexual. Jon was, in a sense, a victim of his own irresistibility: no one could see him without thinking "SEX." Being able to provoke this response is exciting, at first. Being unable to turn it off gets very depressing.

This episode was never brought up between us; I never saw him in that sort of funk again. But I've always regretted not being able to give him what he needed at the moment. I think he brought out a very maternal response in just about everyone he met, just because he was so immature. Everyone wanted to take care of him. Me, too. I kept wishing he'd call me up and ask me for...something. He never did, of course.

I understand he made several more films, in the early 1990s, including a sequel to one of my all-time favorite flicks, *These Bases are Loaded.* I haven't seen any of them, and I'm not sure I want to. I kept hearing occasional mentions of his name, which I took as a good sign; then, in 1995, I heard a rumor that he was HIV positive. I greeted this news with...well, with eagerness, mostly. When there's a man in my sights who I've been lusting after, it makes him twice as attractive to learn that he's HIV positive. Suddenly, I *really* wanted to see Jon again.

Ironically, by the time I heard that rumor, it was already too late. I didn't get the news until June 1996, but he'd died early the year before. I don't know anything about his death. Everyone always wanted to take care of him when he was vital and healthy; I wonder if there was anyone to take care of him at the end. I didn't get the impression that he was someone who had cultivated any deep friendships,. There are drawbacks, you might say, to being the most sexually appealing being on the face of the earth.

The first pornstar I ever met was Chris Burns ("Danny" to his family, but Chris to everyone else): it was October 1, 1993, the day I moved into my Hayes Street apartment. I'd gone down to Safeway— yes, THAT Safeway, the one at Church and Market, where "you can get anything you want" twenty-four hours a day–to stock the kitchen. Of course, I walked out with about six bags. As I was exiting, I noticed a hunky dude in loose sweatpants and a tank top, a cocky little rooster of a guy who looked vaguely familiar. He gave me a very blatant come-hither look, and followed me out to the bus stop. We both got on; when the bus got up to Hayes, he got off the bus with me. He started following me up the hill. I assume he started the conversation, since I've never been any good at that. I invited him home, and he accepted. When he told his name was Chris, I suddenly realized who he was. I'd just seen *Men of the Midway* at the Century Theater a few weeks before, in which he tries to pretend he's an innocent youth. (I'm not sure Chris was ever innocent; Certainly not by the time I met him.) One of the first things to catch his eye when he walked in my door was that doorstop dildo that I'd bought as a joke a couple months previous, and his eyes lit up. Maybe I'd been wearing a red hankie; who remembers? But that night I used dildo, fist, and dick on his ass, and he kept begging for more. He wore me out; that I remember.

I saw Chris pretty regularly, over the next seven years. On a couple of movie sets, at both Black Parties that I worked, and on the streets of San Francisco. We were on the same flight to New York for one of the Black Parties, along with two other pornstars; Chris and I discovered that neither of us had ever had sex on a plane, and decided it was time to rectify that deplorable situation. So we snuck into the john and "did it"; I wasn't able to get really hard, under those circumstances, but we both eventually came. Then, with a line of people waiting, we had to get out of there. Finally, we both just said, "Fuck it, we gotta get out of here before the movie ends"–so we opened up the door and marched out, together, and up the aisle to our seats. The guy sitting next to the toilet, who'd clearly noticed how long we'd been in there, gave us a look that said everything you might expect–*Dirty fags, just can't control themselves*–but what, after all, could he do? It was one of those lovely situations where you really can get away with almost anything, if you're brazen enough. I know a man who tells of sitting on very public benches on busy city streets, at 2 a.m., jerking off in plain view of passersby–but because it's a "dangerous" hour, John Q. Public doesn't want to confront someone who might, in their minds, be mentally unstable–so nobody calls him on it. Now there's a situation in which I do find a definite thrill. Sex should be a public good, an activity provided for in the same way that the city provides water fountains in its parks. Airplanes and trains really *should* have more comfortably padded seats in their johns.

Back in San Francisco, Chris started a self-defense class for gay men (remember those karate scenes in *Below the Belt?* Those were choreographed by Chris), which caused some amount of controversy. Some people didn't think we should be learning to fight back, I guess. I helped to comfort him after his lover, Jim-Ed, died; then, just a month or two later, again, when his new boyfriend Chris was killed in a motorcycle accident. That was the point when I really began to be afraid for his sanity.

He mostly disappeared from my life after that—I was no longer in the City, so I didn't run into him as often. At the 1988 Black Party, he told me, conspiratorially, that he'd just come from realizing his lifelong fantasy of being fucked by a horse—and that he had photos and a video to prove it. I was slobbering with lust; this I wanted to see. He never showed them to me, though. I had to wait until after his death, in 1995, when a mutual friend happened to mention that he'd inherited the "private tapes." My eyes lit up, and I asked, "Including the one with the horse?" He looked startled, but he showed it to me. It's remarkably silly. Oh, sure, the IDEA of getting fucked by a horse (really, in this case, a Shetland pony) is titillating to every gay man, but the reality is more tedious and time-consuming than you would believe. I think Chris probably felt the same way, but, like me, he took a lot of pride in being able to say that he'd tried everything once. Well, Chris tried a lot more things than I ever have, and he was better at them than I would be, too.

When Leo Ford made an appearance at one of the jack-off theaters in San Francisco (after a long absence from "the scene"), I made sure I got to meet him. I don't remember how, but it wasn't difficult. He immediately came up with a business deal for me. Fair or not, that's my primary impression of Leo: he always seemed to have an angle, a way to make money off of anyone. He didn't seem the least bit interested in sex with me; he invited me back to his apartment, but all he wanted to do was discuss his business proposition. Don't ask me what it was, I wasn't listening. I was wondering when he was gonna get around to putting the make on me. He never did. Shortly after that, he moved to Hawaii. A year later, I heard he'd been killed in an accident.

Johnny Dawes was another old-time movie star: his roles all dated, I think, from before I started in porn. He didn't do a lot of films, but at least a couple of them were big hits. *Skin Deep* was one that was particularly affecting to me: it had a message about the dangers of stereotypes and beauty. I liked it.

I met Johnny—Brian Lee, that is—on a bus in West Hollywood. I used to ride the bus when I visited SoCal; all my friends down there thought I was crazy for taking public transit. But he sat down next to me, and again, he looked vaguely familiar; I don't remember whether he recognized me, probably not, but he invited me home.

We talked some; I was very impressed by his collection of 78s, which took up two whole walls of his living room. But he wasn't interested in socializing. That much was clear. He wanted to fuck me; I was agreeable. So we went into his bedroom, and he fucked me for about an hour. He came, got up, and implied that it was over, thanks very much. I'm not complaining; I enjoyed myself. It was just a little more . . . abrupt than I'm used to. I think I called him the next time I was down south, but I don't believe we got together. I was saddened, a couple years later, to read of his death.

Rydar Hanson was a guy who I'd salivated over for several years before I finally met him, backstage at the Mr. Drummer contest. He was Mr. Southern California Drummer; I was an extra, part of the entertainment. He promptly gave me a personal invitation to come down to L.A. to be part of a special event he was planning. It was a big party, at a Bel Air mansion, which was to be videotaped as the background for a video. The video, to the best of my knowledge, was never produced, but I was intrigued enough to make a special trip south to take part. He cast me as a panther. Or was he the panther? Memory fails me. One of us "attacked" the other and ripped his clothes off. There was lots of body makeup, weird lighting, spooky music, and fog machines. Bear in mind, this is all happening in the middle of a crowded party, with a video camera following us around. It was fairly surreal, but fun. I got the chance to play with Rydar's gloriously uncircumcised peepee in the shower afterward, while we were washing off the makeup. That is, until his lover knocked loudly on the door, demanding that we come out and socialize.

I was never sure whether Mike was jealous or not. He claimed to be very open-minded, but he also never left Rydar and me alone for more than a few minutes. He also "confessed" to me, once, that Rydar had AIDS. Something in the way he said it made me wonder (is this weird, or what?) if he was just trying to scare me away. Rydar never mentioned it himself; he always claimed to be in perfect health. I made a habit of visiting them every time I went south, over the next couple of years—their apartment was very conveniently located, right in the heart of West Hollywood—always in hopes that something would develop. It never did. Once, they invited me to come along with them to a house out in Santa Monica that they were house-sitting: it was one of those stunning L.A.-style houses with a view of the ocean and a pool and fabulous architecture, and Rydar's paintings were hanging everywhere. (Not being an art critic, I hesitate to describe them; the term "Cubist" comes to mind, and they were quite vivid. I'm afraid they didn't turn me on.) The pool was heaven, and we lounged around it for a couple of hours, giving me the opportunity (finally!) to take some nude photos of Rydar. He pretended to be shy, but I did get a few excellent close-ups of that mouthwatering meat.

For the past six years, I've heard nothing from Rydar. Admittedly, I was hiding out in Wisconsin for most of that time, but I kept wondering what had happened to him. Had he gone back to Germany? Or just given up porn? Then, this spring, a friend of mine showed me his collection of pornstar obits; Rydar was among them. There's something spooky about reading a seven-year-old obituary, and realizing you've been remembering a dead person as if he were alive, fantasizing about him. It's hard to mourn, after so much time.

Here's one of my most recent contacts: Perry Morton, a Rage video boy, who was out in San Francisco in November 1994, who I happened to run into on Folsom Street. He's one of those obsessive-compulsive sex maniacs: I had an event I had to attend that evening (fortunately, not a formal one), and he tagged along and spent the whole evening rubbing up and down on my leg–rather pleasant, but distracting. I made a date for the next morning, since I was only going to be in town for a few days. We met at Cafe Flore; then we walked over to Dolores Park, sat at a picnic table just uphill from the children's playground (alive with kids and moms), and he reached over and began jacking me off inside my pants. Then he took my dick out. I did the same with him, and jacked him off. Then he leaned over and started sucking me. Okay, sure, I got off on it (and so did at least one passerby who was walking his dog), but that was just a little bit more than I could handle. After just a minute or so, I pulled him upright, and we continued jerking each other off. We both came quickly, and then he had to run to get to a video shoot. ("Huh?" I thought–"He's having sex right before a shoot?" But, well, he did seem to be truly inexhaustible. I suspect it was his ass that was destined to be featured. Pity I never got to explore that, it felt delectable.)

Then–in something of the same vein–there's Taz Action. I don't believe I've ever seen a video of Taz, although there have been quite a number. My first contact with him came when I got a call, late at night, in Wisconsin: he was calling from L.A. to ask me how to get his book published. This would have been, oh, 1993 I guess. I was completely bewildered. First, I'm not an authority on how to get published; second, it was not initially explained how he got my number; third, I'd never heard of him (though he claimed to be a famous pornstar); and fourth (after he'd finally explained that Dave Kinnick had sicced him on me), he eventually admitted, in passing, that he hadn't really written a book, that this was all just an idea, but he was gonna do it, really he was. It was all there in his head, and if he sent it to me, would I read it and tell him what I thought, huh? I sleepily agreed, "Sure, whatever Taz." It took at least an hour, maybe two, to get off the phone. The conversation was brain-bending enough that I didn't really want to just hang up on him. Whether or not he ever wrote a book, I was certain that I could use this episode in one of mine someday.

Shortly thereafter, I did get a letter from Dave, "warning" me that he'd given Taz my number. Yeah, Dave, I know.

He only called me once more; this conversation was similar to the first, but I think it had to do with a brilliant video project he'd conceived, for which he was looking for a producer. I listened, again, spellbound.

Sometime later that year, I believe, I was in San Francisco, and made a dinner date with three dear friends: Howard, Duane, and Kerry. We were meeting at Stars–a fairly toney spot, where ties are not required, but good behavior definitely is. The food is also supposed to be superb. None of us had the opportunity to notice the food that evening, because Taz had shown up at Howard and Duane's apartment–with a friend!–just as they were leaving for the restaurant, and being unable to say "Get lost," they'd invited the two of them along.

I don't believe I'd even known, prior to that, that Howard and Duane even knew Taz. How they met him, well, that's another story. But he regularly does this: shows up on their doorstep with models for Howard to photograph, or asks if he can spend the night (one time this dragged out into a week-long stay), or has other bizarre enthusiasms. On this particular night . . . well, Stars was never the same afterward. Taz practically had hysterics when the waitress delivered him some carbonated water instead of plain water; he claimed that it would induce a heart attack, or something. He offered to demonstrate his cartwheeling abilities in the middle of the restaurant (which, I gather, he'd done at the Patio Cafe a few days previously—but that's a somewhat less formal venue). His enthusiasm on almost any subject was boundless. I don't think any of us got in more than a dozen words the entire evening, and if his friend spoke at all, I don't remember it. Our waitress, fortunately, had a good sense of humor, and the place wasn't too crowded.

I've seldom been so exhausted by a meal.

By and large, though, I have to admit that even when I was "in the biz," I didn't associate with a lot of pornstars. We didn't hang out together. I didn't feel that I had a whole lot in common with most of them. I hate to confirm the stereotype, but it's true: most pornstars don't have much going for them, mentally (there are definitely exceptions, as there are to any generalization). Most of them were concerned more with where they were going to be partying that night, and what drugs to take, than they were with literature and theater. Most of them were not very concerned with their long-term career, or with producing a quality product; they just wanted to get paid. So I didn't pal around with these guys as a general rule. I just ran into them now and then, and some of those stories, naturally, are worth telling.

Geno Gales, for instance. I'm not sure that he ever really made it onto commercial video; when I met him, he was working as a receptionist at Falcon, and he claimed that they'd cast him in a movie. Yes, this was way back when, back at the beginning of my career. He was a cute kid, little, Italian, and enthusiastic—what more could one want? He also liked the fact that I'd been named "Biggest Dick in San Francisco." So we made a date, and I spent the evening fucking his brains out. He was the definition of the term "squealing bottom." True, I felt somewhat like a human dildo, but I wasn't complaining. He was good. We made another date, which didn't pan out quite as well; from then on, we'd greet each other on the street, but never played again. So, you say: "Why write about this here, in a chapter devoted to pornstar encounters?" Because whether or not he ever did that film for Falcon (one of these days I'm gonna have to ask them), he did appear on video. You see, before he'd arrived for that first date, I'd set up my video camera in an inconspicuous spot in the room, and turned it on. For the next three hours, while we talked and fucked and smoked pot and ate and fucked and talked, the camera kept rolling. Hey, the lighting's terrible, but it's still one of the most sentimental videos I own. (Yes, I told him about it, at evening's end; he was thrilled.) Geno was . . . well, I think the proper word is "sweet." And yeah, I would've liked it if he could've been versatile, too, but you take what you can get.

And then there's Cory Monroe. I've written elsewhere about my on-screen contacts with him, but what's most amusing is that I first met him at least a year before either of us had started to do films, at the Steamworks in Honolulu. He was a military boy at the time, and I was just a beach bum, hanging out at the baths almost every night. I'm embarrassed to confess that I do not remember the encounter (there were so many!), but he's described it to me vividly. I have no doubt that it took place. And . . . well, there's a certain charm to having a documented sexual encounter for which I have no concrete memories. I can imagine whatever I want (though, given my subsequent intimate knowledge of Cory, there's not really much left to the imagination), and "remember" the encounter however I please. Having an encounter recorded on video gives a certain degree of permanence, true, but there's a lot to be said for a mutable memory.

Chess

There aren't a lot of secrets in my life. I've lived like an open book, never able to keep quiet about even the things that shame me the most. Because, despite my good Protestant upbringing (never talk about your feelings; never let on that you have emotions), I've cultivated, over the years, a group of friends with whom I feel comfortable: men (for the most part) who, I'm confident, won't judge me for the things I've done that may be less-than-admirable. And, well, I've come to the conclusion that living your life out in the open is safer than living it in hiding. I don't keep secrets because secrets leave a person vulnerable to exposure. I'd rather get them all out there on view, and let the chips fall where they may.

That having been said . . . here is a story that has never been told in its entirety. For once, I don't think I'll leave anything out, embarrassing though it is.

I decided, the summer that I spent in Seattle, that I was tired of winter. I wanted to avoid it. I was fast approaching thirty, and I hadn't yet gone around the world; it was obviously high time. So I bought a round-the-world ticket that had scheduled stops in New York, London, Bangkok, Brisbane, Sydney, Fiji, and Hawaii. I was planning on spending five months in Australia, thus completely avoiding winter. The stopover in Bangkok was primarily so I could say I'd been to Asia. I've never had much of a thing for Asian men (and why else, may I ask, do *you* travel?), but I figured I should at least visit a Far Eastern country–to get a feel for it.

The stopovers in New York and London were memorable. In New York, I got a bright purple cellophane mohawk, about eight inches long, easily the most outrageous haircut I'd ever had; in London I cut most of it off, leaving just a two-inch-long bristle ridge of purple. (Philip didn't like it; in London, punks had gained quite a bad reputation.) In Bangkok, two weeks later, I attracted quite a lot of attention. As in any country without a lot of ethnic diversity, foreigners stand out. Even if I'd had perfectly "normal" hair, I would've gotten stares. As it was, teenagers followed me in the street; I was like a Pied Piper. To my surprise, I didn't mind this in the least. Thai men, I discovered, were absolutely gorgeous. My discovery was not made without trepidation because about thirty percent of these gorgeous Thai males, it seemed, were wearing uniforms and carrying automatic rifles. I'd never been in a country where the military was so ubiquitous. At every significant building, there were dozens of them patrolling. All of them appeared ready to shoot at the slightest provocation. I didn't proposition any of them.

The teenagers were a slightly different matter. They loved me. "You numbah-one punk!" they'd say to me in a somewhat awe-struck tone, or "You Billy Idol!" One group of them surrounded me, asking all sorts of questions about the music scene that I couldn't answer. They then dragged me with them to a little hole-in-the-wall restaurant on a small side street. They ordered a communal dinner, which we all ate with our fingers; they wouldn't let me pay for anything. Nor did my wallet disappear, as some of you may be thinking. (Okay, I admit that the idea did occur to me at the time. But as I recall, my thought was: hey, it would be worth it. This is *real*.)

When I travel, I like to get as close to the everyday life of "the people" as possible. I recognize that it's simply not possible for me to know how the Thai people live, but I rode the public transit to and from the airport, I stayed at the youth hostel, I watched part of a kick-boxing competition over the wall of a public arena, I walked around the city until I was footsore and dog-tired, I ate at restaurants where I thought perhaps the local folks might eat . . . and then, on my last night there, I finally worked up the nerve to go see what the fabled sex scene was like.

I walked around . . . was it Patpong Road? Maybe not, maybe it's something else, but it's an area of the city with more neon per square foot than Times Square, and twice as vulgar, most of it in English. I walked, looking for a bar that said "boys" or something like that; I never found one. Finally, weary, discouraged, ready to go home, I agreed when a pedicab driver offered to take me to a bar. "Real cheap," he promised me. "No pay unless you like." He took me perhaps eight blocks away from the main red-light district, to a dark, quiet street; there were no signs of life around the building. He ushered me inside. I guess he got his kickback from the owner of the bar. He stuck around at the bar, counting on taking me back to my hotel.

There were no boys in evidence when I arrived. Neither were there customers. The owner yelled something, and the boys arrived. They trouped down the stairs, the music started, and they began wiggling onstage in skimpy costumes. There were probably half a dozen of them. The owner was insistent. "You like one, you choose. Very cheap!" I was terribly embarrassed. How can I say this? I didn't WANT to pay for sex. The thought of being with someone who doesn't really want to be with me has always been one of my primary turn-offs. Perhaps it's better described as a phobia. If I'm having sex with someone and I get even the slightest hint that he's thinking about his ex, or his next rent check, or that unfinished book lying on his nightstand, no matter how gorgeous he may be, I lose interest. I'd rather get up and go home. Prostitutes, no matter how good they are, just don't fill my basic requirement that they be turned on by ME–not my wallet or my reputation.

So I sat there, growing more and more embarrassed, as the music kept playing, the boys kept writhing, the owner kept urging. He brought me a drink. Don't ask me what it was. I finally pointed to one of the boys–I think it was the one who had been tending bar when I came in, and spoke to me. The others disappeared upstairs, and the music stopped. My choice came over and sat down next to me, stroking my arm. He was cute, and I might have liked to get to know him, but I didn't want to have sex with him. He kept suggesting that we go upstairs. I asked him how much it would cost; I think it was something like $100. Now really embarrassed (this was my last night in Bangkok; I didn't have that much local currency left on me), I told him, "Look, I've obviously made a mistake coming here, I can't afford this." Thanks for your time, here's a tip–I probably gave him about $5–and good night. I paid the owner for the drink, about $20, and fled, telling the pedicab driver I'd find my own way home.

Outside, in the stifling heat (even at midnight!), I walked the streets, depressed. Scott O'Hara, sex god extraordinaire, had tackled Bangkok, the most infamous den of iniquity on the planet–and lost. *"One night in Bangkok makes a hard man humble . . . "* Yep, that's exactly how I felt. If not quite humble, at least humiliated. As I was walking along, next to Lumpini Park (which, I was dimly aware, was both the cruisiest and the most dangerous spot in the city after dark), I noticed a young man leaning against the wall. As I passed, we exchanged long, searching glances. I slowed down. He started walking after me. I paused. He came right up to me. It was a shadowed street, with only the park on one side and vacant lots on the other. He started rubbing up against me; we kissed, we got pretty worked up, and then he pulled away and said, "I know a place where we can go." Well, okay. My reaction? Relief. Something, anything, I don't care what: just so long as I can leave Bangkok with at least one sexual encounter under my belt.

We walked about two blocks. He knocked at the door of a dark building; it was opened by a middle-aged, suspicious-looking woman. She said something to him; he turned to me and said, "You have money? She wants 500 baht for the room." Well, yes, I had that much. It was, what, maybe $5. We went upstairs. The boy (and he probably told me his name, but I don't remember; and his age, while I never asked, would probably not have gotten him into a bar in the United States) was all over me as soon as we got upstairs and into the little cubicle, equipped with a narrow bed and a cold-water sink. I tried to get into it, and I guess I was reasonably successful. He got me hard; he required no encouragement to raise a hard-on. I sucked him off. It took perhaps five minutes. He didn't linger afterward. The romance had apparently worn off. He even seemed a little bit angry that I'd made him cum. He went to the sink to wash himself off. I made myself ready to go. Then he told me, "I need money."

I didn't know what to say. I mean, I was slightly scared; I was also a little bit pissed. (One of the first rules of honorable hustling is that you settle the price before, not after, the sex. This boy hadn't even mentioned money beforehand, not even in relation to the room.) I asked him how much. He named a figure, perhaps half of what the owner of the bar had mentioned. Now, as it happened, I did have almost exactly that amount of money on me. But I had my dander up now: I felt cheated. My one Thai sex experience had just been taken away from me, soiled, cheapened (while being made, ironically, more expensive). I was angry. I spread my hands wide, said, I'm sorry, I didn't realize you wanted money; I'm just a traveling student, I don't have that kind of cash.

He got angry. He acted as if he were going to physically attack me, then restrained himself. I reached in the pocket of my shirt, where I had some change and small bills. I said, "Look, I'm catching a flight home tomorrow, this is all the bahts I have left. You can take these, but it'll mean that I'll have to walk to the airport." He softened some, but now he looked a little afraid. I wondered if the woman downstairs was his pimp, too, and expected a cut of whatever he made; would she beat him when he came down empty-handed? Still, I toughened myself, and insisted that I had no more money. (The rest of my money was well-hidden in an inside money belt; I wasn't too concerned about his finding it.) Eventually, after another couple of go-rounds, he let me go. I don't remember whether he took the bills I'd offered.

I trudged back to the hostel, this time really depressed, and not at all proud of myself.

I should explain, here, lest any of you be left in any doubt: I wasn't the least bit ashamed of having made it with a prostitute. I've had better sex, but it wasn't bad. I was only slightly guilty over the fact that we had marginally unsafe sex. (Sucking dick? Oh, please.) I was ashamed at the fact that I had lied to him (whatever the justification), and I was ashamed that I, with my relative riches, should be so stingy as to deny him his pay. At the same time, there was a principle involved: he hadn't informed me of the cost before the act; therefore, I would be encouraging fraud by acquiescing—conflicting principles. As usual, since I don't believe in guilt, I felt guilty for feeling guilty. I was also pretty disgusted by the fact that a boy who I thought was as eager for my body as I was for his should turn out to be just a hustler–kind of hard on the ego.

The next day, I was all too eager to leave Bangkok. And of course, British Air had lost all records of my ticket, the flight was sold out, and the terminally bored ticket agent told me I was going to have to wait for the next flight to Brisbane (a week later). I threw a screaming tantrum in the airport, and eventually got on the plane. That's what it takes, apparently, in Bangkok, to get noticed: they're so accustomed to polite Westerners, they just walk all over them.

You have to behave as though you're about to pull out a knife to even get their attention. I'm no good at that sort of behavior.

I have to keep reminding myself that my experiences in Bangkok were probably not typical. I'm sure it's possible to find men there who just like having sex with men, for free. I'm sure there are many Thais with whom I could cultivate astonishing friendships. I suspect, however, that I wouldn't meet them in Bangkok; I'm unlikely to meet them in a three-day visit; and I wouldn't meet them as long as the only language I speak is English. I'm not especially proud of my trip to Thailand ("But it started off so well!" I moan, piteously), but it did serve as something of a warning. To begin with, I'm not quite the Adaptable Adam that I liked to pretend, fitting in smoothly to whatever foreign culture I visit. Second, I'm not really a Big-City Boy. I knew that. In the United States, I can pass. In third world countries, I would be much better advised to visit a small town, where the people would be perhaps a little less jaded. And third, despite what all the magazines say, I'm not much of a sex god.

Chastened, yes, even a little bit humbled, I flew, or fled, to Australia. A country where they speak (more or less) English.

Peaks

Coming into Port Townsend, Washington, on board the ferry Issaquah–having finished the obligatory coffee and clam chowder (and, for good measure, a corn dog)–I was wandering around the ship looking for trouble, when lo and behold, he found me. He came toward me with a grin on his face, gave me that old seductive look of a man in heat, and did a smart pivot across my stern into the men's room I'd just passed. I turned my head in time to catch a glimpse of his neat black-Levi-clad behind disappearing through the swinging door. Having no intention of tricking on the ferry–and really, no time to spare after arrival–I smiled ruefully to myself and continued aft.

About thirty seconds later, I reversed course and headed into the head. I was right behind a young father with his eight-year-old son–the restrooms in these ferries are always busy, they ought to have revolving doors–and the boy went straight for the nearest urinal, while his dad stood and watched. Mr. Devilish Grin–to whom I shall refer as George, a name my father always used to signify any anonymous character–was at the farthest urinal, just zipping up. The bank of three urinals was rotated sideways, occupying the same space as an ordinary toilet stall, crammed tightly together. George looked over at me–I looked at him, and moved to the center urinal–he unzipped again. What did the young dad make of all this? I've no idea. I was far too turned on to tell. Did the boy on my right even piss? Good question. George and I politely waited for them to leave, each of us holding our dicks in pissing position, before commencing a slow stroking action. There was a lull in restroom traffic just then; people had begun returning to their cars, I think. Neither of us said anything–there was someone sitting in the stall right behind us, probably watching us through a peephole–but

---

Originally published in *STEAM*.

we watched each other. His dick was mostly obscured by the fly of his Levi's; I could just see the head, a large, bulbous, mushroom head–shiny and purple. As he stroked, I began to see more, but it never came completely out of hiding. After just a few seconds of this–branded eternally on my memory–he reached over and grabbed my dick, began squeezing and stroking it, and after some hesitation, I did the same. It was nearly hard already, head swollen far beyond the size of the shaft. He dug around in his fly with his left hand and produced his ample balls, either recently shaved or naturally hairless; I did the same, and we each held each others' balls briefly before returning to the main attraction.

All of this seems relatively plebeian as I write it, not to mention cumbersome to relate: he did thus and so, I did the same. How is it that, at the time, it seemed quite possibly the most thrilling sex I'd ever had? Dismiss me as a danger freak if you will (I'm not); I think there's more invested in the episode than that. Yes, the location was thrilling: not just any old men's room, this was the men's room of the ferry Issaquah, a tearoom afloat, awash with salty sentiment. Yes, the fact that when we started, there was a boy standing next to us certainly added to the atmosphere. While I have no actual sexual attraction for eight-year-olds, I know from personal history that they are extremely curious about sex; I wish I could do more to educate them, without putting myself at risk of ten to fifty years in prison. (Now, this boy probably had no hint of what was going on . . . but if he did, and was interested, I'd like to think that he fantasized about our dicks that night, while jerking off.) More important, to me, was the suspense: we'd never met, didn't know each others' names or predilections, and neither of us had a clue of what would happen next–so unlike a dreary old lover, who may well be a stunning piece of work, but who simply *cannot* provide any suspense after a year or two of togetherness! And still, more than any of these, there's another factor: the smile. Oh, didn't I mention that? When he grabbed my dick, in that assertive, hungry way, he looked me in the eye, and smiled. I guess what it comes down to is: a man who can be a perfect stranger to me, grab hold of my dick like it's his own, at a public urinal, and treat the whole affair like it's just good, clean fun . . . well, that man can do just about anything he wants with me.

We didn't have a chance. I'd hardly begun to get hard–although I was incredibly, ecstatically turned on, I find it very difficult to get a boner under circumstances as stressful as those–and George had just bent over to take the head of my dick into his mouth, when the door swung open again. George quickly straightened up; the guy who came in didn't come to the vacant urinal, but I couldn't handle that much tension: I let go of his dick, buttoned up and, with one last smile in George's direction (he was still standing there, hard cock sticking out), I left. The man who'd just come in took my place at the center urinal (and I immediately regretted leaving); when they came out together, two minutes later, I inferred that they were lovers. Both smiled at me; George came over and started chatting. He said he'd like to see more of me. I couldn't have been more sympathetic to the idea, but it just wouldn't work. I had a full day's schedule ahead of me. The ferry started churning, getting ready to dock; I hurried down to my car. I spent the rest of the afternoon with a smile on my face, absurdly pleased with myself and with life in general, all because I'd held a man's dick for a few seconds (and imagined the feel of that bulbous head forcing its way into my throat . . .) in the head of the Port Townsend ferry.

One of the more prosaic reasons I prefer to fuck outdoors is that I don't have to worry about shit stains on the sheets. I'm quite literally anal retentive: shit embarrasses me. Far too rigorous toilet training. I've worked for years trying to overcome this; the net result is that still, regardless of the excruciatingly pleasurable physical sensations, I can virtually never relax and enjoy getting fucked. The exceptions are: when I've thoroughly douched for the occasion (and taking the time and energy to douche before going cruising virtually ensures my inability to find *anyone* willing to fuck me); when I'm with someone who I know to be comfortable with his own and other men's bodily functions, who won't be disgusted by a shit-stained dick; and outdoors, by a rushing mountain stream or an ocean, when we're both aware that all we need to do afterward is jump in the water to wash off. Or, for that matter, fuck in the water, if it's warm enough.

The advent of condoms, you might think, would change all this. Well, it did tone down my phobia temporarily; but even seeing a shit-covered condom coming out of my ass makes me blush with shame. Besides, I don't much like being fucked with condoms. And, just to make the picture complete, I should add that I'm not nearly so phobic about other guys' shit. Oh, it's not a pleasant moment, discovering that he hasn't douched, but it doesn't make me ashamed, anyhow. If we're in the outdoors, next to a stream . . . I have to admit I kinda like it. It makes me feel "rustic." It's downright primeval.

Thus my excitement when I realized I'd be traveling past Jerry Johnson Hot Springs–which, I'd recently been informed, was *the* local hot spot. Wrote my correspondent, "I swear, they're ALL fuckin' butt in Montana and Idaho!" Well, over the past couple of years of domestic bliss, I'd developed a severely unfucked butt, and I was more than ready. I mean, my butt was *achin'* for it.

Wish I could tell you that my every wish was gratified. Alas, no. Arrival at Jerry Johnson was delayed by unexpectedly steep and winding roads; under ordinary circumstances, I would've relaxed and enjoyed the scenery (which was fantastic), stopped to hike along the river, or gathered seeds and fern spores, etc. I was determined to get to the hot springs before dark. I did–just barely. The light was rapidly going. I practically ran down the trail. It was not the leisurely walk it should have been. I bypassed the first pool, which my correspondent had warned was "reserved for straights" (indeed, there were four boisterous males in residence), and headed for the *gai* and *trés gai* pools. To my chagrin, both proved to be deserted and tepid–though, to be fair, both were very stylishly decorated with flat border slabs of granite. Time to clarify my goals: was I here for the waters, as I had steadfastly maintained, or something else? "I need a MAN!" I declared to the empty woods, and headed back downstream.

The population of the straight pool had diminished by the time I returned: just two rednecks remained, both drinking beers. The elder, in his sixties, was regaling the younger with tales of the times he'd visited the Mustang Ranch in Nevada. I asked, politely, if there was room for a third, and they moved over. The light wasn't completely gone yet, but it was pretty dim; I don't think either one could see the "HIV+" tattoo on my left bicep when I stripped.

The pool itself surprised me. The inflow, which gushed from a hole in the cliff face, was intolerably hot; the surface of the pool (large enough to easily accommodate six) was hot, but lower down, the water was downright cold. Swirling the water around with hands and feet, I thought, made it much more pleasant. It also looked pretty faggy, like a water ballet–which was why, I presume, neither of the Real Men were doing it.

Redneck the Younger eventually identified himself as Dan, from New Hampshire; he was in his early thirties, trim and well-built, just finishing up a two-week vacation through Montana, Wyoming, and Idaho. By himself. He was a construction worker by trade. He asked me if I was a deer hunter. I said, "No," and then I lapsed into my Contemplation of the Infinite routine. Eventually, with the fading of the light, I felt confident that I could masturbate discreetly underwater, and did so, in my leisurely fashion.

After forty-five minutes, Redneck the Elder finally gave up and left. I was almost ready to follow him, but I was just too curious about the seduceability of Dan. I mean, he'd been away from his wife for two whole weeks . . . and yes, practically the first thing out of his mouth when I asked how he'd found out about the hot springs was a total non sequitur about how much he liked San Francisco. This is the redneck version of Gay Code, I think: apparently they feel that no one but a fag would admit to liking that sodomitic city. I should've just taken the bait, but I couldn't bring myself to. It seemed too blatant–too easy.

Eventually, after small talk that grew progressively more intimate, I phrased it thus: "So, what about you–do you feel like gettin' off?" There was a long silence, during which I feared he was going to pretend he hadn't heard. I mean, that's the Straight Man's Revenge: to know, but pretend not to know, to leave me twisting in the wind . . . and then he spoke up, very quietly: "It's been a long time." Naturally, I presumed he meant a long time away from the wife–then he went on to tell about how, ten years ago, before he got married, he was involved with a man . . . who died.

He didn't fill in all the details, but he kept repeating, over and over, "It just doesn't seem worth it any more"–meaning the risk of AIDS.

"So," I said, "Do you still jerk off?" He admitted that he did, now and then. "That's completely safe, you know–and I'd really get off feeling your hand on my dick . . . " So that's what we did. He jerked me off, and I did him. For all the years I spent jerking off onstage, all the Monday nights spent at the San Francisco Jacks, I'm not sure I've ever jerked off with someone to a mutual, simultaneous slimax. (Slimax? Freudian slip, perhaps–but oh, so apt!) At least, not on any occasion I can remember. I'm difficult to jerk off; it takes a long time for me to get really excited, even at the best of times. Well, I guess you could say this was the best of times. He had a very good hand, and when eventually we both stood up so that our dicks were above water, visible, I was as turned on as I ever get–I actually had to hold off, hold back, mentally turn my temperature down, so as to wait for him. We slimed together, and then sank back into the pool. I stroked his body, and hugged him–definitely my favorite part of sex, the after-climax meltdown, when intimacy becomes possible even with a straight man, because you've both shot your loads and he knows you're not gonna try nothin' funny with him–and reassured him, in all the ways I knew, that sex with men, whether or not it was worth it, was good, positive, and nothing to be ashamed of. He told me about his wife, the nice Catholic girl next door who he'd dated in high school and then gone back to after his big-city lifestyle went sour; he told me, over and over, that it was "good enough" for him–and that he was afraid for me.

You tell me: at that point should I have told him, "Don't worry about me, I can't get AIDS, I already have it."–or should I have done exactly what I did, smile and say, "Don't worry, I take good care of myself." My goal at that point was to try to make Dan more comfortable with what sexuality he had left. Hell, that's my raison d'être in a nutshell! You only give people what they're ready for. He wasn't ready for the truth, the whole truth, and nothing but the truth; I think the knowledge that he'd just jerked off with a PWA might have sent him over the edge. Okay, I'm rationalizing, huh? I know, but I think I did the better thing.

After we'd been talking and cuddling for perhaps ten minutes, we saw a flashlight weaving around on the riverbank upstream. It was Redneck the Elder, come back to collect some things he'd forgotten. Dan and I separated and watched in some amusement as the old sot got dressed, dropping his towel into the river in the process. He left, and after a few more minutes, we left too. Dan lighted our way back to the parking lot–I hadn't thought to bring a flashlight–and said good-bye, heading for the airport in Moscow, where he'd catch his flight back to New Hampshire and the little woman. I headed just a few miles up the road before finding a pullout where I could spend the night comfortably in the back of my van. I couldn't stop thinking about him . . . and my asshole kept giving the occasional twitch of impatience at being left so totally out of the picture.

Some months before–the last time I'd gotten fucked, in fact-upon meeting a very compatible man who was also HIV positive, we decided by mutual consent to dispense with the rubbers. Being Positive (and totally out about it) gives me that option, for which I'm grateful; we had a fabulous time. Times like that make me actually glad to be infected: there's so much less for me to worry about, you see. Oh, I still have to worry about all the same old STDs that have been around since day one; there are possibly other things that are sexually transmissible among HIVers, too, but I choose not to get too upset about those possibilities. I assume my partner has the same deductive faculties that I have so I grant him the right to make his own decisions about what precautions he thinks are appropriate. And when his level of caution and mine coincide– Yowie Zowie!

Now, most doctors, upon reading the previous paragraph, will gasp in horror: Reinfection! Cofactors! etc. With all due respect to the medical profession, I suspect that most of those gasps (and the theories of reinfection themselves) are based more on the medical profession's long-standing distaste for gay sex than on scientific research. You know: Anal Sex–Icky, Dirty! Remember, most of the doctors now practicing were already in the business when the AMA finally decided that homosexuality was no longer an illness. Some of them probably administered electroshock therapy, or referred homosexual patients to mental homes. It's a conservative profession; I doubt that those deep-rooted prejudices have changed a lot, even among the AIDS docs.

Well, AIDS is certainly a problem in our community (understatement of the year!). I'm grateful for what aid and comfort these professionals provide (though aid and comfort is not really their specialty, in my experience). But my Public Enemy number one is not HIV–but Erotophobia. More often than not, I feel that the medical profession is the number one carrier of that plague. They seem only too happy to make whatever judgments they can to stop people from having dirty, messy sex. In that sense, I find myself in direct opposition to the entire medical profession. Fortunately, I know I have all of Human Nature on my side–so I know that eventually, we will win. People will continue to have sex. People just need to learn what their own personal safety guidelines are. I doubt that the medicos will offer much realistic help along those lines, so it's up to us to use our noggins.

Tony (for that was his name) was a cute little Latino man: chunky, dark-haired, uncut, just the way I like 'em–not hung exorbitantly, but still enough to make me squeal in pain when he porked me. And then, as I got into it, quite enough to make me turn into a wild beast. We'd been through the preliminaries in the bar (it was my once-yearly foray into that foreign territory), and we both knew that we both considered ourselves bottoms, but we were both willing and able to satisfy the other's urges–and yes, he proved more than able, and my hard-on cooperated well enough also, and both of us ended up depositing two loads of cum up each other's butt. Why do I speak so proudly of this one single fact? Why is it so different from the time, a month previously, when I pumped a condom full of cum while fucking another guy? I can't give an objective answer to that, but we all know it's different. If nothing else, our health crisis has *made* it different. Fifteen years ago, I could've fucked a guy wearing a condom and it would've just been kinky; there would have been no emotional baggage around the level of intimacy implied by condom usage. In fact, I remember doing so. It was the first time I'd ever used one (except to jerk off into), and I was wildly turned-on by the idea–but as I recall, I didn't use enough lube (or perhaps I used the wrong kind of lube), and the damn thing broke.

Nowadays, when I make an agreement with a man that we'll fuck uncovered, it's an extreme declaration of trust, knowing that there are potentially lethal diseases that we could be passing back and forth–crypto, meningitis, hepatitis–and we think it's worth the risk. This had only happened for me four times in the past six years (the time I've been actively, publicly aware of being a PWA); each time stands out, diamond-sharp, in my memory, more because of the trust shared than because the sex was extra special. In the past six months, however, I've begun to reactivate my sex life: I've fucked at least a dozen men without a condom, and been fucked by probably twice that number. It feels good. As I write this, in fact, I'm still riding the endorphin high of having been well-fucked last night. There was a time, a few years ago, when I would feel depressed, guilty, angst-ridden, or just plain wretched in my postcoital phase. No matter how safe we'd been, there was always uncertainty: Have I just infected some innocent person? I'm happy to report that I'm over that, thank you. We don't have innocent victims anymore. People know the risks. Those who are getting infected now have chosen to get infected; if I'm the avenue of transmission they've chosen, who am I to demur? My virus is at least as good as your virus.

Sex, at its best, is a mental and emotional exercise. When it's a mechanical, physical exercise, I'd just as soon not bother. I don't need to be fucked, whether bareback or otherwise, every night. Once a week seems excessive. Once a month, perhaps, I get the urge, but I think it's better if I hold off until my hormones are raging, until I'm spending most every masturbatory session rubbing my asshole and fantasizing gang rape–then I'm ripe and ready, and I know it'll be *good*, no matter what my partner is like. Then is also the time when I'm most likely to hook up with some man who clicks all my buttons, but who then says to me, "I'm busy tonight, can I get you to come to dinner tomorrow night–and maybe we could rent a movie, or go bowling?" Sometimes, you know, it would be really convenient to live out the caveman fantasy: bop him on the head with a club, drag him to the nearest dark alley, and do him.

Let me bring in a fourth man: Pedro by name. I met him in an arcade in Billings, Montana, a town under serious construction. (I heard some of the clerks discussing the likelihood that the street construction was actually timed and intended to drive the five adult bookstores out of business. It doesn't seem far-fetched to me–but I doubt it'll be successful. Those cowpokes need relief.) In this arcade, there were no gloryholes, but the booths were large economy size, larger than most bathhouse cubicles, and it was the done thing for two guys to go into a booth. Then it's just a question of who does whom. I have difficulty with that part of the game: of course, my natural position is down on my knees, but my demeanor seems to indicate the opposite to most of my potential tricks. How does one indicate one's Receptivity? Pedro obviously hadn't gotten it–he wanted to do me–but he didn't object when I showed him how good my mouth was, either. He was appreciative, in fact, and friendly. The booths, as always, ate quarters at an alarming rate; after awhile, we stopped feeding the machine, but then a couple of minutes later, we heard someone unlock a door nearby, and he whispered to me, "That's the manager—we'd better put in some more quarters." Ah, a regular! And a living contradiction to the popular notion that "only guys with real neurotic attitudes go to video arcades." Maybe there are some of those guys there, but I guess I just scare them away.

So, after Pedro came, I asked him if he could recommend someplace where I could go to get a meal—a *real* meal, I mean sure that was a great appetizer, but . . . He shrugged apologetically, and said that Billings closed down early: McDonald's might be the best I could do. "Now, if you'd gotten here an hour earlier, I'd've taken you over to my place—I run a Mexican restaurant over on the west side. But the manager's probably just locking the doors."

Was this a "peak?" A few years ago, I probably wouldn't have described it that way. I didn't get a last name or phone number (what would be the point? Billings is not a regular stopover for me), and his foreskin, though tasty, was not exceptional. He spoke English far too well for me to formulate a wetback fantasy around him. He didn't take me to the local nude beach the next day; I didn't get any startling revelations from him, or even any information about the local law enforcement attitudes. What I did get was a spicy load of cum, a smile and a kiss, and a casual, friendly attitude. Those go a long way toward making an encounter memorable; they're characteristics which, if a few million men could learn to emulate, would make the arcades of this world a pretty fine fuckin' place.

Spunk-boy

Spunk is what they call me
when they want me with a mohawk
when they want me up on stage
playing with The Criminal Classes
. . . and they do, some of them
grovelling in the gutter, fawning on my feet
I can give them what they want—
they want a big dick & a foul mouth
a boot on the chest and one at the crotch
they want an old newspaper clipping,
not an 8×10 glossy
and I can dish it out in spades
I can be your Spunk, pig-boy
show you how I play my trade
just don't take me home at night
'cause then I might forget
instead of kicking you out of bed
making you sleep on the floor
might cuddle up against you
fall asleep and—accidental-like—
kiss you on the eyes
When the eyes are closed, the cameras stop
the mirror fades, the lights are cut
even the director goes to sleep
and something changes
Sure I'll be your spunk-boy, mister—
whaddya wanna pay?
Ruffle up my mohawk and I'll curl
like a cat across your chest
You want me for your Spunk-boy?

Chronology

September 11, 1972: first ejaculation. (Actually, this is incorrect. This is the date that I remember, but I *know* it was a Sunday morning. I guess I'll never know.)

Summer, 1976: read Richard Howard's *Two-Part Inventions*

April 16, 1977: first sexual encounter

July/August, 1977: spent in France; no sex

September, 1978: announced to the world that I was a Libertarian

June 19, 1979: left Grants Pass for San Francisco, by bicycle

July 1, 1979: first marijuana

July 22, 1979: arrived in Chicago

September 3, 1979: arrived at the University of Dallas

October 15, 1979: bought first motorcycle

December 23, 1979: Claudia kills herself

April 26, 1980: first fisted; first hallucinogens

May/June, 1980: touring the Eastern Seaboard by motorcycle

October, 1980: first apartment rented, in Chicago

January 3, 1981: met dareK

February, 1981: left Chicago

March, 1981: spent in Memphis

April, 1981: bought first car, a red 1966 MGB; named it Bella

May, 1981: arrived in San Francisco, with Marc

Summer, 1981: worked at Club San Francisco (Ritch Street)

September 23, 1981: flew to Honolulu

1981/82: worked at the Steamworks

November 23, 1981: met Ralph

February 19, 1982: met Basilio Melquiadez Martinez

February, 1983: flew to New Orleans, stayed with Richard in Andalusia, Alabama

March, 1983: bought van in Atlanta; drove west

June 2, 1983: arrived in San Francisco

June 7, 1983: first visit to Savages

June 24, 1983: second (and last) wet dream, involving four bulls

July 15, 1983: first paid performance at Savages; tits pierced afterward, in the basement

July 23, 1983: hired for *California Blue*

April 7-14, 1984: performances at the Follies, Washington, DC

June 5, 1984: totaled Bella in New Mexico

November 6, 1984: decision made to emigrate to Australia

March 15, 1985: met Michael Pietri; shot *The Other Side of Aspen II*

March 17, 1985: premiere of *Juice* at the Castro Theater; met Artie Bressan

May, 1985: "Spunk" is born in *Advocate MEN*

August 11, 1985: won Greasy Jockstrap Contest at Powerhouse, San Francisco; met Al Parker

September 2, 1985: fucked by Al Parker

February, 1986: first fiction published: "Sweet and Sour Pork," in *Advocate MEN*

April/May, 1986: bicycle tour of England, France, Belgium, and the Netherlands

April 30, 1986: met Philip Core

July, 1986: met Bill Webber

September/October, 1987: bicycle tour of Puget Sound, ending at World's Fair in Vancouver

September 21, 1986: met John Gaines

October 24, 1986: premiere of *Jerker*, Celebration Theatre, L.A.; met Bob Chesley

October 29, 1986: Bill moved in

January 4-12, 1987: performances at the Show Palace, NYC

February, 1987: bicycle tour of Australia

March 19, 1987: Black Party, the Saint, NYC

August, 1987: bought 20 acres near Port Townsend, Washington; named it Bog End

September/October, 1987: bicycle tour of Italy/Yugoslavia

March 21, 1988: Black Party, the Saint, NYC

Summer, 1988: spent in Port Townsend, trying to build a house

September, 1988-April 1989: travelled to NYC, London, Bangkok, and Sydney; spent five months in Sydney

October 17, 1988: met Colm

March 2, 1989: met Kosta

July, 1989: eighth (and current) motorcycle, a red '83 BMW R80RT named O. Mores

July-September, 1989: spent touring the United States by motorcycle

September, 1989: recognition of KS lesions

Winter, 1989/90: spent in Oceanside, California

May, 1990: bought 47 acres in Cazenovia, Wisconsin; named it Littledick

November 1, 1991: met Stephen Hemming

June, 1992: idea of *STEAM* is first broached

November, 1992: trip to Italy with Keith Griffith

April, 1993: first issue of *STEAM* is distributed free at the March on Washington

May, 1993-May, 1994: lymphoma, radiation, and chemotherapy

February, 1994: trip to Hawaii

November, 1994: *Scott O'Hara: Nudes, Portraits, and Hard Dick Images* at Mark I. Chester's gallery, San Francisco

June, 1995: moved back to San Francisco

August, 1996: *Do-It-Yourself Piston Polishing (for Non-Mechanics)*, first book of short stories, published

Order Your Own Copy of
This Important Book for Your Personal Library!

AUTOPORNOGRAPHY
A Memoir of Life in the Lust Lane

_____ in hardbound at $29.95 (ISBN: 0-7890-0144-6)

_____ in softbound at $14.95 (ISBN: 1-56023-898-4)

COST OF BOOKS_____

OUTSIDE USA/CANADA/
MEXICO: ADD 20%_____

POSTAGE & HANDLING_____
*(US: $3.00 for first book & $1.25
for each additional book)
Outside US: $4.75 for first book
& $1.75 for each additional book)*

SUBTOTAL_____

IN CANADA: ADD 7% GST_____

STATE TAX_____
*(NY, OH & MN residents, please
add appropriate local sales tax)*

FINAL TOTAL_____
*(If paying in Canadian funds,
convert using the current
exchange rate. UNESCO
coupons welcome.)*

☐ **BILL ME LATER:** ($5 service charge will be added)
(Bill-me option is good on US/Canada/Mexico orders only;
not good to jobbers, wholesalers, or subscription agencies.)

☐ Check here if billing address is different from
shipping address and attach purchase order and
billing address information.

Signature_____

☐ **PAYMENT ENCLOSED: $**_____

☐ **PLEASE CHARGE TO MY CREDIT CARD.**

☐ Visa   ☐ MasterCard   ☐ AmEx   ☐ Discover

Account # _____

Exp. Date _____

Signature _____

Prices in US dollars and subject to change without notice.

NAME _____

INSTITUTION _____

ADDRESS _____

CITY _____

STATE/ZIP _____

COUNTRY _____ COUNTY (NY residents only) _____

TEL _____ FAX _____

E-MAIL_____

May we use your e-mail address for confirmations and other types of information? ☐ Yes   ☐ No

Order From Your Local Bookstore or Directly From
The Haworth Press, Inc.
10 Alice Street, Binghamton, New York 13904-1580 • USA
TELEPHONE: 1-800-HAWORTH (1-800-429-6784) / Outside US/Canada: (607) 722-5857
FAX: 1-800-895-0582 / Outside US/Canada: (607) 772-6362
E-mail: getinfo@haworth.com
PLEASE PHOTOCOPY THIS FORM FOR YOUR PERSONAL USE.

BOF96